Europe's Economy in Crisis

Europe's Economy in Crisis

Edited by Ralf Dahrendorf

Preface by Gaston Thorn
President of the EEC Commission

Holmes & Meier Publishers, Inc.

New York

First published in the United States of America 1982 by
Holmes & Meier Publishers, Inc.
30 Irving Place, New York, N.Y. 10003

First published in West Germany 1981 by Verlag Fritz Molden
under the title *Trendwende*

Library of Congress Cataloging in Publication Data

Trendwende, English.
    Europe's economy in crisis.

    Translation of: Trendwende.
      1. Europe—Economic conditions—1945—   —Addresses,
essays, lectures. 2. European Economic Community—
Addresses, essays, lectures. I. Dahrendorf, Ralf.
II. Title: Europe's economy in crisis.
HC240.T7213 1982   330.94'0558   82-3122
ISBN 0-8419-0806-0   AACR2

Printed in Great Britain

Contents

Contents

The Contributors

Miguel de Aldasoro was for many years Director of Economic Relations in the Spanish Foreign Ministry; since 1979 he has been State Secretary for Fisheries

Samuel Brittan is an economic journalist and the author of several important books on the UK and world economy; he has been assistant editor of the *Financial Times* (London) since 1978

Guido Carli is a member and director of several Italian and international financial organizations; he was Foreign Trade minister 1957–58; Governor of the Bank of Italy 1960–75; since 1980 he has been president of the European employers' organization, UNICE

Ralf Dahrendorf was Professor of Sociology at the Universities of Hamburg, Tübingen and Konstanz; he was a Liberal member of the Baden-Württemberg state parliament and the Bonn federal parliament, and in 1969–70 he was Parliamentary State Secretary at the German Foreign Office; he was a member of the EEC Commission 1970–74; since 1974 he has been Director of the London School of Economics

Etienne (Viscount) Davignon was for many years Director in the Belgian Foreign Ministry; since 1977 he has been the EEC Commissioner for Industrial Affairs, Energy, Research and Science

Jacques Delors has been Professor at Dauphin University, Paris, since 1973; in 1962 he became a member, and in 1971 a honorary director, of the Bank of France; in 1969–72 he was counsellor for Social and Cultural Affairs in the cabinet of prime minister

The Contributors

Chaban-Delmas; in 1974 he became a member of the Socialist Party; he was a member of the National Assembly 1976–79; he was chairman of the European Parliament's Economic and Monetary Committee 1979–81; since 1981 he has been the Economy and Finance minister in the French government

Otmar Emminger has since 1950 been a member first of Bank Deutscher Länder, then of the Bundesbank; he was president of the Bundesbank 1977–79

Horst Knapp has been the proprietor, publisher and editor of the business weekly *Finanznachrichten* (Vienna) since 1960

Francesco Kneschaurek has been Professor of Economics and Statistics at St Gallen University, Switzerland since 1962; he has been president of the St Gallen Centre for Futurology since 1971; he is a member and director of numerous Swiss economic organizations

George Krimpas has been Professor of Political Economy at Athens University since 1976; since 1979 he has been a member of the national executive and political bureau of the Greek Social Democratic Party

Erik Lundberg was Professor of Economics at Stockholm University 1946–65 and at Stockholm School of Economics 1965–76; since 1961 he has been a member of the Swedish Government's Planning Council; he was president of the Royal Swedish Academy of Science 1973–76, and chairman of the Nobel Committee for Economic Science 1974–79

Gaston Thorn was a member of the European Parliament 1959–69; since 1961 he has been chairman of the Luxemburg Democratic Party; since 1969 he has been minister for External Affairs, Trade, Industry, Justice, Education and Sport; he was Luxemburg Prime Minister 1974–79; since 1981 he has been President of the EEC Commission

Jan Tinbergen is Emeritus Professor of Development Planning at Rotterdam and Leiden Universities, and a member of several Academies of Science; he was the winner of the 1969 Nobel Prize for Economic Science

Preface:
An apprehensive Europe

Gaston Thorn

Some people think they are simply having a nightmare. They still believe that our industrialized nations are going through nothing worse than a temporary, though painful, economic crisis. After all, similar situations have arisen in the past and things turned out much the same as before.

But this time everything is different, even the confusion. The first oil crisis, sparked off by a local war, certainly shook the world like a battering-ram. The economies of the European countries, like many others, reacted with a certain amount of complaint and here and there a few temporary restrictions. People wanted to forget it quickly. The only things that changed were that petrol was slightly more expensive, that it became worthwhile double-glazing windows and insulating lofts. Alongside modest changes of habit came numerous energy-saving gadgets. In other words, there was nothing too traumatic about it. Here and there, people were even becoming extravagant again.

But, inexorably, the harsh reality of the situation impinged on most people's optimistic expectations. The first oil crisis had only been a catalyst. The second, in 1979-80, revealed the true nature of the situation, to the public at large at any rate. The effects of the crisis, reaching right into their daily life, disproved earlier optimistic predictions. The international economic climate had suddenly become unrecognizable. People finally began to notice that an increasing number of everyday items were coming from distant countries which before they had only associated with exotic holidays. Meanwhile, in front of our eyes, factories were closing down and unemployment was rising. Whole industries which had previously been symbols of industrial might, were shaken. Their very structure was beginning to dissolve under the effect of aggressive, concentrated and systematic economic penetration from abroad. Huge areas, tactfully referred to as 'declining', saw their industrial fabric being frittered away and added the weight of their problem to the increasing difficulties of other, traditionally more disinherited, areas. Europe was knocked off balance.

Today the crisis continues. Indeed in some sectors it is increasing its grip. Its effects are extending to all levels of the population and all sections of economic life.

But, analysing the situation, we can attempt to draw up a balance-sheet. It is a sad but significant one. Sad because, in relative terms, Europe has become poorer. Each of us has lost a bit, and this must be recognized. Significant because, now, we are identifying the elements of the crisis, and at the same time assessing the road to recovery.

We know that, in a kind of new deal, production factors have been redeployed throughout the world. A new division of labour has appeared and it is impossible for all countries to make the same contribution. Our own countries, concerned to preserve the comfort of our workers and inhabitants, are hamstrung by legitimate social guarantees with which others scarcely bother. Moreover, because of the yoke of energy, our costly supplies of raw materials and the erratic movements of capital produced by monetary anarchy, our countries are hemmed in by fearful constraints.

There is only one way out for them: the frantic search for added value, the race for innovation and productive performance. No less affected than us, many other countries are attacking our traditional markets in a situation akin to commercial war. Forced to produce and sell for their own economic survival, these countries are forcing whole groups of our firms into a decline. Even in areas of sophisticated production, our industrial control is slipping. It is strictly conditioned by the competitiveness of our enterprises.

Despite deserving successes, it is alarming how many production units have disappeared, how many others have been forced to restructure while struggling against unremitting competition.

They all pay a heavy tribute to the crisis in the form of people and materials: workers deprived of their jobs or uprooted, plant and equipment made obsolete or sacrificed. This situation is reflected not only in words but in the attitudes of the people we come across every day. In some of our countries more than one person in ten is bearing its financial and moral burden. And one is bound to ask 'How much longer?'.

It is clear that in this economic climate political laws and circumstances, dominated more than ever by ideological rearmament and partisan violence, no longer allow one to hope for a miraculous solution to these problems. Particularly since, at a time when an extremely promising North–South dialogue should be developing, anachronistic mentalities are returning to the exclusive dialectic of East–West relations.

Nevertheless, at this turning point in modern history, it is Europe which gives its member states the chance of emerging from the crisis. Only European integration incorporates the elements which will allow us to rise above our present problems.

But first it is essential to have faith in this and not to be blinded, not to give in to the instinct of narrow-minded nationalism, of 'every man for himself'. Not to settle comfortably into cosy little habits, be they professional, social or simply attitudes of mind. European integration, in fact, is the opposite of looking inward, of giving up, of demobilization. It is both a daunting economic investment and a feat of political selflessness, the like of which history has surely never yet seen.

If all the European countries are today sunk in the economic crisis, it is through Europe that they will emerge from it. But only if the responsible powers do not get their priorities wrong, do not waste their energies snuffing out individual fires without giving themselves the means of preventing them. The malthusian approach to problems must be rejected. And, above all, they must not discredit themselves in the eyes of the majority by an escalation of theological disputes.

It is clear that first of all Europe must adopt a convincing economic policy and an efficient structural policy, and take coherent action in the fields of manufacturing industry and energy. These combined policies will make it possible to develop internal markets firmly in a continental context, in which economic activity will be freed from all constraints, and to re-establish competitiveness with the outside world and thereby to weave an inextricable web of common interests. Europe will be present at all economic and social levels, involved with industries as well as regions. With or without extra financial resources, it will fulfil its role of stimulating and co-ordinating. In this immense and lengthy undertaking imagination must prevail in the taking of decisions. These must be inspired by generosity and not by defensive national reactions to short-term problems.

At the same time Europe will need to open itself out to the world. This means it will have to resist protectionist temptations (even though this may continue to disturb its own peace of mind), to take an active part in international economic reorganization, and to pursue its commitments to help the underdeveloped nations so that conflict is calmed and defused.

But in order to achieve this Europe will have to be able to master the egocentric forces within it, those very forces which contribute to its richness and vitality. First there are the national forces, always ready to fight over their share of the common heritage. In a crisis they become fiercer and more blind than ever. They will have to compromise, at any rate if they are to hope to respond to the challenge of the crisis. Then there are the institutional forces, often carried away by an excessive self-determination of their power. Henceforth they will have to measure their ambition against operational efficiency. There is no doubt that they will end up by accommodating each other in observing commonly accepted rules. In truth, it is probably at the fringe of the official life of the political and economic authorities that a new direction is emerging. Here at last something significant is happening. Brought to the necessity of sharing common disciplines and sacrifices, similarly affected by the crisis, Europeans are now beginning to perceive individually, and concretely, that their destiny is a common one.

Part I
Introduction

1 Drifting between helplessness and patent cures

Ralf Dahrendorf

Political elections these days are, it seems, lost rather than won. Although the victors may claim a mandate for their policy manifesto, they really owe their victory more often than not to the unpopularity of their predecessors. And even when, once in a while, a government manages to get itself re-elected, it soon proves to have scored a pyrrhic victory. The only apparent exception to these rules is Japan, where one party has been in government since the start of the democratic regime, and where, again exceptionally, the business community – in so far as at all distinguishable from the government – has so far kept up a rate of growth nowadays beyond most other OECD countries' wildest dreams.

There are a number of reasons for this continuous swing of the political pendulum. But probably the most important is that electors are increasingly losing faith in the ability of governments to perform what they have promised. Worse, there is growing doubt about the capacity of any government to solve problems of which the media are as full as campaign speeches.

Those problems are of an economic nature. Since the start of the seventies there have, of course, been far-reaching changes in the socio-economic climate, of which three in particular – each sufficient to lose elections on its own – stand out.

The first is creeping inflation, though on this score there are, among the OECD countries (or Club of the Rich) considerable differences. While memories of past hyperinflation are still very much alive in Germany, in Italy both parliament and people have tried to bypass inflation, by indexation and the black economy respectively. Successive British governments have nailed their

3

flag to the counter-inflationary mast, while resurgent inflation threatens the cause of social reform in France. But we are anticipating; suffice it to establish here that inflation has become the industrialized countries' constant companion.

The effects are numerous. At the personal level, inflation devalues traditional savings and perpetually creates new claims, particularly for higher pay. Trying to keep pace with inflation is fair enough, but it cannot protect against the temptation to move a step faster. At the national level, it is fluctuating inflation that does the damage. It adds an element of uncertainty which plays havoc with any kind of planning, discourages investment and so makes for slower growth. In terms of social policy, inflation involves redistribution, if only from those who are able to protect themselves against its ravages to those who are not.

Not all that long ago, inflation and unemployment were held to be inversely related, with the Phillips curve demonstrating that for decades rising inflation was associated with falling unemployment, and vice versa. Since the seventies, however, this relationship has increasingly been called into question, until in most industrialized countries – there are, of course, some notable exceptions which, as far as Europe is concerned, will be discussed in their appropriate places – high inflation and high unemployment now go hand in hand. Some congratulate themselves merely on being able to hold unemployment down to something like 5 per cent, others battle in vain against rates twice as high.

Unemployment, too, has a number of far-reaching consequences. Its cost in a welfare state is high. Britain in 1981, for example, was spending £8bn, or the equivalent of its entire North Sea oil revenue, on unemployment relief. It is also demoralizing. This is especially so for the widespread unemployment of the young. Young people are responsible for over half of all the violent crimes committed, and whom being unable to get a job is bound to make feel even more unwanted and at odds with the society they live in. Again, it is not merely, or even mainly, the jobless themselves, but also those who fear for their jobs, and especially threatened or displaced members of the middle classes, who – as demonstrated most frighteningly by the rise of the

4

Nazis during the Great Depression – fall an easy prey to political extremism.

The third, and perhaps most important, climatic change since the start of the seventies is, of course, the slowdown of economic growth. The figures speak for themselves. Whereas in the previous twenty-five years growth rates of 4 or 5 per cent had, in most OECD countries, been considered par for the course, and in some cases were substantially exceeded, there is hardly one country which in the seventies did not experience at least one year of negative growth, while by now growth of anything like 2–3 per cent is regarded as a cause for rejoicing.

The consequences of this have been discussed almost *ad nauseam*, so one example, drawn from the social field, will perhaps suffice. All welfare states of the postwar period were based on an assumed growth rate sufficient for the host of their benefits to be maintained – old-age pensions, national assistance, sickness pay and hospital treatment, family allowances, education and housing grants, and much else besides. If growth drops below 4 per cent, the entire fabric is put at risk. But the biggest danger is political – to the credibility of politicians, to law and order, perhaps ultimately to the constitution itself – when legitimate expectations raised by competing promises made in the electoral hurly-burly are invariably disappointed. If many indeed consider growth and democracy inseparable, then all this bodes little good.

Two further points, both taking an illuminating study by James E. Alt on the politics of economic decline as their starting point,[1] may be added. After analysing opinion-poll data in Britain, Mr Alt notes: 'In 1970, 60 per cent [of those questioned] felt that "the Government can do much to stop rising prices". By the spring of 1974, this was true of a quarter of the electorate only'[2] – a proportion unlikely to have risen since. He concludes that 'the history of the mid-seventies is the history of a politics of declining expectations ... not a politics of protest but a politics of slow disillusionment, a politics whose chief characteristic is non-participation in, if not apathy towards, organized party politics.'[3]

Nor is this alienation a purely British phenomenon. There are many other countries whom the economic changes of the seventies have struck like a kind of natural disaster, something for

5

which the governments of today's welfare states are, if not held responsible, at least expected (as in this case they certainly were to start with) to provide a remedy. But governments of all political complexions, trying out a variety of different prescriptions, have conspicuously failed to do so. Small wonder that electors are disillusioned.

The other point is even more serious. To return to Britain, this country has, of course, already a century of (relative) economic decline behind it, whose course and causes Samuel Brittan will retrace later. Others, however, have fared differently. So, in their case, the political consequences of the kind of climatic change now in the making could be much more far-reaching. Samuel Huntington, in a submission to the Trilateral Commission, foresaw this possibility for the United States already in 1975.[4] As the state's activities have widened, so, he argued, its authority has shrunk, a key role in this process being played by the impossibility of satisfying growing expectations. How, one is bound to ask, will a country like Germany – not to mention Japan – respond to a demise of the economic miracle which has almost become part of its life?

One conclusion from all this stands out straight away. On the score of inflation, unemployment and economic growth, the seventies indubitably mark a trend change, inasmuch as the problems they have created are no longer soluble by the comparatively simple means that had passed muster in the twenty-five years before. Governments, like electors, feel helpless. Politicians increasingly vie with each other in disclaiming all intention of promising heaven on earth, indeed in protesting their own impotence in the face of unprecedented difficulties of which they themselves, of course, are innocent victims. Electors, meanwhile, are little impressed, turning away at best disillusioned, at worst hostile and at all events ever-ready to vote against the government of the day.

Diagnoses more plentiful than cures

So far, however, we have merely scratched the surface of the transformation that is the subject of this book. Surely inflation, unemployment and stagnation are interconnected? Do they not have common causes? And what caused the transformation in the first place?

Well, the flashpoint clearly occurred in 1973 – the year of the Yom Kippur War, of the oil embargo and first oil price explosion, of empty motorways and a sudden keen sense of foreboding. Yet in fact, however decisive and traumatic, those events – as pointed out, in the preface to this book, by Gaston Thorn, president of the EEC Commission – just acted as a catalyst. And it was not until the second oil price explosion of 1979-80 that the full extent of the changes affecting our future was revealed.

Those changes, however, transcend the two explosive oil price rises themselves. Rather, the seventies saw a number of other changes and the rudiments of new social and economic insights, which are connected with the oil price only indirectly, if at all. What broke the framework of the international monetary system was not a crushing weight of petrodollars but the floating of the dollar, its linchpin, back in 1971. Though free trade was given a shot in the arm by the Tokyo Round, protectionism now is nearly everywhere in the ascendant. The stir created by the Club of Rome's first report on the 'Limits to Growth' in 1972, and many official and unofficial studies since, have focused the attention of governments and the general public on the environment as well as on the scarcity of natural resources, while the Brandt Report on North-South questions has highlighted the plight of the poor nations of this world and urged the need to help them.

The complexities and ramifications of all this add up to something like the agenda of one of those by now routine world economic summits. But an agenda by itself does not put matters into their proper perspective. To do so, one must begin with the question of economic growth, since this, or rather the lack of it, lies at the root of inflation and unemployment alike. So why, since the seventies, has growth become so much more difficult?

The question can be answered on three levels. The most

obvious explanation – and hence the one that politicians, particularly in Europe and North America, favour most, is that the
trouble is mainly due to dearer oil. After all, as shown by Otmar
Emminger and other contributors to this volume, did not even
economically strong countries like West Germany make heavy
weather of the second oil price explosion, if not the first? But
endogenous factors are blamed also. Rising costs, especially
wages and social charges, have, it is argued, made the mature
industrial countries less competitive. People, it is sometimes
added, no longer work as hard as they should. And there is a
political mood of economic defeatism which discourages investment no less than do high taxes and excessive government intervention. In short, we are presented with a picture of fatigue, of
countries no longer capable of growth because growth is no
longer desired or is, more or less deliberately, being prevented.

Others, like the American economist Walt Rostow,[5] however,
go a lot further. Following the 'wave' theory propounded by
Kondratiev, they portray economic activity moving in long cycles
or, as Rostow prefers, 'trend periods'. From 1790 to 1815, according to him, the trend was downwards, from 1815 to 1848 upwards,
from 1848 to 1873 downwards, from 1873 to 1896 upwards, from
1896 to 1920 downwards, from 1920 to 1936 upwards, from 1936
to 1951 downwards, from 1951 to 1972 upwards – and so, he
concludes, it is hardly surprising that, for the fifth time since the
late eighteenth century, a long-term downtrend is now the order
of the day.[6] Leavening the basic pessimism of his approach with
a kind of synthetic cheerfulness, Rostow credits mankind with
being able to master all problems if so minded, but doubts
whether it will do so before this century is out.

Unfortunately, or rather fortunately for us, neither Rostow nor
others of that ilk explain the mechanism involved in the pattern
they describe, not to mention the significant differences exhibited
by different countries. So we must dig a little more deeply and
ask whether there are inherent reasons for supposing that, as far
as the developed countries are concerned, growth in the coming
decades will be less than it was in the twenty-five years after 1948.
Much of what the Club of Rome said on that subject has, quite
rightly, come in for strong criticism. Absolute growth 'limits' are

almost invariably suspect. To postulate them is to underrate man's adaptability and, above all, imagination. To assume therefore that everything in the garden is lovely, however, would be misguided. There are indeed intimately connected, endemic reasons for thinking that growth in the remainder of this century will be more difficult.

For a start, many major companies have expanded to giant size. The result of past growth, this is also an obstacle to future growth, for capital spending is now of an order which only a few can still afford. Feelings of doubt, even of satiety ('Sufficient unto the day . . .'), offer little investment incentive either. And the aura of uncertainty all this creates is aggravated by government bungling and, of course, by inflation. Investment lethargy, however, is not without repercussions. If the state of the game ceases to be one where every player always wins at least something, then timidity sets in; timidity leads to introversion and, in the economic arena, a heightened craving for protectionism, while protectionism, the hallmark of the siege economy, in turn acts as a further growth impediment – a vicious circle if ever there was one.

This is, of course, to ignore a number of other factors, such as the extent to which the world economy has become an integral whole, or the fact that growing unemployment in part stems from causes, perhaps symptomatic of a society where the established work ethic is being transmuted, which have little or nothing to do with the growth environment. Suffice it to reiterate the apparently amply justified contention that, at least for the old industrialized countries, that environment has become, and in the foreseeable future is likely to remain, less propitious. What, then, are we to do?

Those who consider the present malaise to be of a long-term and intractable ('structural') nature will answer that question by calling for a fundamental change ('U-turn') in economic policy, particularly with regard to mental attitudes. They will argue that we must get used to making do with what we have, and perhaps even be content with less; that the meaning of work and worth ought to be reappraised; and that a sense of community ('solidarity') should take the place of the outworn creed of each man for himself. We must, in short, cultivate new life-cycles of cooperation and mutual help and, instead of worshipping at the altar of size, learn to appreciate that small is beautiful.

A brief, but not wilfully disrespectful, reference to this alternative strategy is all the more necessary in a book where it finds no mention elsewhere. Of course, there is about it a touch of romanticism, though not always necessarily to the degree exhibited by Ed Mishan.[7] Fred Hirsch, for example, has justified the need for a new social ethic on strictly economic grounds.[8] Of course, the alternative strategy overlooks much of what economic growth is all about, though Johano Strasser, for instance, has coupled it with a new theory about social policy and the welfare state.[9] More difficult is the question whether the alternative economy may not really be more about a new kind of humanism, such as expressly championed by Aurelio Peccei,[10] than about a new kind of politics. That Erhard Eppler concludes his *Ways Out of Danger* by 'endeavouring, after years of having allowed himself to be provoked and needled, to escape from some of the constraints of political non-commitment'[11] cannot be entirely fortuitous. But what the alternative economists come to terms with least of all is the fact that, if the alternative life-style they seek at home is to be combined with massive aid for the poorest of the world's poor, there are things in the world environment which cannot simply be swept under the carpet.

The academic debate about the new economic pessimism need not be pursued here at great length.[12] Suffice it merely to point out that the alternative strategy outlined above has numerous adherents in OECD countries, particularly among the young, and that between it and the conventional political wisdom there are few points of contact. Practitioners of that wisdom deliberately avoid, indeed pooh-pooh, profound economic analysis. They stick to the surface of the possible, without worrying whether the possible bears any proper relationship to the needful. They do what they can irrespective of whether or not it fills the bill. The problems of the seventies having reduced many to utter helplessness, moreover, the air is rife with patent cures, among which two are uppermost.

Proponents of the first of these scarcely break new ground, following as they usually do in the footsteps of Keynes (though they may be quite wrong in thinking so because – who knows? – Keynes, were he alive today, might well be a monetarist!). A favourite of the Left, theirs is a position which, through budgetary and fiscal measures, combines Keynesian demand management with a number of other forms of government intervention, notably government direction of investment and various (direct or fiscal) methods of job-creation. Confidence in more, perhaps better, government is the key throughout.

Advocates of the second type of patent cure follow the opposite course of calling for the role of government to be lessened. Its most primitive version, labelled monetarist, prescribes stringent control of the money supply in order first to conquer inflation and then, it is hoped, to create a favourable investment climate for renewed growth. A more sophisticated version, called supply-side economies, combines control of the money supply with vigorous pruning of government activity through reduction of the public sector and, above all, with tax cuts to boost savings – all in the interest of increased investment and hence renewed growth.

Oddly enough, the swings of the political pendulum to which reference was made at the outset have produced a situation where both remedies are being clinically tested – the first in France, the second in its primitive version in Britain and in its more sophisticated guise in the United States – at one and the same time. In Britain, however, much of the pure water of monetarist doctrine has already been adulterated, the Conservative Government having discovered a need both to prop up state-owned industries and to lend its own shoulder to the job-creation wheel. In France, pure Keynesianism laced with socialism runs the gauntlet of recrudescent inflation. And were supply-side economics to work rather better in America than in Europe, this could be due more to something approaching a confidence-trick, or to a rejuvenation of what de Tocqueville called the American tradition of self-help, than to the theory's rectitude. Anyhow, pure theories, however well-founded, butter few political parsnips. Maybe the strongest countries are those which accommodate different theories in their institutions – e.g., by institutionalizing the government/central-bank conflict. But they too are vulnerable, the new socio-economic climate's miasma being proof even against the best pragmatic mixture of present-day medicines. For a time – which for many is a long time – the world may continue to muddle through. But doubts remain. Nor will this book be able to erase the big question-mark which, in the eighties of the twentieth century, hangs over economic policies of every description.

Europe's role

Gaston Thorn, in his preface, makes an important point by arguing that the European countries' economic problems, though national, are soluble only at a European level. But though – or perhaps because – this is the guiding theme of a book devoted, not without good cause, to Europe's economies, its strictly European scenario needs also to be placed in a wider perspective.

The OECD countries continue to be the world's economic driving force, the only others who, in the past decade, could have claimed a share of that role being the countries of OPEC. The Comecon nations trail hopelessly far behind, besides being dependent on the OECD countries not just (as in the case of the Soviet Union) for such things as imported American grain, but also in a more general sense, inasmuch as the American dollar is still the Comecon's sole convertible currency, all efforts to replace it with the rouble so far having failed. They have also suffered more than their OECD and OPEC counterparts from the currency fluctuations of the past ten years, while their contribution to world business activity is minimal.

The same goes for the non-oil developing countries (the Group of 77), at least for those without natural resources of their own, who are the real victims of the two oil price explosions, besides suffering from the world's changed socio-economic climate in other respects. As their poverty increases, the rich countries' willingness to aid them diminishes. Protectionism usually hits the weakest first. While for the European Community to ban imports of handwoven cotton goods from India may have been a bagatelle, a lot of Indians paid for it with their life.

The OPEC countries, meanwhile, though close to the Group of 77, are not part of it. Heading the world league table of per capita income, many of them are at once rich and under-developed. And though they do aid the poor developing countries here and there, joining the Club of the Rich seems, on the whole, to be their supreme objective. Anyhow, riches and largesse in their case do not go hand in hand.

Returning to the countries of the OECD, they have at least three separate components – Europe, the United States and Japan; with Canada, Australia and New Zealand showing, in this subdivision, a rather closer proximity to Europe than to the other two. The triangle of economic superpowers, holding the future of the international economic order in its hands, is nevertheless rather shaky, with each corner of the triangle, moreover, having its own identity problems.

The United States, when it abolished the dollar's convertibility into gold on 15 August 1971, took a step whose consequences are only now fully apparent. Necessary or not, that step marked the end of the Bretton Woods monetary system, born in the closing stages of World War II, which had ruled during the fifties and sixties when world currency stability ultimately depended on the dollar. For this, of course, the United States paid a price – in the form of big balance-of-payments deficits – but the rest of the world benefited. Since 1971, the old order has been replaced by the floating-exchange-rates system, with all the gyrations and uncertainties this involves. More important, the US and the other OECD countries have tended to grow apart, if perhaps less in the currency field where the dollar's position as the world's most important reserve as well as transaction currency has not weakened greatly, than in the sphere of trade, which for the US has never been so important as it is for the OECD triangle's two other corners.

This tendency has gathered further pace under the Reagan Administration, whose economic policy is primarily aimed at putting its own house in order, whereafter all else will, so it is claimed, follow of its own accord. Hence the (for monetary reasons) high, and to European currencies most unsettling, level of US interest rates. Hence, too, a certain disinterestedness in

13

economic co-operation. Small wonder that the other OECD countries, resentful of power without responsibility, have been anxious to recall the US to a greater awareness of where its true interest lies.

In that campaign, Japan, whose economic success in harnessing her traditional culture to the chariot of modern science and technology has been quite outstanding, is something of a stumbling block. Though she herself, a stranger to freedom of the individual, is paying a heavy social price, her success is nevertheless the envy of many, in the United States as well as Europe, who are calling for imitation of her example and for import restrictions on her manufactures in one and the same breath. Turned into the scapegoat of a fear-ridden world, Japan could thus inadvertently become the catalyst of a protectionist tendency she is the least capable of shrugging off lightly.

Hence the first item on the international agenda must be the creation of a new currency and trade system appropriate to the conditions of this decade and conducive to economic progress in the next. That, of course, is easily said, and indeed has already figured on the agenda for quite a while. Nevertheless, the common interest of all sections of the world community in firm rules of the world economic game cannot be stressed sufficiently often. Nothing is more important, and nothing therefore more deserving of the wholehearted attention and energy of the world's potentates and those who advise them.

An agenda by itself, however, solves nothing. The OECD triangle being as rickety as it is, Europe therefore, at least for the time being, has an important part to play. It could become a model for things that one day will be applied worldwide. This book does not mistakenly identify 'Europe' with the 'European Community'; Switzerland and Austria, together with Spain and Sweden figure in it no less than do the EEC member states. Still, the European Community does have a pacemaker function whose job, as the spearhead of European integration, must be to try and inject some stability into an otherwise unstable world.

Take the Common Market, which neither is nor should be an end in itself. The European Economic Community during the Kennedy Round, like the plain European Community during the

Tokyo Round, demonstrated that it takes attempts to create worldwide conditions of unrestricted trade seriously. Today, preservation of the Common Market itself has become more difficult. Or take the European Monetary System, which is no monetary union, but which for all its fits and starts (and subsequent re-starts) does represent an attempt to create within Europe, through systematic co-operation, a zone of currency stability. It is at least a European contribution towards the solution of one of the major, unsolved, world economic problems.

So much then for the wider context of a book discussing part of a part of the world economy, whose larger part – the OECD countries – still calls the tune for the rest, but whose smaller part – Europe – has, unlike either the United States or Japan, the chance to pioneer and propagate the makings of a new world economic order, whether in the field of currencies and trade, in establishing meaningful relations with primary producing countries, OPEC included, or (not least) in developing a responsible North–South dialogue combining respect for the individuality of other cultures with effective aid to the inhabitants of other continents.

The structure of this book

To end this Introduction on a note of euphoria, however, would be misleading. The book's subject-matter, as indicated by its title, is Europe; its Preface is contributed by the President of the Commission of the European Communities (to give him his full title); the other, lengthier contributions will again and again be found to refer to the European Communities and likewise to Europe. But each of those contributions deals with, and its author stems from, one country or one closely related group of countries, so that it is scarcely surprising if the title's (and this Introduction's) wider perspective disappears from view as soon as the first few sentences of the first contribution heave into it. All at once, each country is a special case.

Well, so it is. National economies, for all their interdependence, are still far from becoming an empty phrase. Political frontiers are also economic frontiers. In addition, they are – and may they long remain – cultural ones. Readers, in their perusal of the various contributions, may savour the differences in style no less than in content. The charm of such differences is, of course, the essential spice of a symposium.

The batting order is, as usual, non-alphabetical. It is headed by the four European heavyweights, parading as 'driving forces' or 'locomotives', brakes or even bogymen, whether they admit those titles or not. The opener therefore, and also because much in his figures is of comparative interest for those who follow, is West Germany's Otmar Emminger. Those figures, incidentally, are usefully supplemented with others by Britain's Samuel Brittan, and also of course by the general statistical tables at the end of the book (pages 265–6). The European Community's contribution provides the hinge between the first part and the third, which proceeds to highlight the many special features of the smaller states and concludes with some splendid hitting all round the wicket, including a number of sixes straight out of the ground, by Holland's Jan Tinbergen.

An omnibus volume, of course, needs to be spiced with rather more than diversity, however charming, if it is not to constitute a mere ragbag of unconnected bits and pieces. So, insofar as the individual contributions permit, an attempt to analyse where they differ and what they have in common is made in a concluding summary, which takes up the European theme once again. Europe's diversity, in the cultural sphere a source of strength, is its weak spot in the economic field. Reading this book, it is hard to avoid the impression that Europe is passing through a period of weakness. Yet at the end we shall try to discover on the horizon of national egoism the silver lining of readiness for co-operation.

Notes

1 James E. Alt, *The Politics of Economic Decline* (Cambridge University Press, Cambridge, 1979).
2 *Ibid.*, p. 157.

3 *Ibid.*, p. 270.
4 S. Huntington, 'The United States', in *The Crisis of Democracy* (New York University Press, New York, 1975).
5 W.W. Rostow, *The World Economy – History and Prospects* (Macmillan, London, 1978).
6 *Ibid.*, Chapter 19, pp. 299 ff.
7 E. Mishan, *The Economic Growth Debate* (Allen & Unwin, London, 1977).
8 F. Hirsch, *The Social Limits to Growth* (Routledge & Kegan Paul, London, 1977).
9 J. Strasser, *Grenzen des Sozialstaats?* (Europäische Verlagsanstalt, London, 1979).
10 A. Peccei, *Die Qualität der Menschen* (Deutsche Verlags-Anstalt, Stuttgart, 1977).
11 E. Eppler, *Wege aus der Gefahr* (Rowohlt, Hamburg, 1981), p. 240.
12 cf. W. Beckerman, *In Defence of Economic Growth* (Jonathan Cape, London, 1974).

Part II
The big countries of Europe in search of solutions

2 West Germany: Europe's driving force?

Otmar Emminger

'Model Germany'

Only a few years ago, West German politicians paraded the 'Model Germany' banner to an accompanying chorus of foreign admirers impressed by West Germany's political and economic stability, her social consensus and her strong trade balance and currency. Britain's Prime Minister Mrs Thatcher in 1979 and 1980 more than once held up West Germany as an example; leading French politicians felt increasingly irked by references to West Germany's economic lead; and the US *Time* magazine, as late as April 1980, still hailed the country as 'the world's most successful capitalist society'. This is a testimony to the durability of received ideas; for by that time, as had long before dawned on the experts, that title had been well and truly captured by the Land of the Rising Sun.

As 1980 went on and the mark's weakness on the world's foreign exchanges was hitting the headlines, international opinion changed with a vengeance. When at the start of 1981 the dollar began to climb above the DM2 level, compared with DM1.71 twelve months before, and the mark, temporarily the weakest currency within the European Monetary System, actually had to be propped up by the French franc for a time, Germany's shining model finally lost its lustre. 'The German miracle is just a myth, no longer a reality,' the US business journal *Forbes* noted. 'L'Allemagne en panne,' announced, with ill-concealed glee, the French news magazine *Nouveau Journal* under banner headlines. Whereas at the Bonn economic summit in 1978 West Germany had still been pressurized into assuming, through increased deficit spending, the role of the world economy's locomotive, two years later her currency was such a sorry sight that there was even occasional talk of an international rescue operation being mounted on its behalf.

Just as West Germany's strength had earlier been exaggerated out of all proportion, so, when the tables were turned, was her weakness. In January 1980 (roughly, the turn of the tide) the *Financial Times* still saluted 'a currency whose persistent rise in value and attraction as a reserve currency seems to mirror West Germany's own growing role in the world. ... The process seems bound to continue.' Only eight months later, 'the fall of the mark', declared the French magazine *L'Expansion*, 'signals the end of an era.'

Does West Germany's sudden fall from grace, from a position of persistent surplus to the western world's biggest deficit country almost overnight, represent just a hiccup? Or does it reflect something deeper? Since the economy had been widely regarded as 'Europe's driving force' in the past,[1] the answer to that question is also of crucial economic importance from a European point of view.

Certainly, the days when West Germany could afford to be Europe's paymaster are over. As regards general economic policy, with her monetary as well as her fiscal policies subject to strong external constraints, she finds herself more in the position of a 'caboose' than a 'locomotive'.

West Germany and the European Community

To assess the extent to which West Germany can indeed be said to have been Europe's engine of growth hitherto, let us briefly examine her role within the European Community.

Her economic weight here is indicated by the fact that her share of the Community's gross national product (28 per cent in 1979) exceeds that of any other member state, with France (23 per cent) in second place; taking Western Europe as a whole, her share is nearly a quarter. For most European countries she is the biggest trading partner. Between 1958 and 1979 her imports from other EEC countries[2] expanded from 33.4 to 49.3 per cent, her exports to them from 34.5 to 48.3 per cent, of her respective total imports and exports – impressive evidence of the economic integration achieved in the first twenty years of the Community's existence.

Not least, West Germany is easily Europe's largest importer of services, particularly as far as foreign travel is concerned.[3] Foreign spending by West German tourists, which between 1970 and 1980 climbed from DM10bn to DM38bn, is easily the highest in the world – well ahead of that of the United States, whose population is three and a half times as large. European countries like Austria, Italy, Yugoslavia, Spain and Greece would be in serious balance-of-payments trouble in its absence. When such a large consumer of foreign goods and services gets into deep waters itself, the effects on others can therefore be far-reaching.

Whether West Germany was a driving force for other countries, due to her own economic dynamism, is however, less clear. In fact, her growth rate from 1960 until 1975, unlike the fifties, was no higher than the EEC average and, like her increase in productivity per worker, below that of France.[4] Thus, while West Germany's share of the EEC's GNP stayed much the same throughout (27.6 per cent in 1960, 27.4 per cent in 1975), France's rose strongly (from $19\frac{1}{2}$ to 23 per cent), so that during those fifteen years the latter was plainly, on the score of foreign trade growth as well, more deserving of the title of European leader. There were spells during which Italy, too, was not doing at all badly.

A dynamic interval, 1976-80

Since 1975, however, the picture has altered in West Germany's favour. During the five years 1976 to 1980, her GNP and productivity growth exceeded both the French and the EEC average, largely because of a near-7 per cent (not far short of the average during the golden sixties) annual real increase in investment (excluding building), though as a proportion of West Germany's

GNP fixed investment still nowhere near equalled its 1971 record. At the same time, despite an estimated loss of some 150,000 jobs as a result of the 1979–80 oil price explosion, the number employed in West Germany between 1976 and mid-1980 rose by almost one million. And yet, at least until 1978, West Germans were continually lamenting their loss of economic vigour and the failure of classical growth remedies.

During the seventies, the country also won a special position within the EEC in another important respect. Since 1973 she became a bulwark of at least 'relative' price stability. From 1970 to mid-1973 her inflation rates were roughly equal to the OECD average, but after the transition to currency floating West Germany quickly cut herself loose from the international inflation convoy. In the following seven years (to mid-1980), while consumer prices in the other EEC countries rose by an average 104 per cent, and in the US by 87 per cent, those in West Germany did so by just 39 per cent (less than 5 per cent annually) – which naturally resulted in the mark going from strength to strength, increasingly sought-after as an international investment and reserve currency.[5] Nor has the inflation differential changed very much since 1979 (see Table 1), when West Germany's balance-of-payments position took a sudden and dramatic turn for the worse.

Table 1   **Consumer prices (percentage annual increase)**

	1961–71	1972	1973	1974	1975	1978	1979	1980	1981
France	4.3	6.2	7.3	13.7	11.8	9.1	10.8	13.6	13.1
Germany	3.0	5.5	6.9	7.0	6.0	2.7	4.1	5.5	5.9
Italy	4.2	5.7	10.8	19.1	17.0	12.1	14.8	21.2	19.5
UK	4.6	7.1	9.2	16.0	24.2	8.3	13.4	18.0	11.9
EEC total[a]	4.0	6.1	8.1	12.7	12.9	7.1	9.1	12.9	11.4
Austria	3.7	6.3	7.6	9.5	8.4	3.6	3.7	6.4	6.8
Switzerland	3.8	6.7	8.7	9.8	6.7	1.1	3.6	4.0	6.5
European OECD total[a]	3.7	6.4	8.6	13.1	13.1	9.3	10.6	14.3	12.3
USA	2.8	3.3	6.2	11.0	9.1	7.7	11.3	13.5	10.4
Japan	5.8	4.5	11.7	24.5	11.8	3.8	3.6	8.0	4.9
Worldwide OECD total[a]	3.7	4.7	7.8	13.5	11.3	7.9	9.8	12.9	10.6

[a] Including others.

During the second half of the seventies, then, West Germany achieved within the EEC something of a special position. An EEC group of experts, after a two-year investigation of member states' adjustment to the first oil price explosion, noted in a report published early in 1980:

West Germany has got over the 1974/75 crisis rather better than her European partners. ... By combining a comparatively modest increase in domestic production costs and rapid redeployment of manpower with a favourable foreign trade pattern ... West Germany has held her own with the United States and Japan. ... In terms of investment growth, external balance and inflation, West Germany's economic performance since 1977 is clear evidence of the crisis having been surmounted. ... German industry's lead with regard to productivity and competitiveness has been preserved.

As late as November 1980, in its 1980-81 annual economic survey, the EEC Commission reiterated that 'Germany's competitiveness in relation both to the other EEC countries and to the rest of the world is stronger today than during the last five years'.[6]

Sudden worsening of the current account

This looks like a gross misjudgement. For by then, of course, Germany's external position had altered out of all recognition (see Table 2). Already in mid-1979 she began to run into a current-account deficit which within a year, when the big deficit previously run by Japan began to shrink, had swollen to become the world's largest.

In fact, not only did her 1980 current-account deficit of nearly DM30bn ($16bn), or roughly 2 per cent of GNP, exceed the highest ever recorded, during the slide of the dollar, by the United States (about $14bn in both 1977 and 1978); it also represented a turnround of more than DM48bn, over 3 per cent of GNP, from her own DM18½bn surplus of only two years earlier.

But why did West Germany make such heavy weather of the

Table 2 **West German balance of payments (DMbn)**

	1970	1973	1974	1975	1978	1979	1980
Current balance							
Visible trade	+15.7	+33.0	+50.8	+37.3	+41.2	+22.4	+8.9
Services	−2.7	−5.0	−7.0	−8.3	−7.4	−11.5	−14.7
Tourism	−5.4	−10.9	−12.4	−14.7	−19.0	−21.9	−25.8
Transfers	−9.8	−15.6	−16.1	−17.9	−17.4	−20.7	−24.0
Public sector	−3.7	−6.4	−7.1	−8.8	−8.8	−11.2	−13.5
Total	**+3.2**	**+12.3**	**+26.6**	**+9.9**	**+18.4**	**−9.6**	**−29.8**
Long-term capital movements							
Private sector	+1.5	+15.1	−5.4	−19.4	+0.3	+12.3	−14.5
Public sector	−2.4	−2.2	−0.9	+1.2	−3.3	−1.5	+21.7
Total	**−0.9**	**+13.0**	**−6.3**	**−18.2**	**−2.9**	**+10.8**	**+6.9**
Short-term capital transactions (incl. balancing item)	+19.7	+1.2	−22.1	+6.1	+4.3	−6.1	−4.9
Change in official reserves[a]	**+21.9**	**+26.4**	**−1.9**	**−2.2**	**+19.8**	**−5.0**	**−27.9**

[a] Excluding extraordinary items (allocation of Special Drawing Rights, year-end revaluation of official reserves).
SOURCE: Deutsche Bundesbank.

second oil price explosion when she had fairly easily weathered the first? Clearly it was not, as has been suggested,[7] because she had entered the first period with a bigger trade surplus as a cushion – the trade surpluses of 1973 and 1978 were of similar magnitude (cf. Table 2). Another reason, often cited by Chancellor Schmidt – namely exaggerated 'deficit spending' pressured upon Germany by the 1978 Bonn Summit – is a partial explanation, but not nearly the whole story.

Firstly, in 1973–74 the growth differential between West Germany and other industrial countries had been very favourable for the German trade and payments balance, because at that time she was the first industrial country to fight inflation through a restrictive monetary and fiscal policy. In 1979–80 West Germany had a higher growth rate than the other industrial countries (on average), and the misplaced pressure of the 1978 Summit only added to this differential.

Secondly, Germany's international competitiveness in 1973-74 was still unimpaired, while in 1979-80 it felt the after-effects of the mark's persistent overvaluation and of high labour costs.

Thirdly, in 1974-75 Japan and the newly industrializing countries of the Far East had not yet mounted anything like the present competitive challenge to the older industrial countries – in 1980, West Germany's biggest trade deficit was not with, for example, Saudi Arabia, her biggest oil supplier, but Japan. And, fourth, West Germany's balance of payments had undergone adverse structural changes in other directions too, as can be seen from Table 2.

In short, since the first oil price explosion both the world economic environment and West Germany's own strength have radically altered. The key factors which brought this about call for further analysis.

Debilitating factors

Dearer oil

At first sight, the greater part of West Germany's DM48bn current-account turnabout between 1978 and 1980 could have been accounted for by the doubling – from DM32bn to DM65bn – of her oil import bill. But things are not quite so simple. According to an analysis carried out by the Bundesbank (West Germany's central bank),[8] the net additional burden the 1979-80 oil price rise imposed on the current account in 1980, by comparison with 1978, was only DM16-23bn, depending on whether, in the absence of that rise, oil prices are assumed to have remained unchanged or to have increased by a 'normal' 10 per cent annually. Again, if West Germany had maintained her former share of the OPEC countries' spending on imported goods and services, the net burden on her balance of payments,

27

if not on her real income, would have been considerably less.
Hence, according to this analysis, less than half of West Germany's 1978-80 current-account deterioration is attributable to
the oil price explosion, in the absence of which her 1980 current
account would probably still have been in deficit, although to the
tune of under DM10bn.

The conclusion that oil cannot be solely, or even mainly, held
to blame is also borne out by the less severe payments deterioration suffered by some other industrial countries, whose relative
dependence on oil imports is no less than West Germany's.[9]
Thus, the current-account balances of the US and Japan, whose
oil import bills in absolute terms, as well as in relation to their
export earnings, are higher than West Germany's, did not worsen
to anything like the same extent – that of the US since 1978 has
actually shown a significant improvement in spite of the oil price
explosion.

Growth differential

In 1973, West Germany had adopted an anti-inflationary stance
well ahead of most other countries, some of whom were bent on
expansionary, indeed inflationary, courses instead – hence, despite the 1973 oil price explosion, her record 1974 trade surplus
(cf. Table 2) – whereas after 1976 the growth differential between
her and the rest of the world was reversed.

For West German exporters, the external conditions after
1978, were much more restrictive than they had been in 1974-75.
This was especially so in the UK, which had become one of
Germany's main oil suppliers, where a 2 per cent decline of real
GNP in 1980 was accompanied by a 3 per cent drop in import
volume. But there was, after 1978, also a marked change in
growth differential *vis-à-vis* the US, whose economy had already
begun to slow down in 1979 (while West Germany's then and
through the first half of 1980 was still basking in a boom) and
whose GNP and imports in 1980 both declined, while her exports,
partly thanks also to an undervalued dollar, were abnormally
buoyant ('the sleeping giant is awakening').

Moreover, just as the going was becoming more difficult for

Table 3 **Germany's and other industrial countries' growth rates (annual percentage increase (decrease) in real terms)**

	1975	1976	1977	1978	1979	1980
Gross national product						
Germany	(1.8)	5.3	2.8	3.6	4.5	1.8
Other industrial countries[a]	(2.0)	4.0	2.4	2.7	2.9	(1.0)
Gross fixed investment						
Germany	(4.2)	4.7	3.9	5.8	8.4	3.7
Other industrial countries[a]	(5.7)	2.0	2.6	1.4	2.0	(1.0)

[a] Austria, Belgium, Canada, Denmark, France, Italy, Japan, Netherlands, Norway, Sweden, Switzerland, UK, USA (weighted according to their importance for German exports).
SOURCE: 1975–79 Ifo Institute, Munich (1980 partly estimated).

West Germany's exporters, so her own imports of foreign goods and services were being boosted by the faster real growth of Germany's domestic demand.

Weakened competitiveness

The rapid growth of imports – especially of finished manufactures, which in 1980 accounted for more than half of West Germany's imports – was only to be expected in view of the country's growing economic integration with the rest of the world. What is disturbing is that since 1974, and especially since 1977, imports of goods and services as a proportion of GNP have, unlike previously, been rising faster than exports,[10] at a time when, in order to compensate for the much bigger increase in import than export prices, the reverse should have been the case.

The reasons for the disproportionate import growth are, first, the changed growth differential between West Germany and other industrial countries (cf. Table 3); secondly, increased competition from Japan and the newly industrialized low-cost countries of the Far East (i.e., a change in the world's economic structure); and, thirdly, a general weakening of West Germany's competitive position, as a result partly of the mark's persistent

29

over-valuation in the wake of the 1977–78 slide of the dollar, and partly of excessive wage and other labour costs.

This is also, on the export side, reflected in some decline since 1978 in world market share (cf. also Table 4, p. 33). In particular, her share of the rapidly growing OPEC markets, which had climbed from 13.3 per cent in 1972–73 to 16 per cent in 1977, had fallen back to below 13 per cent by 1980. This was not just because West Germany was harder hit than most by the troubles in Iran, but also because she lost ground in the OPEC country with the highest purchasing power, Saudi Arabia.

Other factors

Another factor in the current-account deficit has been a steady increase, from DM5½bn in 1970 through DM19bn in 1978 to DM26bn in 1980, in her net deficit on tourism. While her national income little more than doubled over this period, spending by West German travellers abroad nearly quadrupled from DM10¼bn to close on DM38bn – a mounting passion for foreign travel which will be hard to restrain.

Again, there has been a rapid increase in net transfer payments (cf. Table 2), notably, of course, to the EEC, to whose budget West Germany and Britain are currently the only net contributors.[11]

Finally, the growth from DM4.4bn in 1973 to DM8.2bn in 1980 in her direct investment abroad, though a charge not on her current but on her capital account in the balance of payments, represents more than a once-for-all foreign-exchange outflow. Not only has it been appreciably greater than the corresponding inflow (DM2.1bn in 1980), but it has also resulted in a permanent transfer of export bases abroad.

External constraints

The West German government was rather slow to wake up to the seriousness of the country's changed external position. As late as June 1980, in reply to a parliamentary question, one of its spokesmen declared that, given the available means of financing it, 'the existing current account deficit presents no special problems in the short term'. Yet, within months, that allegedly harmless deficit was to become a millstone around the neck of German economic policy.

The deficit's size and obduracy had at first been grossly under-estimated. The financing problem was aggravated by the fact that in 1980, on top of the DM29bn current-account deficit, there was another deficit of DM14½bn on private long-term capital transactions (cf. Table 2), for which the record level of US interest rates was largely responsible. The Bundesbank, intent on keeping West German interest rates as stable as possible for domestic reasons, made up for the liquidity drain caused by the external deficit; and in September 1980 – just before another upward surge in US interest rates – it actually made a ½ per cent reduction to 9 per cent in its own 'lombard' lending rate (for loans against eligible securities). Consequently in 1980, far from the current-account deficit being financed through capital inflows as intended, there was a large net capital outflow and – after more than DM21bn of foreign borrowing by the government – an overall reduction of DM28bn in the official reserves.[12]

Obviously, though those reserves were still considerable, this process could not be allowed to continue unchecked. Accordingly, in February 1981, following further large foreign-exchange outflows, the Bundesbank called a halt, by pushing up interest rates all along the line.[13] Even then, however, they were still several percentage points below those of the US – a tribute to West Germany's lower rate of inflation.

The country's high balance-of-payments deficit had to be paid for dearly, by a twofold limitation on its economic policies. First, monetary policy more than ever before fell under the sway of United States' interest-rate movements. As long as there was a large current-account deficit to be financed by foreign bor-rowing, domestic interest rates must be kept sufficiently high both to attract funds from abroad and to prevent capital outflows. Secondly, all economic policies, in particular fiscal policy, had to be directed towards reducing the current-account deficit.

Europe's Economy in Crisis

Balance-of-payments prospects

What are the chances of West German monetary and fiscal policies' dependence on external factors being lessened?

(*1*) Starting with the oil burden, there has been some initial success with oil conservation. In 1980, despite a nearly 2 per cent rate of economic growth, consumption of petroleum products declined by 11 per cent, rather more than the 9 per cent fall registered by EEC countries as a whole. In April 1981, moreover, the government reaffirmed its faith in the price mechanism with a sharp increase in the petroleum tax. It also announced a programme for assisting investment in energy saving.

Longer-term prospects, however, are rather less encouraging. Though West Germany is currently dependent on imports for less of her primary energy requirements (60 per cent) than are France (82 per cent), Italy (83 per cent) and Japan (over 90 per cent), domestic opposition to the use of nuclear energy could result in her falling seriously behind in terms of energy costs, a contingency which is already influencing some investment planning.

(*2*) As far as the growth differential between West Germany and other industrialized countries is concerned, everything points towards a reversal of the former trend, with Germany's growth rate falling behind the average rate of the others. But here the eventual outcome will very much depend on the strength of the economic recovery in the United States.

(*3*) The other, more deep-seated or 'structural' balance-of-payments weaknesses can be repaired only through an improvement in international competitiveness and less spending on imported goods and services. This calls for perseverance in the battle against inflation, including moderation in pay settlements, which is also practically the only way to curb the rampant growth in spending on foreign travel. Here, in the continued absence of exchange controls, it will be necessary to fall back on the price mechanism (i.e., higher inflation abroad no longer offset by a rising deutschmark exchange rate), making foreign travel more expensive. Since foreign travelling ranks so high in the West Germans' list of priorities, however, striking results are not to be expected, calling for correspondingly higher trade surpluses to bridge the gap.

The same goes for the changes in world economic structure primarily brought about by the advance of Japan and the newly industrializing countries of the Far East (see Table 4). In important fields like cameras, optical instruments, many electronic products, cars and, more recently, also in industrial plant and machinery, where West Germany had figured as the world's leading exporter in the past, she has been hit by Japan's triumphant progress rather harder than most other industrial countries.

Table 4 **Shares of total exports of manufactured goods by countries of the Group of Ten and Switzerland (percentage of total)**

	1960	*1970*	*1974*	*1978*	*1979*	*1980*	*1981*[a]
West Germany	19.3	19.8	21.7	20.7	20.7	19.8	18.2
United States	21.6	18.5	17.2	19.1	15.9	16.9	18.6
Japan	6.9	11.7	14.5	15.6	13.6	14.8	18.0
France	9.7	8.7	9.3	9.8	10.4	10.0	9.2
United Kingdom	16.3	10.8	8.8	9.5	9.7	10.2	9.0
Italy	5.1	7.2	6.7	7.9	8.4	7.8	6.7
Others[b]	21.0	23.3	21.8	21.4	21.3	20.5	20.4
Total	**100.0**	**100.0**	**100.0**	**100.0**	**100.0**	**100.0**	**100.0**

[a] Canada, Belgium–Luxemburg, Sweden, Switzerland.
[b] First quarter.
SOURCE: *Economic Review*, National Institute of Economic and Social Research, London.

Recent exchange-rate distortions have played some part in this. Thus, from the spring of 1979 until well into 1980, the Japanese yen – which against the mark fell at times by up to 31 per cent below the third-quarter 1978 level – was grossly undervalued.[14] Following the yen's subsequent recovery, this situation has been partially, if not entirely (having regard to Japan's declining unit labour costs and other structural factors), rectified. Those who look to a full adjustment of this distortion by a further appreciation of the yen, however, may well be disappointed, as Japan's large oil import needs and the interest-rate differential relative to the US weigh heavily on Japan's exchange rate.

So far West Germany, unlike (say) Britain, France and Italy, has ruled out import restrictions on Japanese products – rightly so because, as still the world's largest exporter of manufactured goods,[15] she cannot simply retreat into a defensive posture but must face the Japanese challenge head on. For this, the two countries' relative unit labour costs must, of course, be adjusted to their relative export competitiveness. The mark's 1980–81 depreciation not only against the yen but also the dollar, the currencies of her two principal trading rivals (cf. Table 5), may have done something to redress the balance. But lasting success in the competitive battle demands that the resulting imported inflation be kept to a minimum, through continuing firm measures of domestic price and cost stabilization. The prospects on that score were, at the time of writing, not bad.

Table 5   **Exchange rate indices**[a] (1st qtr 1972 = 100)

Nominal rates	1973	1977	1979	4th qtr 1980	2nd qtr 1981
Deutschmark	111.3	138.2	155.2	150.1	144.5
US dollar	91.3	96.2	84.6	85.3	94.7
French franc	104.9	98.9	98.4	96.3	90.5
Sterling	85.5	61.9	66.7	77.5	75.2
Italian lira	90.6	59.9	54.6	50.6	46.3
Japanese yen	106.4	112.5	127.3	133.0	138.7
Real rates[b]					
Deutschmark	108.9	105.8	108.5	96.9	92.9
US dollar	88.0	95.3	89.1	93.0	109.3
French franc	101.7	93.0	99.0	101.9	96.9
Sterling	85.8	88.8	104.5	127.6	123.3
Italian lira	96.6	99.6	99.9	101.4	98.6
Japanese yen	113.3	107.6	107.6	114.5	102.0

[a] Trade-weighted (against 17 industrial countries).
[b] Effective rates adjusted for average inflation differential on wholesale prices for industrial products (= index of competitiveness in terms of industrial product prices).
SOURCE: EEC Commission.

In the summer of 1981, the mark's real (inflation-adjusted) value was actually well below its 1972 (i.e., pre-floating) level. Continuation of this trend, hardly justified on competitive grounds, would make for a downright undervaluation, and hence heighten inflation and further structural distortions, and so do more harm than good.

To sum up: barring another oil price shock in the near future, there are good grounds for expecting an improvement in West Germany's balance-of-payments position – an incipient reversal of the growth differential, the mark's exchange-rate adjustment against the dollar and the yen, and the chance of maintaining an (albeit reduced) inflation differential in West Germany's favour.

Is the West German 'economic miracle' over?

In 1981, with a still massive current-account deficit, the highest unemployment since the 1950s and an inflation rate fuelled by the external weakness of the mark, the West German economy had to face a dual need for adjustment. On the one hand, its domestic income and cost levels had to be adjusted to the reality of a trebled oil price and other external structural burdens. On the other hand, its manufacturing base had to be restructured to provide the bigger trade surplus that this situation called for. How is it measuring up to that dual challenge?

Adjustment of domestic demand

The task of adjusting real incomes to the worsened terms of trade had, until the middle of 1981, largely been shelved. By financing its current-account deficit out of its reserves and through foreign borrowing, the country and, not least, the government had been living beyond their means. The rise in both real incomes and the welfare state in the preceding years had clearly exceeded the available means.

Leaving most of the adjustment to be effected by a reduction in business activity would be a counsel of despair. A better way has been shown by the Japanese, whose labour unions in 1980 deliberately accepted a slight reduction in real incomes at a time

35

when real GNP was expected to grow by almost 5 per cent, with the extra output used not to boost consumption but to pay for the increased oil import bill and partly also to expand investment.

Now, under rather less auspicious circumstances, West Germany has little choice but to follow suit. The extent of the sacrifice required, however, should not be exaggerated. Reducing real incomes to their 1978 level is probably all that is needed, though admittedly this does confront all concerned with a severe test in self-discipline.

The 1981 pay round showed just how difficult it is, even with the country's continuing social consensus, to divide a cake that is no longer growing. But although the agreed $4\frac{1}{2}$–$5\frac{1}{2}$ per cent pay settlements did allow for some possible reduction in real incomes for the first time in West Germany's postwar history, they were still rather higher than was consistent with improving her competitive position, especially *vis-à-vis* Japan, and with maintaining employment. With productivity stagnant for some time past and, in some sectors, actually declining,[16] the acute pressure on company profits was thus not relieved as much as it should have been in the interest of investment and employment.

The government sector has had even more difficulty in adjusting to the new situation. Formerly, there had been a consensus (also between the government and the central bank) that the net public-sector deficit should average no more than 2 per cent of Gross National Product over the business cycle, implying a lower figure in good years. The chief mistake was to let the net public-sector deficit rise to nearly 3 per cent of GNP in the boom year 1979 – which doubtless owed something to the measures taken under the pressure of the 1978 economic summit in the name of the unfortunate 'locomotive theory'. In the meantime the net public-sector deficit has risen in 1981 to about $4\frac{1}{2}$ per cent of GNP, thus considerably exceeding the relative size of the public-sector deficits of countries like the US and France (cf. Table 7).

It was only very late that it was recognized that the size of the public-sector deficit had something to do with the current-account deficit. Many politicians also failed to recognize that West Germany had begun to suffer from a clear deficit in domestic capital formation since 1979, a deficit which equalled the current-account deficit.

Table 6 **Uses and sources of domestic savings (DMbn)**

	1977	*1978*	*1979*	*1980*
Uses (net financing requirement)				
Public sector[a]	31	35	40	51
Companies (excl. housing)	20	0	30	43
Housing	35	47	58	59
Total	**86**	**82**	**128**	**153**
Sources (net savings)[b]				
Personal sector	85	88	101	109
Financial sector[c]	9	12	16	15
Total	**94**	**100**	**117**	**124**
Surplus/(Deficit)[d]	8	18	(11)	(29)

[a] Federal, state and local governments and National Insurance Fund.
[b] Saving less borrowing.
[c] Banks, building societies, insurance companies and pension funds.
[d] Tantamount to current-account surplus (deficit).
SOURCE: Deutsche Bundesbank.

While net savings were only rising slowly, the private sector's financial deficit was, particularly in 1980, growing at an accelerating pace – in housing because of increased building activity and inflationary price rises, elsewhere because mounting labour and raw material costs in 1980 led to a reduction in industry's cash flow. But the PSBR, far from making room for this increased borrowing need of the private sector, further added to the borrowing pressure – though part of it (DM21bn alone in 1980) has been funded abroad – and, unless reduced, could seriously crowd out private-sector borrowers.

An excessive public-sector deficit is, like an overblown public sector generally, an unquestionably weak spot in West Germany's economic armour. The size of the public sector reflects partly the growth of bureaucracy,[17] partly the escalation of the welfare state. Taxes and social insurance contributions between 1960 and 1980 rose from 32 to 39 per cent, social insurance contributions alone from 9 to 14 per cent of GNP. State expenditure (including social expenditure) has risen from 38 per cent in 1970 to $47\frac{1}{2}$ per cent of GNP in 1980.

37

Though the relative tax burden at 39 per cent is roughly on a par with the EEC average, this proportion is far higher than that of the US (about 30 per cent) and Japan (24 per cent), West Germany's principal competitors, showing that the welfare state has become too large.[18] This has not only unduly increased the tax burden, but worse, it has encouraged excessive expectations all round and reduced the willingness to work.

Competitiveness

Contrary to the EEC Commission's findings of November 1980, West Germany's international competitiveness at the end of the seventies was clearly weakened. Her exporters had been losing foreign market shares since 1978; greater still had been her market-share loss to foreign competitors at home. The mark's over-valuation as a result of the weakness of the dollar, excessive increases in West German labour costs and the growing challenge by Japan and the newly industrializing countries, were responsible for both.

For one thing, the country had suffered a disproportionate increase in supplementary labour costs (social charges and fringe benefits).[19] In 1980 they represented about 75 per cent of basic pay, compared with 39 per cent in the US and 26 per cent in Japan. For another, there had been a steady reduction in man-hours worked,[20] due among other things to the increasing length of paid holidays – a factor which also helps to explain the Germans' inordinately increased foreign *wanderlust* and its mounting cost in foreign exchange.

The second oil price explosion, the competitive onslaught from the Far East and the other catalysts of West Germany's current-account deficit have finally shattered the fond illusion, fostered all too long while the going was good, that shorter working hours, sickness on full pay and all other fringe benefits large and small could be afforded on top of a steady rise in real earnings. The truth now being brought home is that the price of all this, including the insatiable yen for far distant places, is a slower rise, if not a temporary real reduction, in incomes. There are, in short, no free lunches.

In purging past excesses and restoring the competitive balance, the mark's fall from grace (cf. Table 5) has lent a helping hand – but here again there is no painless cure. A weaker mark means higher imported inflation. If this were to permeate the whole spectrum of domestic costs and prices, it would soon cancel out the previous benefit for external competitiveness. Thus the exchange-rate weapon will work only if it is backed by stringent measures of monetary and fiscal restraint.

Industrial restructuring

Meanwhile, the process of adjusting West Germany's industrial structure to the energy price rise is already under way. The fillip this is giving to capital investment has helped to sustain business activity at a rather higher level than would have been the case otherwise – though, since all that this energy-minded investment is doing is to save or substitute energy that had been less costly before, it is not adding to the size of the cake to be shared out. Given the enormous scale of the extra energy-related capital expenditure likely to be required in the future,[21] other (public-sector, house-building, etc) borrowing requirements will have to accommodate themselves to this new situation if financial markets are not to be dangerously overloaded.

In addition, of course, West German industry will also have to gear itself up to earn the higher export surpluses needed both to pay for the country's increased oil import bill and to offset its large deficits on invisibles like tourism and official transfers, as well as to compensate for the fact that its financial sector has grown into a 'structural' net exporter of capital (foreign direct investment, long-term lending) for which the necessary foreign exchange needs likewise to be earned. Needless to say, a country thus forced to run a big surplus on its merchandise trade needs to accord a higher importance to its manufacturing industry, by whom that surplus must be generated in the main, than a country like (say) the United States or Italy which can afford to run a big trade deficit thanks to their traditionally large surplus on services. In fact, manufacturing industry's contribution to GNP is far higher in West Germany (39 per cent) than in France and the US (about 30 per cent) or the EEC average (31 per cent).

Despite the investment boom of the years 1976 to 1980, the level of industrialization as measured by this yardstick has declined from the peak it had reached in the early seventies. Since 1973 there has been a widespread fear that West Germany's economy is subject to a process of de-industrialization. Although fixed investment as a proportion of GNP is rather higher in West Germany than in any other major industrialized country except Japan, a steadily diminishing proportion of it has been going into manufacturing industry, a steadily growing one into the private services sector. Also, partly because more has had to be devoted to anti-pollution measures, capital productivity input has declined. Thus the manufacturing sector's annual growth potential, which at the start of the seventies had been 3 per cent and over in real terms, has more recently been running at $1-1\frac{1}{2}$ per cent only, whereas in other sectors of the economy it has recovered to rather more than 3 per cent.

Consequently, West Germany's export base has ceased to grow as fast as it should. Quite a measurable slice of it, moreover, has itself been 'exported' through the transfer of West German manufacturing operations abroad. If there is to be a lasting, and not just a temporary (cyclical), improvement in her balance-of-payments position, this process needs to be reversed. In order to encourage a greater volume of investment, her economic policy-makers, too, must lend a shoulder to the re-industrialization wheel in every possible way (tax policy, energy policy, etc) – a task which has been aptly compared by economics minister Count Otto von Lambsdorff to Germany's postwar reconstruction. The case for supply-side economics—of a different kind than that of the United States—is nowhere stronger than in West Germany.

Outlook

Early in 1981, there certainly was cause for genuine concern. But only later developments can show whether the widespread conviction that this is the worst slump of the postwar era, is justified. Sometimes one had the feeling that the thirty-year-old Federal Republic had fallen a prey to the pessimism of old age. True, there exist major political as well as economic problems. But the main causes for concern lie more in the social field, although with potential negative consequences in the economic field. They are: the corrupting effect of over-rapidly growing affluence and a welfare state run riot; a consequent tendency for people to think in terms of ever-increasing 'entitlements'; a reduced willingness, particularly among the young, to do a hard day's work; and a growing distrust of scientific and technological progress.

A large public sector and a chronically high public-sector borrowing requirement, absorbing an excessive proportion of the country's savings and thus at once encouraging the country to live beyond its means and making it harder to contain inflation, are other signs of weakness. So is the spectacle of a widespread shortage of labour, and not just of skilled workers only, alongside a stubbornly high (welfare-induced?) level of unemployment. Moreover, in several fields, the technological lead West Germany used to command has, particularly with respect to Japan, been whittled away. Her educational system, too, leaves much to be desired.

And yet the German economy has continuing strengths which should not be underestimated: she still has the edge over any other major industrial country save Japan on the score of inflation, with a majority of her people remaining firmly convinced that growth and prosperity are best secured by price stability; she still also, despite some recent difficulties, enjoys a rather greater degree of social consensus than many other countries; the composition of her export trade, with its high proportion of capital goods, is a favourable one – albeit vulnerable to the Japanese challenge; also favourable, with its widely diversified product range and large number of small and medium-sized businesses, is her corporate structure, except for a 'structural' shortage of equity capital; her innovative capacity, lately manifested in the area of energy-saving products and processes, is of a high order; lastly, the key economic role played by private entrepreneurs is widely, perhaps increasingly, respected.

Table 7 The German economy compared to others (% annual changes)

	Consumer prices		Real GDP growth		Unemployment rate (%)		PSBR as % of GNP	Current account balance ($bn)		Productivity	
	1975–9	1980	1975–9	1980	1975–9	1980	1980	1975–9	1980	1975–9	1980
Germany	4.1	5.5	2.9[a]	1.8	3.8	3.3	3.4	16.4	−16.2	3.4	0.9
France	10.1	13.5	3.1	1.2	5.0	6.5	0.7[b]	−4.0	−7.4	2.9	0.9
GB	15.5	18.0	1.5[a]	−1.8	4.8	6.3	3.2[b]	−7.9	6.5	1.5	0.7
Italy	15.5	21.2	2.3	4.0	4.4	5.3	8.3[b]	10.3	−9.9	1.5	2.5
USA	8.0	13.5	3.5[a]	−0.2	7.1	7.2	1.0[b]	−6.4	3.7	1.0	−0.5
Japan	7.3	8.0	4.7[a]	4.2	2.1	2.0	4.5[b]	21.6	−10.8	3.8	3.2

[a] GNP.
[b] OECD estimate, December 1980.

Basically, then, West Germany's economic constitution – some disturbing social tendencies, particularly in the younger generation, notwithstanding – is still eminently sound. At the same time, there are a number of respects – labour-market rigidity, excessive budget deficits, an overblown welfare state and a diminishing willingness to work – in which she has actually become something of a warning example.

Above all, the days when West Germany acted as a driving force for the European economy are, for some years to come, almost certainly over. Due to her large current-account deficit, she will have to depend on export-led growth, and thus her growth will for a time have to trail behind the rest of the convoy. The role of pacemaker for Europe, no less than for the rest of the world, thus falls even more than before to the United States; and immediate growth prospects there seem rather less rosy than the Reagan Administration's predictions would have led us to believe. Whether North Sea oil could eventually qualify Britain for a similar role as pacemaker is a question others must be left to answer. West Germany, unable to indulge in another import-spending spree on the 1978–80 scale, will have to get down to a far-reaching restructuring of her economy in a more export-oriented direction if she is to get back into her proper stride.

The prospects for West Germany to play a dynamic European role are thus not bright in the immediate future. For all that, it is clearly in the interests of the other European countries that the country which is, after all, still their most important and relatively most stable economic partner should recover its external – and hence also internal – poise with the least possible delay.

Notes

1 'The West German economy was the driving force of this wealth- and welfare-building expansion in Western Europe, and whenever there was a slackening, all looked to Bonn for new steam and acceleration. West Germany has been almost constantly the object of its partners' expectations.' *International Herald Tribune*, special supplement, April 1981.
2 Including the UK and Ireland throughout.

3 West Germany's balance on services has always been in heavy structural deficit (cf. Table 2), while the US, Italy and Britain have traditionally recorded large surpluses.

4 In terms of the increase in productivity per man-hour, West Germany was still somewhat ahead of France. But a larger proportion of West Germany's than of France's productivity gain was translated into a reduction in average working hours, and so did not give rise to an increase in real measurable output, nor therefore, except perhaps indirectly by way of increased foreign travel, in foreign trade.

5 In the spring of 1981, an estimated 13 per cent (around DM80bn) of the world's official foreign-exchange reserves was held in marks.

6 The OECD report on West Germany in June 1980 had expressed a similar view.

7 Interview with Chancellor Helmut Schmidt, *Fortune*, 20 April 1981.

8 *German Bundesbank Monthly Bulletin*, April 1981, pp. 13 ff.

9 In 1979, energy represented around 20 per cent of total imports in West Germany, compared with 22 per cent in France, 29 per cent in the US and 41 per cent in Japan.

10 Imports as a proportion of real GNP: 1977 25.4 per cent, 1980 28.6 per cent; exports as a proportion of real GNP: 1977 28.6 per cent, 1980 30.2 per cent.

11 In 1980 West Germany's net contribution to the EEC amounted to DM4.1bn.

12 Apart from foreign-exchange market intervention by the Bundesbank, this amount also includes operations to similar effect by the US authorities, who required billions of marks both for repayment to the Bundesbank of short-term currency swaps and for subsequent redemption of the mark ('Carter') bonds they had previously floated on the West German capital market for support of their own currency.

13 At the end of July 1981 the yield on West German public-sector bonds averaged 11.9 per cent, compared with 9.2 per cent four months earlier.

14 Contrary to the views of many observers, this was not engineered by the Japanese authorities, who in fact financed virtually their country's entire current-account deficit by employing $18bn of foreign-currency reserves in market intervention to prevent the yen from sliding still further.

15 Since the start of 1981, in the wake of the mark's depreciation, West Germany as an exporter of manufactured goods has been (temporarily?) overtaken by the US and Japan (cf. Table 4).

16 In 1980, though productivity per man-hour worked rose by 2 per cent overall, that per worker did so by only 1 per cent, while in manufacturing industry it showed a 0.6 per cent drop.

17 Between 1960 and 1978 the number of public-service employees increased by some two million, whereas the number of employed overall remained virtually unchanged. Per head of population, the former is the highest among the EEC member states.

18 'In the field of welfare services, we have, I admit, done too much,' Count Otto Lambsdorff, German Secretary of State for Trade and Industry, during an interview in March 1981.

19 During the period 1966-80 this increase averaged almost 12 per cent an-

nually, compared with rather less than 7½ per cent for West German workers' gross earnings.

20 In 1979, compared with the average 1,784 hours put in by West German engineering workers, for example, their Swiss and Japanese counterparts worked 2,006 and 2,094 respectively.

21 For the next twenty years estimates range from DM500bn to DM600bn, depending on the assumptions on which they are based.

3 France: between reform and counter-reform

Jacques Delors

In 1981, six years after the recession of 1974-75, the European economies were still undergoing a recession in economic activity, which had its roots not only in the second oil crisis but also in mistakes in macroeconomic policy. In addition, the sudden rise in interest rates and in the dollar since the beginning of 1981 constituted the equivalent of a third oil crisis. Before examining the recession and economic imbalances in the period following the first great rise in oil prices, it is important to examine the conditions in which the crisis hit France, after a phase of exceptional, but unfortunately incomplete, economic transformation.

The events of 1973 represented a daunting ordeal for the French economy, because of insufficient modernization, although, paradoxically, France's economic structures, still partly pre-industrial, were able to some extent to mitigate and diffuse the shock of the crisis. These mitigating effects were amplified by a policy based on the mistaken belief in a short-lived recession.

Realization was all the more painful in 1976, when the new Prime Minister began to apply a brake to dangerous trends, though less so in regard to prices and foreign exchange. So a kind of liberal counter-reform began, with the two aims of adapting the French economy to the new international environment and significantly lowering the threshold of inflation. It was on this second point that the policy was to founder, particularly since the second oil crisis brought with it a new wave of inflationary expectations.

Large-scale modernization

In 1948 France's net internal production had fallen to the same level as that of 1929, and many observers put forward circumspect analyses of the country's economic backwardness. But despite these doubts the country was on the verge of a period of extraordinary metamorphosis, even though this proved to be unsystematic, partial and incomplete by 1974.

An exceptional transformation

France's growth from 1950 to 1974 appears exceptional compared to that of other western countries (Japan excepted), especially if one considers the unfavourable demographic conditions which prevailed until 1962 – output increased at a rate of more than 5 per cent a year. Compared to that of France's partners, this growth was more sustained (the growth differential was round +1.4) and, more importantly, more regular. The business cycles which could be observed in the United States or in West Germany were not evident in France.

Over a quarter of a century, France saw an unprecedented rise in its standard of living: in constant francs the net national product per head was multiplied by 2.7 and private consumption per head by 2.8.

To describe this period of profound transformation, J. Fourastié has used the expression 'the thirty glorious years'[1] in other words years of globally positive evolution in which growth (economic and demographic), mass consumption and productivity gains were to change the social and economic landscape. Table 1 records this 'invisible revolution'.

The industrial transformation of the French economy was both a direct and indirect agent of change: since it speeded up urbanization, it oriented the transformation and growth in the tertiary sector. One date stands out from this period of industrial restructuring and reallocation of resources, that of the opening-up to the outside world which was decided upon by the signing of the Treaty of Rome in 1957, and put into application eleven years later, in 1968, after a major social and cultural shock. These

Table 1 **The invisible revolution**

	1946	1975
Total population (millions)	40.5	52.6
Active population (millions)	20.5	21.8
Rate of activity (%)	51.4	41.4
Volume of production	84	464
Number of adolescents over 14 studying (thousands)	650	4,000
Distribution of the active population (%)		
primary (agriculture and fishing)	36	10
secondary (industry and building)	32	38.6
tertiary (other work)	32	51.4
Number of houses built during the 7 years preceding the census[a] (thousands)	450	4,000
Number of private cars in circulation (thousands)	1,000	15,300
Percentage of households with a fridge	3	91
Real national income per head of the population (1938 = 100)	87	315
Relative price of a fridge	100[b]	20
Relative price of electrical household fittings as a whole	100	53
Productivity index per head in capital goods industry	100	461[c]
Productivity index per head in consumer goods industry	100	483[c]

[a] War years 1940–45 excluded.

[b] Relative price of an item = $\dfrac{\text{the item's price index}}{\text{cost-of-living index}}$ (1949 = 100).

[c] 1972. (J. Fourastié, *op. cit.*, M. Basle, J. Mazier, J.F. Vidal, for the calculation of productivity indexes.)

SOURCE: J.H. Lorenzi, 'La Crise du XXème siècle', *Economica* (after J. Fourastié).

changes affected the sectoral direction of investment in production and its nature, the evolution of employment, as well as the organization of labour, and were made manifest through the concentration and increasing internationalization of capital. The introduction of the French economy into the worldwide exchange network was a historic decision in the light of the tradition of protectionism;[2] it was also a gamble which paid off, thanks to the efficiency of market mechanisms.

Inflation as a sign of confusion

The transformation of the French economy did not come about without creating imbalances. Sustained and continuous growth did not prevent the appearance of unemployment within structural and inegalitarian prosperity. Meanwhile inflation, which was accelerating throughout this period, was the most obvious sign of confusion and the central problem of macroeconomic policy.[3]

Though we cannot ignore factors linked to the rise in prices (synchronization of cyclical movements in industrial economies, international monetary crises, the cost of raw materials, etc.), inflation in France has a specific character for structural reasons. These reasons played their part in other mixed economies[4] but in some respects more deeply in France: the process of price-freezing by large firms, the maintenance of rigidities which prevented gains in productivity from being transformed into lower prices, the importance of margins in the distribution sector, and, more generally, the shackles on competitiveness. We must add to these the continual granting of concessions to certain social groups whose electoral behaviour was strategic.

Inflation in France can thus be interpreted as the means used by the socio-political system of the time to find a provisional solution to its contradictions, born of the concentration of capital, of resistance to change on the part of the middle classes, and of allowances made to the protected sector of the economy. The system resorts ultimately to inflation in response to the pressure from social groups and in particular from the workers, whose aspirations to a different sort of society became more and more pressing from 1968 onwards.

Specific socio-economic structures

The economic structures in France are more diverse than those observed in other industrialized nations. Despite a great decrease in the number of farms, France has remained more rural than its major commercial partners; more than 10 per cent of the active population is still engaged in agriculture.

The large number of mergers and restructuring operations have not affected the maintenance of an industrial network with firms of very different sizes. Though the position of small and medium-sized firms is comparable to that in Japan or Italy, it remains more important than in other western industrialized countries. These differences betray a greater continuity in French economic life.

This dual aspect helps to explain the numerical and sociological importance of non-wage-earners (20 per cent in 1974 in France, compared to less than 10 per cent in the UK or the USA).

The social structure is more inegalitarian. Though international comparisons of inequality are difficult, they all point to the same conclusion of greater social disparity in France. A report of the Centre for Studies of Prices and Incomes (CERC)[5] shows that the dispersion of wages is clearly more marked in France than in Great Britain or West Germany. The appreciation of inequality in incomes, however, is a subject for controversy. In 1976 the OECD[6] outlined the degree of inequality of incomes in France. As regards unemployment, access to education (and therefore the reproduction of inequalities), and inheritance, social disparities remain strong in France and are accumulating.[7] The households with the smallest incomes are also among those where nothing is inherited, which have uncomfortable homes, which suffer most from unemployment and from inequality as regards illness and death.

There is no doubt that rapid economic expansion and a raising of the standard of material life have brought about improvements: access for many people to a more decent level of life; the extension of social insurance for illness, retirement and unemployment; a lengthening of the education period and access – still tentative – for working-class children to higher education. Nevertheless this has not been enough to convince the French people that there is both effort and will towards greater solidarity between the social groups.

An incomplete evolution

This incompleteness is particularly noticeable as regards social relationships.

Until 1968 our system of social relationships was fairly unchanging: long periods of stagnation followed by dramatic but short-lived explosions, which produced some innovations before giving way once more to a climate of cold civil war, with limited, if any, dialogue.

The events of May 1968 achieved a breakthrough and gave rise to hope. The 1968 law finally recognized the role of trade unions in firms, but without giving them the means to conduct effective negotiations. This also explains the emphasis placed today on the necessity for more intense and organized relationships within firms.

After May 1968 it was possible to conduct regular wide-ranging two-way negotiations on the subject of contractual policies. Simultaneously, in the private sector, a series of interprofessional agreements reflected important social progress (monthly payment, permanent training schemes, etc.) and gave rise to hopes of positive results throughout the economic and social network. But things did not develop in this way and, as force of habit won the upper hand, France was once again plagued by immobility on the part of the employers' organizations and excessive trade-union preoccupation with political matters as opposed to practical needs. Apart from certain inevitable agreements, such as those on indemnity for total or partial unemployment, the very spirit of the contractual policies became etiolated, each party finding an excuse, some to do nothing, some to complain about the trade unions, some to sit back and wait for the political change which would, miraculously, solve all their problems.

The belief in a short-lived crisis

At the height of prosperity, the crisis of the 1970s arrived like a bolt out of the blue. Whatever the diagnosis of the crisis, there is general agreement that the brutal quadrupling of the price of oil in 1973 by the OPEC countries caused a very significant rupture in the growth of the developed countries. In the short term, this oil crisis had a dual effect, a 'price effect', in the form of direct increases in prices for imports and the consequent increase in production costs, and a 'revenue effect', in the form of a net transfer of revenue towards the exporting countries.

Nevertheless, without entering into the complex debate on the causes of the economic crisis, the increase in the price of oil does not provide the whole explanation for this profound and long-lasting crisis.[8] Indeed, calculations of the order of importance of consequences during this first phase converged, for all countries in the OECD, around these figures:

Increase in the oil bill	+ 1.8% of the GNP[9]
Direct deflationary effect	− 1.2% of the GNP
Effect on general price level	+ 2-3% over about 2 years.

Serious imbalances had already been evident, not the least of which was the acceleration of inflation in France from the middle of the 1960s. This had been the most significant indication of an upset in the mechanism for internal regulation, aggravated by the incapacity, even the unwillingness, of some to sort out the confusion in the international monetary system.

As P. Dubois remarks, 'the oil crisis only had such long-lasting and important visible consequences on the western economies as a whole because their health had already been undermined'.[10]

A postponed, less savage but more inflationary reversal

The effect of the oil crisis in France was delayed not only by the political situation in 1973-74[11] but also by the existence of a very diversified economic network.

The break in the evolution of economic activity was a major one: expansion was reduced by half and became highly irregular. However France, which had the benefit of a constant, positive growth differential compared to its principal partners, main-

Table 2 **The fall in output after the first oil crisis**

	A: quarter showing highest production	B: quarter showing lowest production	Fall in production from A to B (%)
USA	4th quarter 1973	2nd quarter 1975	− 14.4
Canada	1st quarter 1974	3rd quarter 1975	− 6.9
Japan	4th quarter 1973	1st quarter 1975	− 19.8
West Germany	4th quarter 1973	3rd quarter 1975	− 11.8
France	3rd quarter 1974	3rd quarter 1975	− 13.6
Great Britain	4th quarter 1973	4th quarter 1974	− 10.1
Italy	2nd quarter 1974	3rd quarter 1975	− 15.5
Netherlands	1st quarter 1974	3rd quarter 1975	− 11.7
Belgium	1st quarter 1974	3rd quarter 1975	− 17.1
Sweden	3rd quarter 1974	2nd quarter 1975	− 4.1
Switzerland	2nd quarter 1974	1st quarter 1975	− 20.3

SOURCE: *OECD Economic Perspectives, no. 19*, July 1976, p. 47.

tained this advantage (+0.9 per year, compared to +0.8 from 1963 to 1969, and +1.3 from 1969 to 1974).

Inflation, on the other hand, had nearly doubled and appeared to be inflexible (10.4 per cent on average 1973–80, against 5.8 per cent 1969–73). A higher propensity towards price increases also persisted, the differential being +1.7 in relation to the price rises in our six principal commercial partners.

Unemployment more than quadrupled[12] and reflected the combined effects of unemployment in times of prosperity (unequal and structural) and of crisis unemployment, which affected the hard core of the active population, i.e. men between 25 and 45. Crisis unemployment was also directly linked to the industrial cycle.

Finally, foreign trade was thrown out of balance and recovered only in 1978, on the eve of the second oil crisis, before declining again in 1980.

A new kind of economic mechanism?

A comparison of the present crisis with that of 1930 shows that though the setback in activity was the same, the macroeconomic chain of events worked very differently. Although the fall in production in both cases was more than 10 per cent, and although it was even more delayed[13], there is a fundamental difference in the non-cumulative nature of the reversal of autumn 1974.

After the shock of 1930, the following cumulative process had taken place: drop in production–drop in workforce–drop in salaries–drop in demand–drop in prices, and underutilization of productive capacities–collapse of profits and investment. Three things explain why this chain of events did not take place in 1974–75: a relative maintenance of international trade, a smaller fall in investment and, most of all, a substantial increase in consumption by households, which remained clearly positive. This apparent paradox between the fall in industrial output and the rise in consumption is not explained by the growth in real wages, which was comparable for the two periods studied here.

What does differ is the adjustment of the workforce to the level of activity. In 1930 unemployment began from the very beginning of the recession (-8 per cent). In 1974–75, it was limited (-2.4 per cent), both by socializing the cost of partial unemployment, by the willingness of firms to maintain their workforce for social (or political) reasons, and, finally, by the resistance of the workers, who were able to oppose redundancies. This meant that household incomes were kept up, and this was reinforced by better redundancy payments than in 1930.

One wonders whether the specific nature of the present crisis reveals a change, from a competitive approach to what some call a monopolistic one, in the regulation of industrial economies. This is the hypothesis put forward by the CEPREMAP[14] in the context of their historic studies of inflation and the crisis. The authors put forward the opposition of these two types of regulation to explain the difference between the two crises.

Competitive regulation is associated with the heyday of capitalism. It is characterized by the great sensibility of nominal prices towards fluctuation in the market; the key role of the industrial outlook (notably on the formation of wages); the speed of adjustment to a fall in output, employment and prices; and the strict constraint imposed by the gold standard in monetary matters. In this context, prices and production develop side by side[15] and one can associate inflation with expansion, recession with deflation.

Monopolistic regulation limited the cumulative effects of the rupture by expanding new institutional forms (programming of wage increases, indirect incomes, development of buying on credit, a programmed obsolescence in fixed capital, a monetary system based on an artificial rate), which imply new procedures for the formation of prices and incomes. Prices were set artificially, and their disconnection from market imbalances then supposed the existence of social procedures for validating prices and incomes.

Social and political constraints reinforce the belief in a temporary crisis

In a book written in 1933 J. Duret noted the incapacity of those responsible for the economy to deal with the consequences of Black Thursday on Wall Street in 1929: 'The acute crisis is less frightening than the chronic illness it reveals. There is no shortage of healers, but for a few serious practitioners, how many charlatans, quacks, grotesques! They want to cure the cancer in society with an elixir of youth.'[16]

One wonders whether the same judgement cannot be made in 1975-76 on the capacity of political leaders to face disruption, since social and political constraints seem to be the main factors explaining their behaviour.

Indeed, after the presidential elections of 1974 France seemed to be divided down the middle, since only a small margin separated the two candidates: Valéry Giscard d'Estaing was elected president on 15 May 1974 with 50.6 per cent of the votes, against 49.4 per cent to François Mitterand, candidate for the left.

The fear of a strong wave of union demands dominated the political debate, all the more so because the presidential election reinforced the unity of the trade-union movement. One month after the election of the new president, two of the main unions, the Confédération Générale du Travail (CGT) and the Confédération Française Démocratique du Travail (CFDT), reached an 'agreement of offensive' on the objectives, the methods and the consolidation of united action between the two headquarters. If this agreement renewed the union agreement of 1966, which had been restated in 1970, it also covered up the numerous quarrels between the CGT and the CFDT which had been particularly animated since 1973. This was a *rapprochement* both on objectives and on methods of action.

Moreover, social and trade-union life saw many conflicts (the numbers of days lost through strikes increased by nearly 20 per cent in 1975), which were often violent and of a highly political nature: Post and Telecommunications, strikes of non-qualified workers protesting against poor working conditions, but, most of all, conflicts over redundancies and the closing of firms, such as LIP at Besançon (followed by many others). Finally, the prevailing economic policy was marked by the failure in December 1973 of an explicit attempt at an incomes policy to fight inflation, the last time an effort was made to link it with contractual policy.

In this economic and social environment, the new president's problem was to try to increase his majority. The policy of stabilization which he adopted cannot be compared with those of 1963 and 1969, which under very different political and social circumstances had tackled the risks inherent in excessive demand and an exorbitant increase in money wages. For the first time since 1946, the investment of firms was denounced as being inflationary. Two fiscal measures were to deal with this directly: companies paid a sum equal to 18 per cent of the tax they had paid in 1973, and the scale for depreciation payment was modified in a way which made it less favourable for firms.

Not only did these measures penalize firms at a time when western economies were entering a long restructuring crisis, but they were also by their nature inflationary. In a period of high inflation, since depreciation is calculated on the cost price of capital expenditure, it is only by rapid depreciation that firms can avoid losing money. If the opposite happens, the firm pays taxes on artificial revenue. Since a phase of restructuring was just beginning, firms were particularly sensitive to this impoverishment. The only way they could cope with it was by raising their prices. Aware of the perverse effect of its policy, the government intended to limit this by instituting an *ad hoc* levy, penalizing excessive nominal increases in added value. But, in the face of resistance from employers and trade unions, this authoritarian incomes policy was not applied.

The policy came up against a contradiction: unable to convince the opposition, its announcement aroused the suspicion and discontent of part of the electorate which had voted for the new president. Despite the defeat of the project in parliament, the president continued in his chosen course by announcing a series of reforms and opening the way for what was to be called the 'Republic of Reports': the reform of firms (the Sudreau report), social inequality (the Méraud report), decentralization (the Guichard report), etc. Here too the unwillingness to give these reforms a concrete form failed to convince the opposition, and increased suspicion among the president's political majority.

Moreover, the worsening of the crisis and the growth of unemployment caused the government in 1975 to reflate the economy on a grand scale by acting strongly on demand: in a matter of months, 45 billion francs (or about 4 per cent of the GNP) were swallowed up in the economic system.

The reflation was based on a desire to limit social and political problems by assuming that the crisis was a cyclical and short-lived one. The results were not slow in coming: output in 1976 reached the level of 1974. This confirmed the optimism of the president,[17] who announced that 'the most important event to have taken place this year is an economic one, the picking up of economic activity, signifying the end of the crisis' (televised speech 25 May 1976).

Nevertheless inflation worsened (increasing towards 13 per cent in mid-1976), as did the foreign deficit; the foreign value of the franc went down considerably,[18] and after a period of strong speculation it left the European monetary snake. Regulation by demand, which marked the first phase of the crisis in France, resulted more from social and political constraints than from a rational economic policy. Deflation, by acting on investment, and reflation, via demand management, resulted in stagflation. The time was ripe for an era of liberal counter-reform.

The liberal counter-reform

The relative failure of conventional management policies lent a new impetus to the theoretical debate and favoured the liberal counter-reform. Without exaggerating its importance, the publication of the McCraken report by the OECD[19] in 1977 revealed the development of thinking both on the diagnosis of the crisis and on the cure.

The counter-offensive was based on monetarist theories which viewed the recession as an essentially cyclical phenomenon, resulting partly from exogenous shocks (like the rise in the price of oil) but mainly from the excessive laxity of an economic policy which had produced inflation. 'Involuntary' unemployment, it was said, was a transitory situation, due to lasting inflation, false expectations and resistance to a drop in real wages. If people were prepared to restore free market forces and to rigorously apply a monetary policy, the economy would again find the natural balance from which it had been temporarily led astray by excessive interventionism.

It is in this climate of counter-reform that one must judge the action of Raymond Barre,[20] though economic policy from 1976 onwards was not dogmatic and by no means ignored the political and sociological constraints of French society. 'France's policies ... are not the fruit of an exclusive doctrinal approach. They have been elaborated from facts', Barre declared at a conference in New York in 1980. Nevertheless, these facts were viewed through then prism of a liberal doctrine, even if it was modified.

Confronted with the seriousness of the situation, these policies were first of all directed towards avoiding economic backsliding and then towards adapting France to the new conditions of the international economy. However the ultimately negative balance-sheet of this policy was to mortgage the future.

Stopping the slide

The situation in France in autumn 1976 was so worrying (the growth of inflation, the threat to the currency, the imbalance in foreign trade, public finances in the red) that the new government's first task was to put an end to the adverse results of the economic policies of its predecessor.

As Christian Sautter remarks, 'The Barre plan was primarily a refusal, a refusal of nominal and *a fortiori* real devaluation of the franc, a refusal to bolster up demand by means of a budgetary deficit.'[21] This refusal, at least at the discussion level, included some innovatory aspects: never had a hierarchy of objectives been put forward so forcefully, and the analysis of inflation was a new one since it defended the necessity for a strict maintenance of buying power by means of a unilateral incomes policy. The whole gamut of a policy of regulation was made use of, but in a degree which underestimated the positive aspects of a voluntary investment policy and an active employment policy.

The priority was clear: the main thing was to fight inflation, 'not the inflation of autumn 1976, but the permanent and pernicious evil of inflation in France'.[22] At this stage all the aims of economic policy were the consequence of the fight against inflation.

The explanation for inflation was a new one. The analysis made by Raymond Barre rested on the distinction between causes on which the government could act and those which were imposed on it, in particular international causes. Among those on which the government could act, 'the most important is the excessive growth in incomes . . . the increasing growth of salaries constitutes under present circumstances the vital factor in the rise in prices'.[23] 'France is living above its means. For several years, incomes have been rising faster than production. Indeed, whereas during the world recession of 1974–75 the nation's real income went down by 1.5 per cent, the buying power of household incomes went up by more than 4 per cent.'[24]

In the initial presentation of his policy, Raymond Barre insisted both on earned and unearned income. In fact he was to institute a unilateral incomes policy which slowed the growth of buying power. The implementation of this policy raised two problems. First of all, Raymond Barre had to create a psychological rupture. Three main methods were adopted:

(1) A prices policy, and in particular a price freeze, for four months by a reduction in VAT at the time of the freeze in January 1977.

(2) A fiscal policy, and in particular measures of fiscal law and morality. Among the methods used let us mention: the 'drought tax'[25] on large incomes as well as on large-scale farmers, a freeze on high salaries, the special contribution levied on companies, the special tax on certain styles of life, etc. On the other hand, even though the parliamentary majority of the time was clamouring for it, the idea of a tax on capital was abandoned.

(3) The announcement of the implementation of ambitious structural policies. Four main ones were mentioned: re-establishing healthy competition, re-examining public expenditure, re-establishing a balance in the social security system, and improving knowledge about the existence, formation and evolution of incomes.

The second problem was to know whether firms, professional people and the purveyors of services and recipients of fees would play the game. Aware of the difficulty, the government imposed certain controls which were quickly abandoned, but they practised more rigorous monetary controls, to prevent this policy from becoming a source of inflation. For the first time in the history of credit policy in France, a norm for the growth of the amount of money in circulation was explicitly set.

This policy of stabilization was a coherent one and prevented France from sinking into a situation of increasing imbalances. Nevertheless, though the worst was avoided, we were, at the beginning of 1978, far from a return to equilibrium, either in employment, where the situation continued to deteriorate, or even in the other variables in economic policy; the rate of inflation was slowed down[26] but it was still close to 10 per cent, foreign trade remained deficient, and production was stagnating.

Though the fever had abated, the patient was still very weak and this explains the difficulties which were encountered in improving the efficiency of the French economy in the face of very strong international competition.

Adapting to a new international deal

After the legislative elections of 1978 the policy defined in 1976 still prevailed: to achieve economic and financial recovery. But since this rested essentially on educating people to the idea of disindexation (by means of a unilateral incomes policy) and stabilization, which could lead to unemployment, it was necessary from 1978 onwards to encourage 'the adaptation of France to the new conditions of the international economy'.

This policy was clearly expressed at the time of the adoption of the Seventh Plan in November 1978 and again at the presentation of the preliminary options of the Eighth Plan in May–June 1979. According to d'Albert,[27] the policy (following the example set by West Germany) has a theory behind it: 'Employment is linked to growth. Growth is linked to the external balance. The external balance is linked to our adapting our industry.'

The policy was to be implemented in two main ways: freeing prices and maintaining a strong currency. The freeing of prices which had come about in most sectors since 1978 was conceived as a structural reform contributing to a transition towards liberalism.[28] After the legislative elections of 1978, the decontrol of prices took place in several stages, albeit rapidly: prices in industry were eased in two months. The professionals concerned made 'commitments of moderation'. Commercial margins were freed from the beginning of January 1979, in exchange for 'commitments of stability' for three months. The process was complete on 1 July 1979. Freeing of rents began on the same date. In May 1980 nearly all service prices were freed. Only energy prices, rents on old housing, certain transport costs and pharmaceutical products remained frozen.

According to the government, the process should involve not only a freeing of prices but also a strengthening of the compensating powers of competition and of organized consumption so as to avoid any risk of inflation. In practice the policy rested on one postulate: 'Action which favours competition progresses as price control subsides.'[29] If price control was not a desirable measure, the experience of price-freezing did reveal in retrospect that the inflationary consequences (alignment on ceiling prices, commercial behaviour, etc.) could equally well be ascribed to the absence of true competition as to intervention. Instituting price freedom could not iron out these malfunctions unless traders or firms were encouraged to lower their prices by competition, i.e. by re-establishing the role of the market. But the measures which accompanied the freeing of prices were too timid to make this possible.

In this sense one wonders if price freedom was not extended too quickly to the service sector, where market forces have much less impact, given the nature of benefits and the absence of real competition.

The government was aware of the ambiguity inherent in a policy which involved a rapid freeing of prices, and so adopted the approach of having a strong currency so as to impose the necessary disciplines from the outside. From this point of view the government benefited from the USA's lowering of the dollar. The fall began in about mid-1977 and continued until November 1979, despite the various measures which were taken to cushion it. This policy explains the sharp criticism which was addressed on 18 April 1979 by Chancellor Schmidt towards Washington's monetary and energy policy, which he called 'irresponsible'. The Japanese monetary authorities were simultaneously following the same policies. These two devaluations made American and Japanese competition even stronger, presenting the European economies with serious problems of structural adaptation.

The advantages of a strong currency, often put forward by the government, are threefold. The first advantage, frequently underlined by Raymond Barre, concerns the oil bill. Like most countries, France pays for a great deal of its imports in foreign currency (particularly in dollars); an appreciation of the currency automatically reduces the price paid for these imports. This argument is particularly relevant to energy prices.

The second effect concerns the domestic management of the economy. A strong currency makes it possible to contain inflation better, since imports are cheaper. In a country such as France, where the share of imports is over 20 per cent, imported inflation is reduced. But Raymond Barre also expected the appreciation of the franc to bring about external constraints which would limit the growth of wages. And in fact because of the appreciation of the currency, firms ran into difficulties over prices both in the domestic and export markets, and they were therefore obliged to limit wage increases and to increase productivity. The level of the currency thus contributed to reducing the inflationary wages–prices spiral. The effect of this policy was perfectly illustrated in Switzerland, West Germany and Belgium. These three countries, which adopted policies of high exchange rates, had a lower rate of inflation than their partners. This obviously does not mean that incomes did not rise, but that the increase in income could only be the fruit of gains in productivity. Finally, a strong currency has an important effect on industrial structures.[30] It gives a boost to firms, encouraging them to increase productivity and to specialize.

An analysis of these advantages led to the belief that an increase in the exchange rate brings only advantages and must be sought at all costs. But an appreciation of the exchange rate also entails perverse effects. Higher-priced exports run the risk of weakening competitiveness. A strong exchange rate can impede internal growth. This is the case at the moment in Great Britain, where the currency has gradually increased in value because of the country's oil production. The British economy is experiencing serious industrial difficulties in connection with this, along with a great increase in unemployment, and it is still unable to effectively contain the level of inflation. This also applies to some extent to France, which has not during this period made the necessary effort towards research and investment.

Mortgaging the future

Up till the beginning of 1981 Raymond Barre's policies had fully succeeded in only one field, the exchange rate and monetary reserves, and this in a situation which was very favourable because of the weakness of the dollar and of the yen, and then of the deutschmark, in 1980. As for the rest, even if he avoided economic shipwreck in 1976–77, the final balance-sheet was negative. Indeed, in three fields it was distinctly worrying: the structural resistance of inflation, the risk of a shrinking industrial base and, most of all, unemployment and its effects.

The structural resistance of inflation can be observed in the cycles of price increases which have led to higher and higher price levels. Since 1950 we can observe five cycles of inflation; comparing them, we notice higher and higher levels of price rises: 2.5 per cent between 1953 and 1957, 3.8 per cent between 1963 and 1973, 9.9 per cent between 1975 and 1979. As the national accounts for 1980 have noted, the difference between the general movement of prices in the 1970s and the 1950s lies not in the size of the largely exogenous inflationary shocks, but in the subsequent limiting of the ensuing *dis*inflation. On this level, the policies adopted only increased the tendency towards rigidity in lowering prices, for lack of a policy to attack the structural causes of inflation.

The risk of a shrinking of the industrial base is also a worrying one, both as regards the economy's sensitivity to imports and the weakness of our investment in production. Since 1968 the French economy has largely been open to the world. Our exports have made strong progress and today represent about 20 per cent of the GNP. The natural counterpart to this growth is the penetration of our domestic market. Nevertheless, despite a noticeable slowing down in economic activity since 1974, this penetration has continued to increase at almost the same rate as before the crisis.

Table 3   **Rate of penetration of the domestic industrial market (per cent)**

	1974	1975	1976	1977	1978	1979
Industry as a whole	24.1	22.4	24.7	25.4	25.8	27.3
Capital goods	27.6	25.4	29.1	29.6	30.3	32.8

SOURCE: INSEE.

This phenomenon is particularly noticeable in the fields of capital and consumer goods. Demand is shared out to the advantage of imports and to the detriment of internal production. This evolution results from the unfavourable specialization in French industry and the relative tightness in output capacities, but most of all from insufficient competitiveness.

These developments are related to the weakening of the effort to invest in production since 1974, which characterizes the bulk of firms other than large national enterprises, and in particular the industrial sector. Our backwardness in this field is noticeable in comparison with some of our commercial partners, especially West Germany (see Table 4).

Table 4 **Annual percentage increase in investment in the private productive sector**

	1976	1977	1978	1979	1980
France	+8.3	−3.3	+1.0	+ 0.7	+ 2.7
West Germany	+6.4	+7.7	+8.1	+10.0	+10.0

France is the only industrialized country (with Italy) to have a declining share of investment in the GDP. This poor record of investment in production has led to manufacturing industries becoming obsolete. Thus, France's place today in the international division of labour is not satisfactory. Despite an improvement in the financial situation of firms up to 1979, they did not invest, due to the lack of a rigorous industrial policy and of a minimum of selective planning. The only alternative could have been a stronger growth in internal demand, but in this case inflation would have been higher.

However, unemployment, because of its terrible effects, has remained the most troubling economic problem. Even the expansion which took place in the 1960s did not prevent a doubling of the rate of unemployment. And slow growth was certain to unbalance the job market. At a time when the workforce was greatly increasing (principally because of the greater number of young people and a higher rate of activity among women), the employment offered by firms has considerably slowed down, given the stagnation in economic activity and the early effects of new technology. The result is massive unemployment, which has quadrupled in seven years.

This unemployment has several characteristics which have evolved during the various cycles of recession. At the lowest points, or troughs, in 1975, 1978, 1980, the increasing number of redundancies in industry, as well as the various cases of 'pruning', made for higher unemployment among the male industrial workforce of mature age. This is what is called 'crisis' unemployment, and is reminiscent of the conditions prevailing in 1929. At the highest points, or peaks, the resumption of activity benefits only this group and so increases inequalities, since women and young people suffer most, making up respectively 60 and 45 per cent of those seeking employment; unemployment thus becomes 'prosperity' unemployment, but of course on a much higher level.

Unemployment is also deeper-rooted. The average period out of work becomes longer, and this accentuates imbalances: 7.6 months in April–May 1975, compared with 11.7 months in March 1980. The job market tends to operate like a waiting list[31] which grows as recruitment declines. But the older people are not the first to be satisfied. Age (more advanced) and sex (female) appear to be the most discriminated against. This is an unemployment of exclusion[32] which, combined with the various schemes for early retirement, has contributed to the expulsion from the work market of older people: the rate of activity among men over 60 has fallen from 26 per cent in 1975 to 17 per cent in 1980.

The adaptation of employment to slow growth has also taken place in a less measurable way by the modification of criteria for recruitment: temporary employment and short-term contracts have become common. The result is enforced and depressing mobility, with an increase in temporary employment which turns the labour market into a sort of sucking and blowing pump, with smaller and smaller scope and whose filter system produces marked inequalities.

These kinds of unemployment cause particular concern because of their effects. First of all there is the problem of the position of the unemployed within society. It is certain that job instability, the feeling of being excluded from society, as well as the feeling of injustice, will, if employment trends are not altered, produce a deep change in the concept of work and responsibility held by several generations. But the effects can be even more serious. The medical pathology of the unemployed is a specific one, as shown by the centre for studies of the CGT. The consequences can be dramatic. In a study on suicide and the economic crisis, the Institut National d'Etudes Démographiques (INED) comments: 'In 1980, for the first time in France, the yearly number of deaths by suicide exceeded 10,000; this rate had been unknown since before the war years. It is during the last four years that the number has risen sharply, from a level of about 8,000 a year. This phenomenon cannot be related to the present crisis.'[33]

Young people are particularly affected by this development, hence the question posed by INED:

Can we relate this phenomenon to a rise in unemployment among young people? Without a doubt there is a certain correlation between the two. But it is not possible to establish a simple relationship between unemployment and suicide. On the one hand the economic crisis gives rise to a good many difficulties other than unemployment (bankruptcy, failure in careers, inability to bear responsibilities which have become too heavy: rent, debts, etc), but also the influence of unemployment on suicide is certainly not limited to a direct, individual relationship. The anxiety caused by the general atmosphere of crisis no doubt counts as much as the direct loss of a job.

Less dramatic but quite as brutal are the results of under-employment on public finances and social institutions. Unemployment constitutes a financial cost for the country as a whole, it is a levy on the state budget and contributes to the wage bill paid by firms.[34]

It is clear that public expenditure on unemployment provides support for household incomes. But a financial circuit is thereby created which weighs on the competitiveness of the economy, and one wonders whether this money would not be better directed towards more productive uses, i.e. towards creating jobs.

Conclusion

All things considered, the French economy is at a stage of its evolution which is similar to that of the other European economies. The analogies are striking and need no underlining. France's special features are today less remarkable, thanks to thirty years of working towards modernization and adaptation to the facts of an industrial society.

Like its European neighbours, France is faced with a dual

challenge: an internal challenge, linked to the increasing difficulty of administering a mixed economy which is marred by inadequate functioning of its markets, growing rigidity and disorderly state intervention; and an external challenge, as a result of the profound change in the world economy and the outbreak of a new industrial revolution.

In order to face the external challenge, our country must not only speed up its adaptation to the new facts of the 1980s but also find support in relaunching European co-operation, in particular in the fields of industry, energy and research, relying on a truly common market. Equally, the European Community desperately needs a foreign policy if it wants to reinforce its autonomy and assure its future.

To face the internal challenge, which is basically a social problem, France needs a social dynamism which it has lacked for too long. This can be achieved by a reduction in inequalities, a gradual decrease in unemployment and the development of a vigorous system of industrial relations. It would be possible on this basis to build a more mobile and productive economy. Particularly since there are cards to be played: the reduction in the country's dependence in the field of energy, the high quality of many firms, a workforce which is qualified and keen to work.

The central conception of economic policy can only be made up from a judicious blend of different instruments, leaving none of them out: prudent stimulus via the budget; a fiscal structure geared towards greater social justice, and the encouragement of saving and entrepreneurial initiative; an active employment policy (training, mobility, placing); a counter-inflationary monetary policy; and a more selective financing policy, particularly as far as long-term bank loans and the provision of risk capital are concerned.

But this policy of regulation will fail to achieve its aims unless at the same time indispensable structural reforms are carried out, to achieve real decentralization, effective competition in the market, and flexible planning oriented towards stabilizing structures, as well as towards grasping the potential of the new industrial revolution. The liberal counter-reform has come up against the traditional state control of French society, resulting in an incoherent mixture of *laissez-faire* and interventionism. We must substitute for this a largely decentralized economy, housing both an efficient market and a system of planning which will stimulate the economy and clarify national priorities.

Notes

1 J. Fourastié, *Les trente glorieuses ou la révolution invisible de 1946 à 1975* (Fayard, Paris, 1979).
2 As Boyer and Mistral remark: 'With the exception of the short interlude decreed by Napoleon III, public intervention was the rule in matters of international economic relations. From Colbert to Méline all forms of protectionism have been tried.' (*Accumulation, inflation et crise*, PUF, 1977.)
3 The annual rate of price increases oscillated between 3 per cent in 1963-64, after the stabilization plan, and 7 per cent in 1969, with a peak of 12 per cent in 1958.
4 cf. Report of the study group, *The Problems of Inflation*, under Mr Maldague (EEC, Brussels, March 1976).
5 CERC, *Distribution and Differences in Incomes Abroad, in Comparison with France* (CERC no. 29-30 I and II, 1976). The inequalities of income measured by the relation of the 9th decile to the first decile seem clearly greater in France than in Great Britain or West Germany. Dispersion of wages (D9/D1) in the wage-earning population as a whole:

	Both sexes	Men	Women
France 1972	3.8	3.9	3.1
Great Britain 1972	3.3	2.5	2.6
West Germany 1972	2.4	2.05	2.05

6 M. Sauyer, *The Distribution of Incomes in the OECD Countries*, Economic Perspectives of the OECD, 7 (OECD, Paris, 1976).
7 Strauss-Kahn, 'Les inégalités en Europe. Rapport an Premier Secrétaire du Parti Socialiste.' (roneoed document, Paris, 1979).
8 EEC, *Economic and Social Conceptions Prevailing in the EEC* (December 1979, Brussels). Report of a study group presided over by the author.
9 The figures calculated for France by C. Sautter give the same results.
10 'La rupture de 1974', *Economie et Statistique*, 124, August 1980.
11 The illness of President Pompidou, followed by the presidential elections of April 1974 postponed all decisions of economic policy, and the first significant measures to deal with the oil crisis were taken in July 1974.
12 The number of people seeking employment went from 400,000 in 1974 to more than 900,000 in 1976, reaching 1,600,000 at the beginning of 1981.
13 Essentially because of the smaller size of firms and a smaller overlap between financial structures than in the USA, which suffered from the recession from 1929 onwards.

14 CEPREMAP (Centre d'Etudes Prospectives d'Economie Mathématique Appliquées à la Planification), *Approches de l'inflation. L'exemple* français. (Paris, 1976), Vol. 4.

15 J. Mazier, *Revue du CORDES* (Paris, 1977).

16 J. Duret, *Le marxisme et les crises* (Gallimard, Paris, 1933). Reprinted in 1977 in Editions d'Aujourd'hui, Collection Les introuvables.

17 Jacques Chirac was of the same opinion, declaring that at the economic level the end of the tunnel was in sight.

18 The exchange rate, which had appreciated to nearly 110 per cent during the first quarter of 1976, had fallen to below 90 per cent by the third quarter.

19 P. McCraken *et al.*, *Towards Full Employment and Price Stability* (OECD, Paris, 1977).

20 Raymond Barre was initially on the committee directed by McCraken, but was replaced by Robert Marjolin when he was appointed minister for foreign trade.

21 C. Sautter, *L'economie française*, Centre d'Etudes Prospectives et d'Informations Internationales, January 1981 (due to appear in C. Allsopp and A. Boltho, *The European economy since 1950*, Oxford University Press).

22 Valéry Giscard d'Estaing, televized speech, 25 August 1976.

23 Barre, 12 October 1976. Loi de finances rectificative.

24 Barre, televized presentation, 22 September 1976.

25 The idea was, by transferring revenues, to compensate for the very damaging consequences of the exceptionally dry climate on farm production.

26 The rise in consumer prices fell from 11.8 per cent in 1975 to 9.6 per cent in 1976, 9.4 per cent in 1977, and 9.1 per cent in 1978.

27 Theory announced by the Commissaire Général du Plan, Michel Albert.

28 A. Vianes, 'L'expérience française de liberté des prix: bilan économique provisoire et enjeux sociaux', *Economie et Humanisme*, March/April 1981.

29 Blue note from the Service de l'Information du Ministère de l'Economie, January 1980.

30 See Ramses, 1981: *Coopération ou guerre économique*. Annual report of the Institut Français des Relations Internationales.

31 R. Salais, 'Le chomage; un phénomène de file d'attente', *Economie et Statistique*, no. 123.

32 Cf. the report of R. Lion, *Vieillir demain* (Documentation Française, 1979).

33 INED, '*Le Suicide et la crise éonomique*', *Population et Société*, May 1981, no. 147.

34 A current estimate roughly equates loss of receipts with the amounts given by the state and Unedic towards indemnifying unemployment. These have increased very rapidly, particularly since 1974. The system of unemployment insurance installed in 1958 and jointly run by the national council of French employers and the five national federations representing the workforce has seen its expenses increase from 1.2 billion francs in 1972 to 15.1 billion in 1978, and about 20 billion in 1979. Parallel to this, the contributions paid by firms and workers, which between 1964 and 1972 did not go above 0.4 per cent of wages, have progressively increased, reaching 3 per cent of

wages in 1978, and 3.6 per cent in 1979. State expenses on unemployment indemnity have also increased considerably. (Source: *Profil économique de la France au senil des années 80*. Under the direction of Jean-Pierre Page. Documentation Française, 1981.)

4 A transformation of the English sickness?

Samuel Brittan

Underlying problems

During the course of a short sabbatical at the Chicago Law School in 1978, I had the honour of being invited to give the Henry Simons Lecture; and it was suggested to me gently that I might like to choose as my subject the British economy.[1]

There was little point in either repeating, or trying to repudiate, criticisms of British performance which would be all too familiar to a sophisticated American audience. But the invitation did give me an incentive to stand back from immediate problems and controversies and ask two questions. First, what is so special about the British economy, as distinct from other Western economies? And secondly, are its special features due to some unique entity such as the 'national character', not susceptible to further analysis? Or are its stresses and strains susceptible to some more general explanation with wider relevances?

The first question about the special features of the British economy is possible to answer in a reasonably factual way, although some of the answers seem to surprise some people. To begin with there is the long-standing gap between the growth rate of the United Kingdom and that of other industrial market economies. This goes back over a hundred years. Alfred Marshall remarked that by the 1860s and 1870s 'many of the sons of manufacturers' were 'content to follow mechanically the lead given by their fathers. They worked shorter hours; and they exerted themselves less to obtain new practical ideas.'[2]

One estimate made by Angus Maddison suggests that the average level of output per head in sixteen industrial countries rose sixfold between 1870 and 1976, but only fourfold in the United Kingdom.[3] Neither the study of alternative estimates, nor that of subperiods, nor attempted corrections for working hours, upsets the relative orders of magnitude. The estimates are of course of output, not of happiness or welfare.

During the nineteenth century and the first three-fifths of the twentieth century the United Kingdom remained ahead of nearly all the main European countries, and the low growth rate was a matter for concern only to sophists, calculators and economists. Since 1960, however, an absolute gap has emerged – whether measured by output, or real wages, or whether the comparisons are made at market or purchasing parity exchange rates, or by the fallible impressions of personal travel. One comparison of gross domestic product (GDP) per head at purchasing power exchange rates suggests that by 1973 most European Economic Community countries were 30 to 40 per cent ahead of Britain.[4]

International corporations are in a good position, compared to merely national concerns, to minimize productivity differentials between plants in different countries. Yet a study of such international corporations showed net output per head to be about 30 per cent higher in German and French plants than in corresponding plants in the United Kingdom. Only about half the Anglo-German difference could be attributed to product-mix, scale, or capital equipment. The remainder was due to 'differences in efficiency'. Much more lurid comparisons could be given by selective evidence from particular industries, or anecdotally.

Recent problems

Although the lag in the British growth rate is historically deep-seated, the country's special troubles on the inflation and unemployment fronts are, by contrast, recent. The 1949 devaluation of sterling was part of a common adjustment of the parities of most war-devastated countries relative to the United States dollar. Between then and 1967 there was little out of the ordinary in the UK macroeconomic experience. The British inflation rate was only very slightly above the average of the twenty-four nations of the Organization for Economic Co-operation and Development

(OECD). Registered UK unemployment averaged scarcely 2 per cent, and even in the worst recessions, seasonally adjusted adult unemployment rarely touched 3 per cent.

British inflation rates began to rise substantially above the average of industrial countries only in the decade after the 1967 devaluation of sterling. It was in the second half of that decade, from 1972 to 1977, that the British inflation rate really soared. This was a highly inflationary period for the world economy. But while the OECD price level rose by 60 per cent in five years, the British level rose by 120 per cent, or twice as much.

Suggested explanations

Why has British performance fallen so far behind other countries? A great deal of fun could be had from the many and often contradictory suggestions offered. Both the inequities of British society and excessive egalitarian zeal have been blamed; so too have inadequate competition and insufficient government intervention. Some people cite the enormous institutional obstacles to change and others the excessive ease with which policies are reversed under a two-party winner-takes-all system; and one could go on indefinitely.

Some of the suggested explanations of British economic performance may shed light on recent years, but cannot conceivably explain the long-term lag in growth rates. Some dwell on transitory phenomena already disappearing or unlikely to last. Some are factually dubious on any basis whatever.

For instance, a once-popular diagnosis was that British growth was held back by cyclical fluctuations in output, caused by stop-go financial policies. Numerous studies have, however, shown that deviations in UK output, measured in relation to trend, were less than in most other countries.

A related explanation was low investment, especially in manufacturing, in the post-World War II period. Close examination reveals, however, that gross investment in manufacturing, as a percentage of value added, was for many years higher in Germany than in the United Kingdom. Where the United Kingdom did come clearly at the bottom of the league was in the effectiveness of investment in terms of output generated, as Table I shows. It is therefore not surprising that profitability and the return on investment were low by international standards.

Table 1 **Investment in manufacturing 1958–72**

	Investment ratio[a] (*per cent*)	Increase in net output per unit of investment (*Index nos., UK = 100*)
UK	13.0	100
USA	12.2	145
Germany	13.0	190
Sweden	14.4	145
France	16.3	163
Japan	24.6	157

[a] Manufacturing gross investment as percentage of value added.
SOURCE: Confederation of British Industry, *Britain Means Business 1977* (1977), p. 38.

One aspect of a relatively slow growth rate has been the fall in the British share of world trade or world exports of manufactures. Repeated investigations have shown that this decline cannot be explained by any special features of either the commodity composition or market distribution of British exports. It is simply that if the United Kingdom has a lower growth rate than competitor countries, one would expect, other things being equal, a declining share of world exports relative to those countries' share. It is thus a consequence rather than a cause.

There is a more specific doctrine relating Britain's slow growth to trading performance. This is that the country has a special difficulty in earning enough overseas to support a full-employment level of activity. This is the theme song of the annual reviews of the Cambridge Economic Policy Group. The essential argument is that, even if exchange rates move so as to keep British money costs competitive with other countries', imports will be too high and exports too low to maintain full employment. This would imply that British products are not merely inferior in design, performance, or delivery, but are continually deteriorating in these respects. The Cambridge Group's case rests on the very strong assumption that the annual fall in terms of trade required to stay in equilibrium would be so steep and meet such strong union resistance that it could not be brought about without an inflationary explosion. The Cambridge Group attributes the large current balance-of-payments surplus attained in 1980–81 to the severity of the prevailing recession and maintains that a deficit would re-emerge if home demand were restored to full-employment levels.

Many other analysts would dispute, however, the whole diagnosis of output being limited by a demand or balance-of-payments constraint. The rise in import penetration in the 1960s and 1970s took place in a series of jumps during periods of boom and supply bottlenecks. The increase in British exports, relative to any given increase in world real incomes, has it is true been substantially less than that of exports of other countries. But such ratios are unlikely to give a true measure of the income elasticity of demand for British exports. Bottlenecks on the supply side – even when the unemployment statistics have been high – have limited the response of British industry to increases in overseas demand.

Government spending

The level of government spending is also often blamed for recent poor performance. But on any comparable international measure of government ratios, the UK has been for some years in the middle of the international league and far from the top. On British definitions, public spending as a proportion of the Gross Domestic Product reached a peak of 46½ per cent in the two-year period 1974–76. As a result of the cuts made by the last Labour Government, it fell in the later 1970s to 41 or 42 per cent, only to rise to 44 or 45 per cent in the second year of the Thatcher Government – which was regarded by friend and foe alike as having an anti-public-spending bias.

It is in fact likely that public spending, which was rising from the early 1960s and reached its peak in the mid 1970s, has since been on a slightly declining trend. The high figures for the early 1980s, as for 1974–76, reflect (a) recession, which boosts social-security spending and industrial subsidies and at the same time reduces GDP – the denominator of the public-spending ratio, and (b) the public-sector pay explosions following the demise of the Heath and Callaghan pay controls. The figures for both periods are likely to prove temporary bulges.

Let me not be misunderstood. Large parts of public expenditure are not devoted to genuinely public goods and do little to transfer resources to the poor. These expenditures take place only because of the imperfections of the political market. But there is no need to claim that public spending is (a) out of control, (b) higher than in other countries, or (c) in itself a likely cause of economic breakdown or political collapse.

Tax perversities

Not surprisingly, international tax comparisons lead to a similar picture. One of the great myths spread by the British themselves is that they are an overtaxed people. But as Table 2 shows, tax receipts (including social-security contributions) are lower in the UK than in France and Germany, and much lower than in the Scandinavian countries and the Netherlands.

When it comes to the tax treatment of corporate enterprises, especially overseas ones, there is still less cause for complaint. Several years ago a Treasury Minister in the last Labour Government privately described Britain as a 'leading tax haven'; and an Economist Intelligence Unit Special Report (No. 85, 1981) concludes that this country is a 'fiscal paradise', which in some respects has left places like Jersey, Monte Carlo and Lichtenstein far behind. An unofficial estimate suggests that more than 4,000 non-resident companies enjoy tax-free stakes.

Where there is smoke, there is usually some fire. The trouble with the British tax burden has not been its size, but its incidence. Until the 1979 Budget there was a top marginal rate of 83 per cent on earned income and 98 per cent on unearned income. These percentages are now down to 60 per cent and 75 per cent. The highest marginal tax rates are now at the bottom end of the income scale. Because of the interaction of the tax and social-security systems, the implicit marginal rate of tax for a family man a little below median income, on return to work after unemployment, or on promotion inside a job, can approach or even exceed 100 per cent. The 1981 Budget, which failed to adjust tax thresholds for inflation, aggravated this 'poverty trap'.

Table 2 **Total tax revenue (incl. social-security contributions) as percentage of GDP**

	1978	1979		1978	1979
Sweden	53.50	50.27	Italy	32.58	30.09
Luxembourg	49.88	46.17	Switzerland	31.47	31.12
Norway	46.94	46.06	Canada	31.13	31.01
Netherlands	46.79	47.42	New Zealand	30.36	31.18
Belgium	44.18	44.69	United States	30.19	31.32
Denmark	43.59	44.09	Australia	28.81	29.82
Austria	41.43	41.36	Portugal	26.15	25.82
France	39.67	41.16	Japan	24.06	24.77
Germany	37.82	37.34	Spain	22.76	23.27
Finland	36.54	35.03	Turkey	22.53	20.84
United Kingdom	34.45	34.02	Greece	NA	27.69
Ireland	33.38	33.82			

SOURCE: *Revenue Statistics of OECD Member Countries 1965-80* (OECD, Paris, 1981).

Another problem, not confined to the United Kingdom, is that the tax base is too narrow and rates are too high. The basic rate of income tax, which is also the marginal rate for most people, is not 30 per cent but nearly 39 per cent if employees' National Insurance contributions are added. On the other hand because of tax concessions on home-loan interest payments, and on pension-fund and life-insurance policy contributions, most people are paying a very much lower effective rate. This combination of tax subsidies for institutional investment and high rates on individual investment is one of the main reasons for the disappearance of the small investor. A shift towards a broader tax base with lower rates would do more to help small firms than the many special schemes in the Budgets of the last few years.

What proportion of the lag in Britain's growth rate do recent high marginal tax rates and other perversities explain? We can only guess. But two facts are worth pondering. One is that these confiscatory rates cannot explain any of the lag before World War II. Secondly, the Western country which most nearly approaches the United Kingdom in the severity of its tax progression, Sweden, has been much higher in the growth league for most of the postwar period. Despite its recent setback, Sweden has a level of GNP per head which is comparable to that of the United States.

State intervention

Nor can we really ascribe the UK growth lag to any generalized fault known as state intervention. For the greater part of the postwar period, there is no evidence that there was more state intervention in the marketplace in the United Kingdom than in other Western countries. During the 1950s and most of the 1960s – even during the Labour governments of 1964–70 – most industrial decisions were made in the marketplace. Moreover, among industrial economies there is little connection between growth rates and the degree of state involvement in the economy. Germany has prospered under free-market doctrine, while Japan and France have prospered under a sort of right-wing *dirigisme* – a common front between government and industrial organizations designed to bypass the market wherever possible. At the level of specific industries, agriculture has been subject to more government intervention than almost any other industry in most Western countries. Yet it has been characterized by a high rate of productivity growth.

A generalization worth venturing is that a country can get away either with a great deal of state intervention *or* with a great deal of egalitarian social policy, but not with the two together. Sweden, for instance, had a high level of social services and fiscal redistribution but, until recently at least, was a model market economy. Industrial policy was geared to encouraging workers to shift as quickly as possible to the most profitable industries, and investment was guided by world markets rather than by government planning. In France and Japan, on the other hand, 'planning' was combined with a highly unequal distribution of income and the bulk of taxation tends to come from sales and turnover levies.

One further tentative generalization may be suggested. The

79

more democratic a country's institutions, the more likely is government economic intervention to hold back rather than encourage growth. Growth depends on change; and change can be disturbing. The general citizen has a dispersed interest in change and efficiency spread over thousands of different decisions. Particular industries and interest groups have a much more concentrated interest in stopping change or in securing inefficient decisions for their own narrow benefit. In a highly democratic society, geographically or professionally concentrated groups have much more influence than do general citizen interests. A concrete example of what I have in mind was the decision of Conservative Premier Harold Macmillan in a conflict over the location of a steel mill between Scotland and Wales at the beginning of the 1960s. The resolution was to have two smaller, suboptimal mills, one in each area.

In its time, the steel-mill decision was untypical. Most such decisions would then have been taken in the marketplace. But after 1972 there was a notable increase in the quantity of government intervention in the United Kingdom and a deterioration in the quality. We have had a multiplication of discretionary subsidies to individual concerns with no realistic prospects of paying their own way and with no genuine spillover benefits to justify subsidy. The standard of living of UK consumers has been reduced and the development of poorer countries impeded by putting barriers on low-cost imports. There have been laws which seem deliberately designed to price out of work the less skilled, the less able, the victims of prejudice, the young, the old, women, and coloured immigrants – all in the name of high-sounding principles such as 'the rate for the job'.

A provisional summary

To summarize so far. The lag in the British growth rate goes back at least a century, although it took on a new dimension in about 1960 when the level as well as the growth rate of British real income began to fall behind similarly placed European states. In addition, the United Kingdom has shared in the poor output and employment performance of the post-1973 economic cycle.

British inflationary excesses are recent, and may be on the wane. They are not the most fundamental aspects of the British disease. Many other much-criticized British policies are also followed to a comparable degree by other governments, working under similar political pressures. Moreover, these errors are too recent to explain the longer-term weaknesses. The tax rates of the 1970s hardly shed light on weaknesses of British management which worried Lord Haldane before World War I.

Can then anything be said of the deep-seated lag in the British growth rates? And does British experience throw any light on the stagflation problem, which still remains serious, even if it is likely henceforth to show itself more in Britain in stagnant output and employment, rather than in runaway inflation?

These broader questions bring us to two subjects which are always raised in any discussion of long-run British economic performance. These are the class system and the trade unions.

The class system

Contrary to travellers' tales, the United Kingdom is *not* more stratified than other societies in any obvious statistical sense. Yet, there is a sense in which Britain is more class-ridden than other capitalist or mixed economies. But it is to be found in the features of British society furthest removed from pecuniary matters. They lie in such things as emphasis on the social pecking-order, concern with subtle differences of speech and manner, and the educational segregation from an early age of a so-called elite in fee-paying and often unpleasant residential institutions, strangely known as public schools. In all societies people care about their status in the eyes of their fellow men. The exceptional feature of Britain is that social status has less to do with merely making money than in almost any other Western society.

Union power

The other old-established British institution, which needs to be mentioned, is the trade-union movement. But here again we must be careful of misdiagnosis. The number of days lost in British industry through strikes, even in the troublesome period of the early 1970s, was less than in the United States or Canada. The quantities involved are insignificant – just over one day per man-year on average; and strikes are overwhelmingly in large concerns.

Monopolistic union practices are a different matter. Their effect on productivity is difficult to quantify, although the international productivity comparisons cited earlier may give a clue. Let me quote from a profound analysis of the logic of contemporary unionism. The writer shows that unions derive their influence over wages from the power to exclude and that the main losers are other workers. He cites severe restrictions on entry such as:

... high initiation fees, excessive periods of apprenticeship and restrictions upon numbers of apprentices, barriers to movements between related trades, and, of course, make-work restrictions, cost-increasing working rules, and prohibition of cost-reducing innovations, not to mention racial and sex discrimination ... Investors now face nearly all the disagreeable uncertainties of investors in a free-market world plus the prospect that labor organizations will appropriate most or all of the earnings which would otherwise accrue if favorable contingencies materialized.

But even this is not the worst of it. Partial unionism is 'a device by which the strong may raise themselves higher by pressing down the weak'. It makes 'high wages higher and low wages lower'. This works when 'everybody does not try it or when few have effective power. Attempts to apply it universally are incompatible with order.' He goes on:

In an economy of intricate division of labor, every large organized group is in a position at any time to disrupt or to stop the whole flow of social income; and the system must soon break down if groups persist in exercising that power or if they must continuously be bribed to forgo its disastrous exercise ... The dilemma here is not peculiar to our present economic order; it must appear in any kind of system. This minority-monopoly problem would be quite as serious for a democratic socialism as it is for the mixed individualist–collectivist system of the present. It is the rock on which our present system is most likely to crack up; and it is the rock on which democratic socialism would be destroyed if it could ever come into being at all.

The author I am quoting does not pretend to have a remedy, but talks about the possibility of 'an awful dilemma: democracy cannot live with tight occupational monopolies; and it cannot destroy them, once they attain great power, without destroying itself in the process'.

This sounds like a despairing British economist writing in the aftermath of the 1974 miners' strike, when union power broke one government and demoralized the whole governing order. In fact the author was an American writing of US trade unions, and the passages cited were composed before 1946 by the US economist Henry Simons.[5] His remarks can be regarded as an elaboration of Dicey's contrast at the beginning of the twentieth century between the effects of individual pursuit of self-interest and its collective pursuit.[6]

Democracy and interest groups

Simons's forebodings were followed in the United States by over three decades of unparalleled prosperity in which the membership and influence of US trade unionism, if anything, declined. Unfortunately, a premature prediction is not necessarily a wrong one. We still do not know whether the gloomy forebodings of Dicey and Simons were averted or merely postponed.

The underlying question concerns the impact, not merely of unions, but of all producer and special interest groups on the functioning of the economic system. The problem is not one of inflation, as is so often wrongly supposed, but of unemployment. If the total effect of the monopolistic activities of producer groups is to price so many people out of work that the resulting unemployment rate is higher than the electorate will tolerate, then our system of political economy is doomed. If the government in such a situation tries to spend its way into full employment, the result will be not just inflation, but accelerating inflation. So there is no escape that way – as I believe British policy-makers are at last learning. We do not know if the sustainable unemployment rate is too high for democratic stability or, if it is, what the role of union-type monopoly is in making it so. The fact that we cannot rule out the pessimistic hypothesis is itself important.

A great deal depends on things such as the proportion of the population unionized – which is much greater in the United Kingdom than in the United States – as well as on the degree of toleration of undercutting of union suppliers by others. Much also hangs on the electorate's toleration of higher unemployment in today's circumstances. This is clearly higher than it was, given the social cushions now available; but we have yet to test its limits on either side of the Atlantic. Nor have we any real idea how high is the sustainable rate of unemployment consistent with avoiding merely an acceleration of an existing inflation rate.

Moreover, we should not conceive the producer-group threat too narrowly. Collective action to secure real wages incompatible with full employment may come not just through the strike threat alone, but also through political action. The real danger is that the end-result of action taken by people through collective activity will be unacceptable to the same people in their capacity of consumers and voters – a perverse invisible hand. The fact that Simons was premature in his forebodings in the case of the United States does not mean that they can be dismissed.

The costs of stable institutions

Why have restrictive policies, not only by unions, but by all producer groups, had more impact in the United Kingdom than in many other countries? An interesting hypothesis has been suggested by Professor Mancur Olson.[7] This derives from the old problem of the free rider (i.e. someone who benefits from the efforts of others without participating himself), which Professor Olson has recently applied specifically to the United Kingdom. The point is that there is very little personal incentive for an individual to participate, whether financially, or by direct action such as striking, or by political lobbying, in group activity, since the gains spill over to others while he bears the costs himself. Long periods of peace and established institutions are necessary for producer groups to overcome this constraint. The passage of time enables such groups to build up selective benefits for their members which will persuade them to participate in collective action. As the years proceed, political linkages become established, voting lobbies become organized; and the biggest allies of all – instinctive habit and group loyalties – have time to become established.

The central conclusion that Olson draws is that 'the longer the period in which a country has had a modern industrial pattern of common interest and at the same time democratic freedom of economic organization without upheaval and disorganization, the greater the extent to which its growth rate will be retarded by organized interests'. Thus it is not surprising that the British disease should have come first to the country which both pioneered the industrial revolution and has the longest record of civic freedom and settled institutions. On the other hand, countries 'where common interest organizations have been emasculated or abolished by foreign occupation, totalitarian governments or political instability' experience rapid rates of growth 'after a free and stable legal order is established'. The Olson explanation has the great advantage of not having to suggest that Germany gained in a physical sense from having had her industrial plant destroyed in the war. Among Continental countries it was Italy, where the traditional culture was most deep-rooted, and the wartime destruction was most superficial, that saw the earliest end to the period of 'miracle' growth, and the earliest infection by the 'British disease'.

On this interpretation there is nothing peculiarly British about the British sickness, but it is something which will come in time to any country with a settled record of free institutions. It came to New England before California, and it is coming to California before Alaska. As World War II and its aftermath recede, and settled democratic institutions move into their second generation, producer interest groups might be expected to gain ground in Western Europe as well. The countries now experiencing the most rapid growth in the Pacific basin are those where industrial development is still a novelty and untrammelled by collective or political constraints.

The United Kingdom's problems are thus likely to become

typical of mixed, advanced democratic economies in general, rather than confined to a particular country. The British disease pertains not to a particular country, but to a stage in political and economic development. The disease is that of collective action by special interest groups preventing a reasonably full use being made of economic resources.

Self-correcting forces

But it is not necessary to wallow in pessimism. For the so-called 'English sickness', even though it may infect many other countries, may eventually, like many other diseases, produce its own cure. For there are such things as self-correcting forces, automatic stabilizers and built-in regulators. And there is every reason to suppose that they apply to long-term trends, such as relative national decline, as well as to trade cycles and specific disturbances.

Nor is the nature of the corrective forces all that mysterious. A slowly growing country, held back by restrictive interest groups, experiences a steadily growing gap between its own output per head and that of other countries employing best-practice techniques. But the more this happens, the greater the incentive to catching-up activity.

The more atrophied become a country's techniques and habits, the greater becomes the return to innovation. Restrictive practices are never of the same severity across the economy, and if innovation is blocked in traditional or well-organized sectors, talent and capital will drift to newer areas, where group loyalties have not yet 'solved' the free-rider problem. In the last resort the returns to political entrepreneurship from trying to change the institutional or political rules in favour of better economic performance may become so great that the changes are made.

These self-correcting forces can take a very long time. Spain began to lag in the seventeenth century and did not start to recover lost ground until the boom of the 1950s. The reversal in the British case could come much earlier. Indeed it may already have started, judging by some recent developments. The rapid growth rates of Continental Europe in the two-and-a-half

decades up to the first oil price explosion of 1973 were exceptional because they reflected progress in bridging the gap that
then existed with best-practice American techniques. It could
now be the turn of the UK to benefit from such gap-bridging.

Comparative pay rates suggest how large the possibilities are.
Going rates of pay reflect, by and large, average productivity
levels. Labour costs per man-hour are less in Britain than in most
advanced industrial countries – whether one looks at wages alone,
or total costs per man including social insurance overheads. For
a company which can employ best-practice international techniques the UK is a very low wage country indeed. Indeed it has
been called by some wit an FDC – 'formerly developed country'.
The greater the gap between existing productivity and that ob-
tainable with best international practice, the greater is the profitability of action to reduce the gap.

Latest trends

Policy changes

The attempt to rethink British economic policy goes back well
before the election of Mrs Thatcher's Conservative Government
in 1979. The first big change was the abandonment of Keynesian
demand-management policies – which would be summarized by
sceptics as the attempt by a country to spend it into target levels
of employment. Under the last Labour Government adult unemployment rose from less than 600,000, or $2\frac{1}{2}$ per cent, in 1974
to a peak of 1.4 million, or nearly 6 per cent, in 1977–78 without
any serious attempts to pump extra spending money into the
economy. (Indeed in terms of the headline figures, which included
school-leavers, the peak was even higher, over 1.6 million.)

This failure to apply orthodox Keynesian policies was partly a
negative decision not to take 'reflationary' action. It was also,
however, a positive decision to impose limits on public-sector
borrowing and monetary growth, which precluded the use of
these instruments for stimulating output and employment. Both

positive and negative decisions owed a great deal to pressures from the International Monetary Fund (IMF) and fears about international confidence which came to a head during the sterling crises of 1976.

To some extent the IMF was a convenient pretext. As a result of the inflationary explosion of the early 1970s, a belief grew in governing circles that control of the money supply was at least a necessary condition for controlling inflation; and in turn this required a limit on public-sector deficits, if it was to be accomplished without soaring interest rates. This 'practical monetarism' was the policy of Mr Denis Healey, the Labour Chancellor; and his commitment to it increased when even the limited demand stimulus of 1978-79 in the period up to the election led to a flood of imports and only a modest increase in output. The fierce attacks by Mr Healey on monetarism - not merely when Mrs Thatcher came to office, but even when he was carrying out similar policies himself - were a smokescreen which obscured the timing of the change, and the degree of agreement between leaders of different political parties.

The shift in policy objectives was presented in an unnecessarily mystifying way under both governments. The basic shift was from the attempt to control *real demand* and output, to controlling *money demand* only - or, in symbols, MV, money times velocity. This is identical under national accounting conventions to money GDP, or 'nominal GDP' as it is sometimes called.

Misfortune and mistakes

Despite the would-be monetary rectitude of both the outgoing Labour Government and the incoming Conservative one, there was a fresh inflationary spasm in 1979-80. Inflation, which had fallen to 8 per cent in 1978, rose to a peak of 18 per cent in 1980. This was below the previous peak of 24 per cent reached in 1975; but it was still higher than in other OECD countries. The higher inflation rate was especially remarkable and dangerous in view of the 20-25 per cent appreciation in the effective sterling exchange rate in 1979-80.

The most well-publicized reason for the fresh inflationary upsurge was the switch from direct to indirect taxes by the incoming Conservative Government, which added 3 to 4 per cent to the retail prices' index in order to finance a reduction in the basic rate of income tax from 33 to 30 per cent. The switch was particularly harmful because it coincided with the second world oil explosion of 1979–80, following the deposition of the Shah, which had a knock-on effect on UK prices of another 3 or 4 per cent. It was unfortunate that the full extent of the oil crisis became apparent only during the course of the 1979 election campaign when party leaders were in no mood to adjust programmes and prospectuses.

On top of these two misfortunes came a third. The Labour Government had combined 'practical monetarism' with pay controls negotiated annually with union leaders and imposed by *ad hoc* expedients. By the pre-election winter of 1978–79, the unions, who had already overturned the pay norms in the private sector, were in full revolt in the public sector against the suggested Callaghan pay norm of 5 per cent. In order to buy off the public-sector workers, the Labour Government offered them post-dated pay cheques to be awarded on the basis of 'comparability' studies by the Clegg Commission and other bodies, a commitment in which the Conservatives joined for vote-maximization reasons. Fourthly, there was in 1979–80 a temporary loosening of monetary and fiscal policy due *inter alia* to the financing of the Clegg awards, and the initial reluctance of the new Conservative Government to raise interest rates to a level consistent with its monetary objective.

As a result of these cumulative misfortunes and mistakes, cost-push forces were at their height in early 1980. In contrast to their opposite numbers in other OECD countries, British union leaders attempted to maintain and increase living standards, despite the worldwide rise in real oil prices (some 150 per cent in 1979–80). At first they managed to do so for those of their members who remained at work.

The Medium Term Strategy

As 1980 progressed, the inflationary forces wore off and went sharply into reverse. Sterling M3, which was the monetary aggregate used for target-setting purposes, became subject to numerous distortions from 1980 onwards, first due to the lifting of exchange control, then to the lifting of the direct controls on bank deposits under the 'corset' scheme, and finally to the large amount of corporate 'distress borrowing' from the banks in the 1980–81 recession. Thus the overshoot of the official money supply totals (which rose by 20 per cent in the course of 1980, or twice as fast as intended) gave an impression which was almost the opposite of the truth.

The one potentially important economic innovation of the Thatcher Government was the Medium Term Financial Strategy (MTFS) (see Table 3). This was inaugurated in 1980; but few people in political or industrial circles woke up to its significance until 1981, when taxes were raised in a recession to cover part of an overshoot in public spending. The purpose of the MTFS was to remedy a crucial defect in the hand-to-mouth monetarism of earlier years, the basic defect of which was that it provided no basis for long-term expectations by economic agents. Thus it

Table 3   **The Medium Term Financial Strategy expressed in terms of money GDP**

	Money GDP percentage increase per annum	
	Actual	Target[b]
1969–74[a]	13	
1975–76[a]	22	
1977–78[a]	14½	
1979	15	
1980	17	
1981	10½[c]	10½
1982		10
1983		9½
1984		9½

[a] Compound average.
[b] The targets for 1981–85 inclusive are based on the Medium Term Financial Strategy set out in the 1982 Financial Statement and Budget Review ('Red Book').
[c] Estimate.
SOURCE: CSO and Financial Statements, 1980 and 1981 (HMSO, London).

tended to magnify the effects of monetary squeezes on output and employment and delay the effect on wages and prices, as there always seemed a possibility that inflationary awards would be ratified by subsequent increases in monetary demand.

The MTFS was stated as a series of declining monetary growth targets up to 1983-84. Its true significance was not the exact numbers, but the suggestion that total spending would be limited in money terms and that cost-push forces, whether from pay increases, oil price shocks or any other source, would not be accommodated. The underlying idea was to reduce inflationary expectations and introduce more modest ideas of the pay and price increases people could hope to obtain.

If successful, it would be in advance of anything attempted in almost any other country. Indeed it would amount to a new domestic monetary standard, comparable to the gold standard or Bretton Woods. But it is much too early to celebrate the Strategy, which was introduced in the teeth of the scepticism, not merely of the bulk of the Cabinet and Conservative MPs (some of whom signed a very foolish report on the subject, led by the nose by a Labour MP who blinded them with supposed science and managed to exercise a key role in the choice of advisers). It was opposed even by supposedly Thatcherite Ministers who regarded a week in economics as a long time and who were so confused by anything to do with numbers that they could not distinguish between statements of intention, forecasts, 'fine-tuning', adjustments to new information and policy reversals.

Those members of the Opposition parties who saw the point of it kept very quiet indeed, as they had no wish to look as if they were on the 'right' of the Conservatives. Thus the MTFS is still an experiment as these pages go to press. In any case it came too late to lessen the 1980-81 recession.

Oil and sterling

The development which had the biggest effect on the economy was one that was neither predicted nor desired by any school of politicians or economists: it was the appreciation in the real exchange rate for sterling in 1979-80. Over these two years the trade-weighted sterling effective exchange rate rose by nearly 25 per cent. As British costs rose faster than those of competitor countries, the real exchange rate rose even further. The IMF index of relative unit labour costs pointed to a deterioration of 40 to 50 per cent in cost competitiveness. It is unnecessary to take such figures at face value to appreciate the intense squeeze imposed on exporters and producers of goods and services, subject to import competition – which in total covered about half the economy.

Part of the reason for sterling's appreciation was North Sea oil, which displaced oil imports and allowed the UK to balance its current account with a smaller volume of manufacturing exports, relative to imports. But the direct terms-of-trade effect of North Sea oil (accounting for a sterling appreciation of perhaps 10 per cent) was not nearly large enough to explain all the rise of the pound in world currency markets.

Riding on the back of North Sea output – like an elephant on a camel – was a much larger flow-of-funds effect. The combination of large OPEC surpluses, political and financial uncertainties about Germany and the US, and political stability and assured energy supplies in Britain, were all making the UK into a magnet for footloose international funds. These were boosting several-fold the direct impact of North Sea oil output.

Despite agreements to 'phase out' sterling's role as a reserve currency, exchange reserves held by overseas national authorities in sterling rose by £1.4 billion, in the four years to the end of 1980, to reach £4 billion. Sterling liabilities to non-official overseas holders rose by £6.5 billion to reach £10 billion, easily a record. Moreover, the *ex post* figures do not tell the whole story. The pound had to rise to balance the increasing demand for sterling with the available supply. (At an unchanged sterling rate, the build-up of overseas balances would have been even higher.)

These shifts in overseas demand explain why sterling rose and inflation fell much faster than expected in 1980-81, despite an overshoot in the domestic money supply. The combination of North Sea oil and huge footloose OPEC surpluses led to an increase in the demand for sterling even bigger than the increase in supply.

As always when demand exceeds supply, the price rose. A rise in the price of sterling in terms of marks or dollars meant that German and American goods were much cheaper to buy with pounds than before. This very fact put pressure on profit margins and made the recession in the UK worse than elsewhere. At the same time it induced British producers to hold down their own costs and prices if they were to stay alive in the international market. Companies were caught between the large wage increases of 1978-80, following the collapse of the Callaghan incomes policy, and the exchange-rate pressures which prevented them from passing on these increases in higher prices. These pressures led to a drop in the inflation rate to about 10 per cent in 1981-2. The deceleration exceeded all earlier forecasts, and was accompanied by a drive to reduce costs and improve efficiency of a severity which no British government committed to 'gradualism' would have dared to attempt consciously.

The main contribution of the Thatcher Government was the passive one of allowing sterling's real appreciation to take place, without intervening in the foreign-exchange market or panic reductions in interest rates. Even after the fall in sterling in the later months of 1981, British costs were still high relative to other countries and profit margins were still under pressure. Thus corporate resistance to wage claims continued, as did the drive for improved productivity.

A productivity miracle?

The motivation for government policy – negative although much of it was – was the desire to reduce inflation. By 1981 inflation was down to near the OECD average, but with many questions about how much further inflation would fall. As the near-hysterical attacks on 'monetarism' showed, British political, journalistic and business opinion still remained highly inflationist and clamoured for what it called a U-turn, i.e. a return to large Budget deficits, money creation and the deliberate downward manipulation of the exchange rate. It was unlikely that either Mrs Thatcher *or any likely successor* would grant these wishes. The question was more how far the anti-inflationary momentum could be maintained in the face of normal pre-election pressures. (A general election is due by the spring 1984 at the very latest.)

The most interesting results of the squeeze were not however on the inflation front but in terms of productivity. Although wage increases in exposed competitive sectors were down well into single percentage figures by 1981, the main change which allowed international trading companies to survive in business was a fierce attack on overmanning and restrictive practices.

There had earlier been a false dawn. By the early 1970s, output per employee in manufacturing, if not in the whole economy, was growing at the same rate as that of the main European countries. This improvement was lost in the inflationary slump ('stagflation') of the middle 1970s, when if anything the growth gap widened further. In the 1980–81 slump, however, the most severe since the early 1930s, employers made a determined and success-ful attempt to reduce labour forces which had become inflated over decades and to insist on realistic manning levels for new equipment. Even heavily subsidized public-sector concerns such as British Steel and British Leyland hit the headlines with labour-shedding agreements and with low single-figure wage settlements.

Several questions needed to be answered before an 'economic miracle' could be proclaimed. The exact size of the improvement in productivity would take a long time to be established and could be measured only when the economy emerged from reces-sion. One question was whether the productivity improvement would continue once the UK emerged from recession, and the immediate pressures were reduced. Nevertheless, the real appre-ciation of sterling up to the end of 1980 had been so great that quite a large recovery in output and depreciation of sterling could occur without restoring profit margins to normal. Moreover even a once-for-all productivity jump would affect the productivity *trend* over a decade; and contrary to the old saying, nature sometimes moves in leaps.

Jobless prosperity?

The biggest threat to the British economic miracle was the emergence of a severe unemployment problem, exceeding that of other countries – where unemployment had also been on a rising trend. Towards the end of 1981 seasonally adjusted adult unemployment was near 2¾ million, or 12 per cent, and official forecasts pointed to no more than a levelling-off in 1982–83 (with still higher figures of '3 million' in newspaper headlines).

These figures did not quite mean what they seemed. A large outflow from the unemployment register continued and about 7 million people found new jobs even in 1981. Thus the '3 million unemployed' were not one group but an ever-changing constellation.

Moreover living standards held up despite the recession, as Table 4 shows. In the winter of 1980–81, real GDP was about the

Table 4 **Change in real personal disposable income in the UK, after allowing for tax, benefits and inflation**

1948–57 (average)	2.6	*1976*	−0.6
1957–64 (average)		*1977*	−2.1
(*'Never had it so good' years*)	3.8	*1978*	8.3
1964–70 (average)	2.2	*1979*	5.7
1970–74 (average)	4.2	*1980*	2.0
1975	−1.7	*1981*	−2.0[a]

[a] Estimate.
SOURCE: Central Statistical Office, London.

same as in 1975, the trough of the last recession. Manufacturing output was 13 per cent down compared with that previous low point and nearly 20 per cent down compared with the 1979 peak – a contraction not seen since the interwar depression. On the other hand real personal disposable income was 15 per cent up on 1975 and nearly 18 per cent up on 1977. There were several reasons for this discrepancy. Manufacturing was much harder hit than the rest of the economy both by the recession and by a longer-term decline. Yet the purchasing power in international markets of a given total GDP increased. The rise in the exchange rate was associated with an improvement in the terms of trade and, despite the recession, the real value of the national product ('national disposal income') rose by 8 per cent between 1977 and 1980, not too bad a performance even by Continental standards.

The truth is that, for all the hysteria in the media and among panic-stricken Conservative backbenchers, the mass of the population had 'never had it so good', in the immortal words of ex-Premier Harold Macmillan. Unfortunately some of them had had it a little too good and priced their fellow workers out of jobs. The high level of unemployment was both a social and economic waste; and it posed a threat of make-work policies designed deliberately to slow down productivity growth or take people forcibly out of the working population.

The spectre of jobless prosperity was not due to any absence of 'demand' in any normal understanding of these words. The MTFS provided implicitly for a growth of monetary demand, as measured by money GDP, of 10–11 per cent in 1981–82, gradually declining to $9\frac{1}{2}$ per cent in 1983–84. These rates were quite sufficient to ensure a recovery in employment, even on very optimistic views of productivity, so long as demand was not siphoned off into higher wages and prices. Past experience suggested that boosting demand growth would lead mainly to more inflation and a fresh application of the economic brakes. Moreover, rough estimates of the underlying non-cyclical unemployment rate (Friedman's 'natural rate') suggested that it was well over 2 million, or not far from 10 per cent.

The jobless problem was due to a combination of severe structural change and an ossified labour market. The British economy has had to adjust to (a) the sharp increase in energy prices which has made many processes and products obsolescent; (b) the drift in the most efficient location of many traditional manufacturing industries to the newly industrializing countries; (c) the effects of North Sea oil in crowding-out non-oil exports; (d) the long delayed attack on overmanning; and (e) the rapid reduction in inflation. The first two are common to other industrial countries, the last three unique to Britain. They have combined to produce very heavy manpower losses in manufacturing industry.

The demand for labour is not fixed either by technology or by the government. It depends crucially on the price of labour, that is wages: both the general wage level and relativities between different kinds of workers. The sharp rise in unemployment was hardly surprising considering that the earnings index rose by $15\frac{1}{2}$ per cent in 1979 and $20\frac{1}{2}$ per cent in 1980, at a time when the pound was rising sharply and earnings in other countries were rising by smaller amounts.

According to the new specially adjusted earnings index published in the Department of Employment *Gazette*, the increase in earnings in 1981 was down to an annualized rate of about 10 per cent – and by several percentage points less in manufacturing industry. Taking into account productivity improvements, British competitiveness was beginning to recover. But the earnings deceleration needed to go further in order to price people into jobs; and relativities needed to shift a great deal to reflect market forces more closely.

Union pressures priced people out of work, not only in particular industries, but in particular categories. One of the worst examples was the insistence on young people being paid the full adult wage, irrespective of productive performance. An OECD Report[8] attributed the low level of youth unemployment in Germany compared to other countries not only to the apprentice system, but to the fact that wage levels of new entrants are 'adjusted to their productive capacity'. Denmark had a German-type apprenticeship system, but the rate of youth unemployment there soared suddenly at the age of 18 when a minimum wage corresponding to two-thirds of average manual earnings became obligatory.

More generally, union pressures led to workers being priced out of the more heavily unionized sectors and being crowded into other sectors, where the level of wages was forced down towards the social-security minimum. This unionization effect was estimated by the Liverpool model (*Lloyds Bank Review*, April 1981) to raise unemployment by up to 3 per cent, or nearly three-quarters of a million. The Wages Council System, which established minimum pay in low-wage industries, worked in the same direction.

Market distortions with which people can live in normal times cause particular damage in periods when rapid change is required.

The Manpower Services Commission (MSC) pointed out that only one per cent of the working population moved household for job or training reasons each year. Such movement has been heavily discouraged by rent controls which led to the disappearance of one-third of privately rented units in the last decade.

Wages can be too low as well as too high to clear the market. Wherever employers are prevented from paying more for people of special skills or in particular regions, labour shortages will co-exist with unemployment elsewhere. The MSC warned in 1981 about skill shortages developing in the upturn, even while employment generally was still depressed.

Assessment

My own guess is that in the competitive private sector, wages will very gradually adjust towards market-clearing levels, despite union obstacles. It is in the public sector that the religion of uniform grades prevails most strongly and where it is impossible to vary pay in accordance with regional or occupational variations in supply and demand. It is also the area where monopoly employers and monopoly unions confront each other, with the Exchequer as banker of last resort.

If the public-sector industries, responsible for a third of total employment, could be broken up – whether by denationalization, devolution, local workers' control or any other method – the worst distortions in the labour market would be removed. The Labour Party is too tied to the unions and the Conservatives are too guilt-ridden to tackle this nexus of problems. But it is in the political arena, nevertheless, that the main grounds of hope are to be found.

Political innovations

Without raising false hopes, it is possible to point to a great change for the better in the political environment. A new reformist group, the Social Democratic Party, without the Labour Party's attachment to outworn dogma or the union connection, has been formed – the biggest political change in the lifetime of most Britons. Their task is made more difficult by the peculiar bias of the British voting system which can lead to an enormous discrepancy between seats and votes and which is particularly loaded against new and smaller parties. But despite this formidable obstacle, the new Social Democrats have, in conjunction with the Liberals, at least a chance of holding the balance of power, if not more, in the next Parliament.

The trouble with the traditional two-party system is that under it people had no alternative but to vote for almost any Labour or Conservative leadership, irrespective of quality or programme, if they were sufficiently frustrated to want to dismiss the existing government – which they very often were. This gave party activists and interest groups a disproportionate influence relative to normal voters because their leaders could afford to indulge them, for example the mass of pro-union legislation by Michael Foot when Employment Secretary in 1974–76, or the policies favouring the armed forces and the farmers under the Conservatives since 1979.

The arrival of a third group could change the character of the political market. The new group will make less likely the arrival of a Labour government completely opposed to – or having to make a show of being opposed to – the profit motive and the market system. The Labour Party itself will no longer be able to run on such policies just to please its activists, and hope to arrive in office on the basis of disillusionment with the Conservatives.

The breakdown of the winner-takes-all system will also be beneficial when the Conservatives are in the lead. Indeed, one reason why Thatcherite policies ran into such heavy political weather is that they were the result of a takeover of the Conservative leadership to which the old guard were still unreconciled. Not being able to sell their policies to their own Cabinet or Party, economic ministers were unable to reach out to a broader political spectrum. Thus, arguments about policies were bogged down in theological dispute about the nature of Conservatism, just as arguments about nationalization or nuclear arms were once conducted in terms of 'the meaning of socialism'.

There is thus a very good chance that we shall see the end of the notorious policy switches between, and within, every Parliament which makes the British political environment so much a curse to the business community. Any enacted changes will in the end have broader support and be less likely to be reversed than under the present system of elective dictatorship. This favourable prognosis does not depend on any wildly optimistic view of the Social Democrats – or even agreement with all their policies. It arises rather from the prospect of new rules of the political game and a changed political market.

Even then utopia is far away. The most that is likely is a shift from the English sickness to a share in the general problems of the Western industrialized countries, which remain reasonably affluent but have still to recover from the shock to their self-confidence and optimism triggered off by the first oil price explosion of 1973–74, and the subsequent check to growth and employment in the years that followed.

Notes

1 I am grateful to *The Journal of Law and Economics*, Chicago, for permission to draw extensively on the text of the seventh Henry Simons Lecture, 'How British is the British sickness?', vol. XXI, October 1978.
2 Memorandum on Fiscal Policy of International Trade (1913), reprinted in *Official Papers* (London, 1926), pp. 404–6.
3 Angus Maddison, 'Phases of Capitalist Development', *Banca Nationale del Lavoro Q. Rev.* (1977), 103.
4 Daniel T. Jones, 'Output, Employment and Labour Productivity since 1955', *National Institute Review*, 1976.
5 Henry C. Simons, 'Some Reflections on Syndicalism', in *Economic Policy for a Free Society* (Chicago, 1948), pp. 121, 130–31, 146–8.
6 A.V. Dicey, *Low and Public Opinion in England* (reprinted Macmillan, London, 1963).
7 Mancur Olson Jr, 'The Political Economy of Comparative Growth Rates' (1978) (mimeo, Univ. of Maryland).
8 'Youth Unemployment', *OECD Observer* (HMSO, London, March 1981).

5 The Italian crisis

Guido Carli

During the 1970s the Italian economy suffered the consequences of changes in both endogenous and exogenous factors, which affected both its performance and its development prospects. These changes involved some of the conditions which, during the previous two decades, had directly contributed to turning Italy into a modern industrial country.

Most of the changes occurred on the supply side of the economy: firms became less flexible in reacting to external shocks; the economic policy decision-centres lost a good deal of their ability to perform an autonomous role in steering the economy. Furthermore, the interaction between economic policies and constraints on firms and market operations made policies ineffective as instruments of growth and instead confined their effects to deflation.

At the end of the 1970s and the beginning of the 1980s, the Italian economy is characterized by severe restriction of profits and a sharp reduction in the resources employed in investment.

In the last ten years, both the share of available resources used for export purposes, and the general conditions in which the industrial system operated underwent significant changes. The system suffered a drastic change in the relative prices of inputs and outputs, while the social and economic framework in which it operated was rapidly transformed. Private and public agents and policy-makers often intervened in a disorderly fashion in promoting or offsetting short-term adjustments. This contributed to changes in the economic environment. Events and corrective policy actions interfered negatively with each other, in an economy largely deprived of its ability to function according to traditional economic rules.

The Italian economy proved very successful in achieving short-term adjustments. But it was much slower to adapt its institutional and productive structures to the new internal and international situation. Success in bringing under control the deficit in the external balance, the exchange rate and inflation was offset by largely negative consequences in the medium and long term for the structures of production.

The Italian economy in the 1970–77 period

Over the last ten years the fall in growth rates and the rise in unemployment – problems largely shared by other industrialized economies – was paralleled by a progressive deterioration of the conditions required for continuing capital accumulation. The quality and quantity of productive real investments fell steadily and it appeared increasingly difficult to attract them. This limited the possibility of labour force re-absorption, and of reforming the structure of the productive system, though the exposure of the economy to external shocks required both.

Various exogenous factors, operating in different ways and with differing intensity, affected the development opportunities of the Italian economy during the 1970s. The rise in raw-material prices and in the price of imports generally, reversed the condition which had contributed most to the expansion of output. In 1963–64, for example, this element had actually offset the pressures arising from other, endogenous costs. Later, it became a cause for disequilibria in the accounts of firms, especially after 1973.

The impact of the exogenous factors was dramatic, particularly in view of simultaneous trends in the cost of labour. Wage rises added to increased import prices from 1969 on. After 1973 pressures on firms' accounts became stronger because productivity growth, which had been steady and sustained until 1969, declined further, thus strongly pushing unit labour costs upwards.

Productivity was primarily affected by institutional factors associated with wage bargaining. They became an autonomous force in the crisis, perhaps of greater importance than nominal wages; they introduced rigidities in the use of plant and in the modifications of factor combinations. In 1975, the introduction of new forms of wage indexation introduced an automatic mechanism for the almost complete protection of money wages. This mechanism prevented any recovery from the previous rise in exogenous costs caused by the first oil shock, and they worked as a vehicle for the diffusion of inflationary processes of whatever origin. Their introduction was accepted in view of the expectations of improved productivity due to better industrial relations. However, these expectations were largely disappointed by the unions' behaviour, which proved inconsistent with the constraints imposed by the interdependencies of the productive system, and indeed with the results of indexation itself.

The continuous and large fall in profits experienced by firms in the 1970s indicates the difficulties they met in transferring to prices the rises in costs, and in changing the factor combinations in order to restore efficiency. Another sign of the same difficulties was the worsening of the 'terms of trade' as between productive inputs and outputs.

Both phenomena show how the Italian economy inherited from the past some specific features: it continued to be based on first transformation processes and remained conditioned by wage developments which often conflicted with the need for the competitiveness of Italian products in domestic and export markets.

The use of largely imitated technologies and the relatively low added value of production made the external constraints to the expansion of output more significant. Because of the need to increase the value of exports, mostly by increasing the quantity of goods exported rather than by higher unit values, competitiveness became a necessary condition for the enlargement or even the preservation of the Italian share of international markets. From 1972 on, in spite of the currency devaluation as well as the strong dependence of the Italian economy on external factors, the Italian share of world trade decreased slightly.

The profit shrink was further worsened by the economic policy aimed at the solution of the 1974–75 and the 1976 crises. The measures to bring inflation, the exchange rate and the external deficit under control conflicted with the need for structural reforms of the productive system. Increasing capital investment, which started after the rise in the relative cost of labour and thus the necessity to offset rising costs with higher productivity, was robbed of its effect both by policies and by the consequences of public-sector activity.

Public-sector behaviour proved very important, both through the combined effect of expenditures and revenues, and by the impact of growing deficit financing on the financial markets.

The increasing inefficiency of public expenditure brought about a decline in capital-account expenditure and a lower incidence of public expenditure on aggregate demand. Larger current transfers had small multiplier effects on private investment, but contributed steadily to disposable family income. Together with indexation, this made the control of internal resources and the equilibrium in the balance of payments increasingly difficult; it thus led to adjustments mostly based on investment restrictions.

The government deficit also had a negative impact on the financial markets. A growing absorption of credit by the public sector kept private investment low. This effect was enhanced by the combined impact of public-sector financial needs and the behaviour of monetary authorities with respect to interest rates. The way the public sector affected liquidity and credit control, by way of enlarging the monetary base, delayed the normalization of the interest-rate structure.

This situation in the capital markets, together with many institutional constraints, largely determined the supply of capital in the medium and long term. Interest rates on short-term funds were volatile, and banks contributed to their rise in order to make up for the loss in revenue they were suffering because of portfolio constraints.

Such a situation, leading to a persistent high cost of money and to increased distortion in the structure of firms' liabilities, had a strong effect on the financing of firms and thus on their balance-sheets, especially after 1973. This affected production costs and hence capital revenues, and thus increased the obstacles to investments and restructuring of plants. While the latter consequences were less immediate they were very important for growth prospects. Changes in factor costs increased the need for structural reforms, while government measures made their realization more difficult.

The effect on the Italian economy of the oil shock of 1973-74, together with the modification of the wage-indexation mechanism of 1975, was a sharp reduction in profits and investments, in a situation of a generalized fall in external and internal demand. Economic policy and firms relied on credit, and the pressures of private firms on the credit market contributed to rising interest rates. The cyclical recovery of 1975 pushed interest rates further upward. From the first quarter of 1976 on, this movement continued and reached a climax at the end of the year with credit restrictions by which the monetary authorities tried to control the fast rises in the level of prices and the balance of payments, which was rapidly deteriorating because of the expansion of real demand.

Currency devaluation was an important part of the economic policy followed during 1976. It helped to sustain profit margins of the trading sector of the economy. It also contributed to worsen inflationary pressures, because it transmitted faster rises in imported inputs costs into labour cost by way of the new indexation mechanism. The financial stability of firms deteriorated further.

Policy interventions were intended to deal with the structural aspects of the crisis, leaving aside short-term policies. A number of laws were enacted and some proposals were made concerning, for instance, the financial restructuring of firms and medium-term plans to accelerate the reform of the Italian economy. Their effect was very limited.

By the end of 1976 all the factors which had contributed to the 'economic miracle' seemed to have been reversed. The social and political conditions which had previously allowed for economic policies designed to bring about internal and external equilibria, were rapidly changing.

The productive system was progressively losing its vitality while remaining extremely vulnerable to the external situation as well as economic policy. Monetary policy, for instance, imposed sudden stops to economic activity, while public expenditure and trade unions were independently contributing to increase inflationary pressures and produce macroeconomic disequilibria.

Distortions in prices and in market behaviour, sometimes introduced with the purpose of moderating the effects of stabilizing manœuvres, made the results of economic policies unpredictable. Stimuli to the recovery of activity were actually stunted and distorted by mechanisms operating in the various markets and by institutional factors which, by making the productive system more rigid, transformed them into inflationary pressures, thus requiring further stabilizing monetary actions. In this framework of uncontrolled and disorderly expectations, traditional Keynesian interventions became largely ineffective.

The 1978-79 recovery and the new oil shock of 1979

In spite of this situation, in December 1978 the conditions of the Italian economy were assessed by many in an optimistic retroperspective, that is, by comparing them to those at the end of the 1950s and the beginning of the 1960s, the time of the so-called 'economic miracle'. Discussions about the structural weakness of the Italian economic system were replaced by forecasts of growth rates of 5-6 per cent for 1979, and for large surpluses in the balance of payments, even after Italy had joined the EMS, which tied the lira to the strongest European currencies, and even in the presence of a considerable inflation rate.

The general concern for the structural aspects of the Italian crisis became attenuated after the temporary fall in the real price of oil and after the reduction of the OPEC countries' current-account surplus. The decreased importance of structural problems at the international level was matched by their reduced incidence at the national level. In Italy, medium- and long-term borrowing declined to slightly above 1.5 billion dollars in December 1978; the official debts were all repaid at the end of 1979. A single short-term intervention package, approved in September

1976, and some financial interventions, like changes in the port-folio constraints imposed on the banks, and credit ceilings, were apparently sufficient to solve the structural crisis of the Italian economy, even before the introduction of more effective medium- and long-term measures.

Such improvements in the real and financial conditions of the international economy facilitated the 1978–79 recovery more than the austerity measures imposed by the government in 1976, which, on the contrary, depressed the level of economic activity. The improvement in the terms of trade started, in 1978, a period of growth, associated with a surplus in the balance of payments. This fast recovery was achieved without particular short- or medium-term policy measures.

This does not mean that there was a total absence of economic policy. The most careful manœuvre was the control of the ex-change rate. The depreciation of the dollar *vis-à-vis* the EEC currencies allowed the Bank of Italy to keep the lira tied to the dollar, from late 1976. This policy was, in view of the weakness of the US currency, a compromise between appreciation relative to the dollar and depreciation relative to the European currencies. In other words, the position of the lira was largely dominated by movements of the US dollar. It was almost impossible to pursue an independent policy for the Italian currency. But, from 1976 on, the position of the dollar in international monetary relations was such that it allowed for conditions highly favourable to the Italian economy.

Along with a large increase in government participation in the social-security contributions of firms, in February 1977, the exchange-rate policy restored some of the conditions present during the years of the 'economic miracle': low nominal price rises of industrial imported inputs, mostly quoted in US dollars, and improved competitiveness and profitability in industry. It would be wrong to believe that the lack of any medium- and long-term policy for the Italian economy involved no changes at all in its structure. As a matter of fact, the short-term policies themselves had, as we shall see, some structural effects.

At the very moment at which spontaneous adjustment mech-anisms had removed the need to concentrate all efforts on structural interventions, the stability of the price of oil was suddenly shaken. Between the end of 1978 and the end of 1979 the oil price rose by 75 per cent in nominal terms. A large current-account deficit reappeared and recycling problems again became urgent in 1979. It also became clear that the OPEC countries were now more inclined to keep the real price of oil constant by controlling the quantity supplied and exported. Thus, any inflationary adjustment used to reduce the real price of oil had less chance to be successful.

The new oil price rises struck Italy at a moment of sustained growth and exchange-rate stability. Many believed that anti-inflationary measures like those of 1976 would be sufficient to control the impact of the new oil shock on the inflation rate and the balance of payments. In addition, policy options were reduced by increasing difficulties in controlling aggregate demand because of the effects of wage-indexation and of rigidities in the use of labour, quite apart from the difficulties in restructuring public expenditure.

Possibilities for an effective monetary policy were not great. The rigid defence of revenues from savings had been attenuated, while the extension of the public debt maturity structure, through interest-rate manipulation, excluded any possibility of using this instrument. Control of the total money supply was the only possible action, but it was hindered by the difficulties arising from balance-of-payments movements and the public borrowing deficit.

Thus, the exchange rate was the only readily usable instrument. However, membership of the EMS, in March 1979, reduced the national possibilities of taking advantage of international conditions and of adjusting the exchange rate in order to improve terms of trade and export competitiveness. After joining the EMS, the lira appreciated in effective terms. This increased the positive differential Italy had accumulated with respect to the rise in price and cost levels of competing countries, thus contributing to its real appreciation. This policy, which West Germany and the UK followed in 1978–79, was aimed at using the appreciating exchange rate to control the internal rate of inflation. However, this was hardly tolerable in the conditions imposed on firms by the new cost shock, without further compromising export competitiveness. Meanwhile structural interventions and medium-term policies were neglected once again.

The sustained growth of 1979 was associated with a higher-than-expected rise of inflation. This confirmed the impression that the system was now largely out of control so far as economic policy-makers were concerned, since both price and output levels were dominated by exogenous factors, i.e. import prices and external demand. The interaction of these impulses triggered a demand-production-expectation mechanism which exerted strong inflationary pressures on the price level.

After the worsening of the terms of trade, and accession to the EMS, the Italian economy, characterized as it is by strong structural rigidities, became more dependent on international developments and lost the use of a policy instrument which had previously proved very effective. The economy appeared to have escaped any short-term control at a moment when external shocks were highly destabilizing. The OPEC decisions and the economic policy of the United States affect Europe directly. The lack of a common policy *vis-à-vis* the dollar makes the EMS countries very dependent on changes in the US currency value and less capable of controlling external pressures on prices by an exchange-rate policy. The fast and strong impact which the new oil shock of 1979 had on the Italian economy was directly caused by the fragility of the adjustment to the first oil shock, by the lack of any lasting structural adaptation to the change which had occurred, and by the progressive loss of efficacy of the economic policy instruments. Therefore the response of the economy to the changes deserves some further consideration.

Structural rigidities and adjustment

The transformation of the Italian economy from an agricultural economy into an industrial one had taken advantage of favourable terms of trade as between imported raw materials and finished output. The reversal of this fundamental condition could have been absorbed by the economy, if policy-makers had grasped the need for structural reform, and if the consequences of a permanent change in the terms of trade for productive factor combination and for the behaviour of the economic agents had been appreciated.

In the absence of a policy of this kind, the response of the Italian system had to be either of the inflationary or of the deflationary kind. An inflationary adjustment was a simple response to the monopoly power exerted by the oil-exporting countries. This required either an improvement of the political relationship or spontaneous acceptance of this reaction by the OPEC countries.

The inflationary solution was partly followed. This was the result of the lack of effectiveness of economic policy and the lack of international cohesion among the industrialized countries. The latter further worsened the crisis of the dollar, which made inflationary adjustments easier for economies heavily dependent, like the Italian one, on the US currency.

The deflationary solution would have meant acceptance of the new international distribution of resources. The social cost of this adjustment could have been reduced by a strong rise in labour productivity and larger capital investments with lower energy consumption. This would have been the way to obtain more products to pay for less quantity per output of more expensive energy. This strategy failed because of rigidities in the use of labour and insufficient investments.

The adherence of Italy to the EMS was an attempt to prevent the continuation of the inflationary process. It was intended to remove some of the conditions favouring inflation which were created by international monetary relations. Nevertheless the consequences of the EMS for the Italian economy were significant, especially in terms of its effects on economic policies. The lack of a defined relation between the EMS and the dollar allowed for a period of dependence on the strong currencies mostly used to pay for Italian exports, while the US dollar which determined the price of imports underwent a period of depreciation. By reducing preoccupation with production cost, this delayed more effective policy interventions.

The inflationary adjustment brought about a sustained demand for real goods. This, as we have seen, resulted in an improvement in the level of economic activity in the period 1978-79. However, the positive aspects of the good economic performance were largely of a short-term nature, and could not be reproduced by economic policies. The negative aspects, particularly the cost of financing debts, accumulated by firms after the rise in the cost of money, were bound to have structural consequences.

The role of the market in the adjustment process led to general agreement that market forces could solve the problems arising from the oil crisis. This attitude began to prevail in many western countries.

However, the Italian experience shows that the reaction of the market is too slow with respect to the intensity of the crisis and the rate of adjustment of our competing economies. Furthermore, spontaneous adjustment does not generate deep changes in the sector composition of industrial output and in the relations among sectors, as observed in other countries, like Japan.

Rigidity in the sector composition of industrial output reflects the lack of any strategy of structural intervention of economic policy; it also reflects differences in the way in which obstacles to the adjustment process affect the various sectors. The 'traditional' sectors, where small and medium-sized firms prevail, did most of the real adjustment. These sectors proved extremely dynamic. Evidence is provided by the so-called 'submerged' or 'black' economy, which is at least at the margin a part of these sectors, though it provides a solution to problems of the dimension of firms and to institutional aspects, rather than to output composition. However, it might well be that the real dimension of the 'traditional' sectors is larger than official figures show, given the role of the 'submerged' economy.

Productivity performance of medium and small firms was far better than that of large ones. Small industry and even the black economy does not necessarily work with backward technology. The elasticity of small industry, together with its advanced technology, permitted better adjustments. To the extent to which this was an alibi for private and public decision-makers not to intervene in the medium- and long-term problems of the productive structure, this seriously damaged the prospects for growth.

It is probably not unrealistic to say that rigidities in the composition of Italian industrial output were also the result of governmental budget policy. This proved to be oriented, as far as the productive system is concerned, to the principle of defending employment in a static sense, almost as a 'social value'. This policy, which was certainly influenced by the trade unions' behaviour, is unsuitable for the dynamism of a developed modern economy, which is largely dependent upon foreign trade.

Italy's inflationary adjustment to changes in the terms of trade had its own peculiar features due to the existence of the black economy and a charitable economic policy. Prices increase more than the growth rate. Productivity gains are more than offset by price rises. In the presence of high growth rates and high inflation, the system does not improve any of the sectors in crisis, but only the areas which are already performing well.

The disequilibrated financial structure of indebted firms has been identified as the reason for the insufficient extension of productivity and price benefits to the sectors in crisis. The unbalanced financial situation generates, in presence of inflation, a financial burden which cannot be re-absorbed in costs. This hampers the replacement of plant and hence the main vehicle for productivity growth.

In asking what kind of policy could improve the adjustment provided by market forces, one should remember that the exogenous character of the determination of cost neutralizes most of the possibilities otherwise open to the public authorities. The effectiveness of stabilization policies themselves is today limited by the trends in unit labour cost, the cost of capital and the cost of raw materials, all of which are removed from any control.

Unit labour cost is determined, through wage-indexation and productivity, by international inflationary pressures and by the demand for exports. The first effect does not require further examination. The second one depends upon the link between internal demand, current-account balance and the exchange rate, which leads to the connection between external demand and any productivity growth beyond the spontaneous tendency of our system. Unit labour costs are thus largely determined by international inflation and external demand, i.e. by factors dominated by forces uncontrolled by the authorities.

The same is true for the cost of capital, whose components, reinvestment and external financing, are also conditioned by international factors. Global demand and inflation, in the presence of static product and sector composition, determine the capital revenue. International interest rates determine the cost of money.

The exogenous character of the cost of imported raw materials can be partly offset by an exchange-rate policy, of the kind followed after the first oil shock, which requires a weak dollar. But the US currency exchange rate is characterized by large fluctuations, and participation in the EMS obliges the lira to follow its fluctuation in relation to the dollar.

Any economic policy should first of all bring under control the mechanisms of inflation diffusion, exchange-rate determination and productivity growth, in order to play an active role in the adjustment process. An effective economic policy also requires a drastic change in the budget policy, so as to restrict its contributions to production, in defence of the existent employment level, to increase those to investment and to reduce the 'crowding out' effect of its financing needs. Any other budget policy would be ineffective with respect to structural strategy and non-inflationary adjustments.

Absence of an effective policy, restricted margins resulting from previous devaluations, and a probable policy to defend the real price of oil by the producing countries, can lead only to new balance-of-payments crises. A further devaluation of the lira occurs at a time of already high inflation, and can only generate even higher inflation. The benefit to our exports from a devaluation can, at this stage, be no more than temporary. Participation of the raw-material-producing countries in a production structure similar to the Italian one, in competitive conditions, reduces the possibilities of counting on the performance of traditional sectors.

The effectiveness of monetary policy in preventing inflationary adjustments is reduced by the tendency to 'escape from money', due to the high inflation rate. The only instrument left is then the manipulation of interest rates; but any recourse to this has to take into account the financial conditions of firms.

In summary, the oil shock of 1973-74 had the following effects: the diminution of real resources through the sudden increase of the value of imports brought about an adjustment process based on lower investment, higher inflation and increased exports. The inflationary adjustment was facilitated by the reform of the wage-indexed mechanism introduced in 1975. Higher imported inputs' costs, transferred into prices, pushed nominal labour costs upwards. In the presence of low productivity, this brought about higher unit labour costs.

This exerted further pressures on prices. Structural problems of the Italian productive system turned inflation into the only possible kind of adjustment. The structural propensity to inflation, determined by the public-sector deficit, by its financing needs and by the indexation of the system, together with institutional limitations to changes in the employment structure and with the discouragement to investment due to the profit squeeze and to the use of resources by the public sector, all made the 'productive' answer to the oil shock not viable.

Nevertheless the favourable situation in the foreign exchange market allowed for an exchange-rate policy which proved very convenient for the defence of the competitiveness of Italian exports. The latter was better defended in the so-called 'traditional' sectors, or even in the 'submerged' economy, where productivity is higher.

The unexpectedly fast recovery of Italian exports, due to the contingent causes mentioned, made it possible to ignore the disadvantages of an inflationary adjustment and indeed to disregard completely any kind of structural policy to provide lasting solutions to the problems posed by the first oil crisis. The answer to the crisis, thus, was short-sighted, or, rather, it was no answer at all, since it was left to the system to adjust spontaneously.

The insufficiency of this adjustment revealed itself dramatically when all the favourable conditions which had permitted the 1978 recovery, started to disappear. When the exchange-rate situation again deteriorated, when the real price of oil started to rise once

more, and when the competition from newly industrialized and
primary producing countries in the low value-added export sectors became more aggressive, the same old answer to the first oil
shock was no longer possible.

Part III
The contribution of the European Community

6 The end of the road for Europe, or a new beginning?

Etienne Davignon

The 1970s: the great upheaval

Since the signature of the Treaty of Rome in 1957, and particularly during the 1970s, Europe has experienced major changes. Its international environment has been greatly modified, its appearance has changed, its social structures and its institutions have evolved. The second oil crisis struck Europe just as it was beginning to take real stock of the harmful effects of the first oil crisis of 1973. All the countries in the European Community were confronted with the same problems related to balance of payments, inflation, the budget, unemployment and, most of all, a youth which understandably wonders what the future has in store for it.

Some people state categorically that Europe is on its last wind. The expression is a convenient one, but I think that it is exaggerated and completely unacceptable. Democracy teaches us that citizens are to be governed and not abandoned to their fate. In particular, faced with these new challenges, Europe cannot allow itself to disappoint those who will be twenty in the year 2000.

During the last decade we have seen a new deal in the card game of life, one which requires more co-ordination and solidarity, and less confrontation. Whether it is the opening up of China, the industrial take-off of certain developing countries, the formation of cartels among oil-producing countries or the expansion of multinational firms, the truth is that today new actors occupy the international stage. The old economic order and world politics no longer exist, and the new – if there is anything new – are trying to take their place, even though one of the most important international negotiations, the North–South dialogue, is taking some time to get going.

This state of affairs poses serious constraints on the future of our societies, because the gap between the understandable aspirations of the different groups in this multifaceted world and reality, is growing daily for lack of the right machinery to regulate this new political deal.

The overlapping of the world economies, which is both cause and effect of this new deal, has become much more noticeable. World trade has increased in volume far more than production during the last twenty years. This shows as clearly as it is possible to do so, the increase in international specialization and its corollary, interdependence.

A second wind for Europe

The challenges which face us – even though some people pretend to ignore them – call for an original response from Europe in particular. At the level of the European Community, preparations are being made to take up the challenge. Starting with the budgetary impasse posed by the position of the United Kingdom and its contribution to the expenses of the EEC, the European Commission has proposed to the governments an in-depth study of the future construction of Europe.

True competition exists between the industrialized countries, and the emergence of new competitors only reinforces and stimulates it, thus accelerating the process of industrial readjustment, of withdrawal (naval construction, textiles, steel) and of redeployment (micro-electronics, space, bio-industry) etc. We are all being forced to search for the poles of competition, so as to be able to export and pay for compulsory imports. Nevertheless, the international division of labour which results from this must not be the result of fate or chance, but of coherent industrial and financial policies founded on innovation and judicious decisions in investment and research.

The course adopted by Japan in this context is particularly

enlightening. To adapt to this situation, to make better use of one's own strengths and resources without however withdrawing inwards – interdependence excludes a return to protectionism – these are the imperatives for the present and the future, dictated by interdependence and competition.

The evolution of the balance of power brought about by world-wide geo-political changes has been accompanied by profound changes: the ups and downs in the international monetary system, where the dollar henceforth plays a more perturbing than regu-lating role, the brutal evolution of the price of energy and of raw materials, contrasting growths in balances of payments, inflation, the increasing debt of the third-world countries – all these factors contribute towards destabilizing the world economy.

More and more countries are searching for palliatives of all kinds and trying to lessen their sensitivity to the international environment: the birth of the European Monetary System, the search for a lesser dependence in the field of raw materials, agreements of co-operation, are all positive routes. Will they be enough to fight the temptation to protectionism?

Above and beyond these considerations, more fundamental doubts are added to these constraints: the change in values, the questioning of the role of the state, the growing awareness of certain ill effects of growth (environment, urbanization, waste).

It is on our capacity for adapting and transforming economic and social systems that the possibility of finding a new road to growth will depend, rather than on our capacity for resisting change or withdrawing into ourselves.

The lessons of the past, or the price of a non-Europe

The difficult period which Europe is going through should serve, for those in positions of responsibility, as a valuable moment of reflection on past errors. We must not, as we have too often done in Europe, simply analyse, with an attention to detail which verges on masochism, all the tactical or strategic errors we have made. We can no longer allow ourselves the luxury of nostalgia. If it is clear that those responsible for politics and economics on national and European levels have made numerous mistakes over the last twenty years, we must nevertheless avoid moving straight from arrogance to uncontrolled panic.

It is clear, for example, that in traditional industries such as steel, shipbuilding and textiles, Europeans – industrialists too – have failed to notice certain warning signs which from the end of the 1960s onwards announced important changes in the world economy and the European economy in particular. Even in the past few months I have met, in certain parts of Europe where the decline is hitting centenarian industrial concerns, heads of firms who have obviously not understood that times have changed. They continue to believe that everyone else is wrong.

This arrogance is suicidal. Let us take the example of the Japanese motorbike in Europe. Ten years ago European industrialists announced the end of the growth of this means of transport, which was judged to be anachronistic, inconvenient and unsuitable for the European market. They thought that small cars on the one hand, very light motorcycles on the other, would fill this gap. The Japanese proved that they had a better understanding of our market, and of the motivations and tastes of European youth in particular, than their European counterparts. They triumphed spectacularly. Let those who complain about what Europe is costing them take note and ask themselves rather what the cost is of what I call 'non-Europe'.

Let us reflect on the costs, industrial and social, involved in the disappearance of an entire industry in Europe for lack of a common strategy. There are other examples to illustrate this foolish arrogance. Thus in shipbuilding the accumulation of national subsidies initially thwarted any industrial strategy and then led to a regrettable wasting of the last public shipyards. One result is that all the European countries without exception are practising a policy of subsidies, which means that right from the start one has to accept that the true cost of ships built in Europe will be 10 per cent more than those built elsewhere. This, too, is the price of a non-Europe.

One can certainly also criticize those in the European Commission, who have not always insisted on a European dimension in the Community's industrial structures. On the other hand, there is no lack of examples in the 'golden sixties' of industrialists and national politicians, if not refusing, at least preventing the implementation of European strategies. That was a period when everything was going well, when expanding economic activity was reflected in clear social advantages. It was also the period, alas, of a quasi-theological quarrel between the supporters of unbridled liberalism and the advocates of sterile interventionism. Europe itself was the greatest loser in this pointless debate.

Steel: the hard lesson of the indispensable European solution

Without mentioning success – a brave word in the midst of the deep crisis in the industrial sector – we must recognize that in 1981 no one any longer contests the fact that the European answer is the only one which will help us to overcome these problems.

At the end of the 1960s industrialists, governments, unions and European authorities all misjudged the future. They all thought that the 'engineer's dream', with more and more steel, could go on indefinitely. Several phenomena tore us away from these dreams: the fall in steel consumption in the world, the arrival in the export markets of new steel-producing countries and the ageing of certain factories brought about a structural overcapacity equivalent to 25 million tons of steel for Europe alone. In the middle of the 1970s the crisis resulting from the first oil shock hit this traditional sector very hard. The mistake was to believe at that point that this was one more passing storm and that all we would have to do was to weather it for a while. The steel crisis, however, was not a crisis of circumstance; it was structural and worldwide. Faced with this new situation, the producers judged it best, to prevent their production from decreasing too much, to engage in a suicidal price war.

The European Commission had its back to the wall: in 1951 the Treaty of Paris, in creating the European Coal and Steel Community, had put an end to conflicts between the European nations by deciding to put on a common level within Europe the 'sinews of war', i.e. steel and coal. Since this common market was now quite simply in danger of disintegrating, the very credibility of the EEC structure was in doubt.

The Treaty of Paris conferred on the supranational organ which was the European Commission important powers to maintain solidarity between the countries within the Community. In 1977 the Commission launched an anti-crisis plan for the steel sector which was meant to deal with three main problems: to end the steel price war, to provide industrial and financial means to restructure this vital sector, and to safeguard the interests of the principal victims of the crisis, the workers. This programme was founded on a respect for common European interests, because it required in certain circumstances that the 'strong' elements should not compromise the survival chances of the 'weak'. The European foundry-owners learned the hard lesson of market sanctions: they had to learn not how to produce steel, but how to sell it in economically viable conditions. All things considered, the European steel-makers played the game quite well. Indeed at the end of 1979 most of them were in the black.

However, the second oil crisis, the deterioration of the economic environment and insufficient restructuring were once again to demolish a solidarity which had been achieved with difficulty. During the second quarter of 1980 all the warning lights were flashing: the world recession was once again hitting the steel industry hard. Consumption of steel was in a free fall, prices were collapsing, and the average rate of capacity utilization of European steel fell sharply from slightly over 70 per cent to about 55 per cent in a few weeks. Rather than make use of their solidarity, the steel producers once again tried, in a depressed market, to sell their product at any price, in the mistaken belief that the crisis would hit their neighbour harder. Several attempts by the European Commission during the summer and early autumn of 1980 to restore confidence between the producers failed. In October 1980, for the first time in the history of the Treaty of Paris, the Commission decided to restrict the production of steel in Europe to strict quotas, declaring what was called a 'manifest crisis'.

Disgruntled people often accuse the EEC of being a bloodless bureaucratic machine, ignoring the human dimension of problems. I categorically refute this: in the case of steel it was the fate of individuals, of the regions which depended on steel, which was the prime motivation of those in the European Commission. It was not the interests of the industrialists but those of a basic sector which concerned us.

Discussions were difficult. They had to be: ambiguity would have been fatal to the effort for rebuilding. But at the end of the debate the governments of the Ten *unanimously* supported the Commission's action. The solution to the industrial and social problem of steel must come through joint European action. This is the main lesson of the many hours of often difficult negotiations between the European Commission and the ministers of the ten countries in the Community: we are resolutely engaged in a strategy of solidarity and lucidity.

In practical terms this means: all member countries undertake to put an end, in stages ending in 1985, to the competitive and costly state intervention; workers affected by the restructuring will be assured a decent standard of living by the Community while waiting for new jobs to be created; and resolute action to ensure that the regions particularly affected can start the necessary industrial diversification.

The road is full of pitfalls. But the European Commission will not allow itself to be caught up in making more and more rules. The primary responsibility for the modernizing of European steel lies with the industrialists and though the thing must be tried no one can guarantee that the operation will succeed everywhere and in all circumstances. How could it be otherwise? What a Europe it would be if the Community's only aim was to eliminate the risk in enterprise!

The challenge of energy, or the grasshopper and the ants

'The second oil crisis, born of the Iranian revolution, has once more underlined the vanity of the hopes periodically provided by some surpluses on the market. Rather than the rise in prices, it is the appearance of new sources of fragility which seems to us to deserve attention.' This quotation, taken from the annual report of the Institut Français des Relations Internationales (Ramses, 1981: *Coopération ou guerre économique*), exactly expresses the concern of the European Commission about the energy challenge.

The Iranian crisis set oil prices alight when there was no world shortage. This could have been avoided. The head-on clash between Iraq and Iran highlighted one of Europe's particular problems: because of their dependence on one of these two states for their oil supplies, certain EEC countries went through a difficult period for their supplies. This was of course less serious than a total turning-off of the oil 'tap', but worrying situations arose for some member states. In the autumn of 1980, first the Council of Ministers of the EEC and then the International Energy Agency worked out a plan of action. They decided to use their stocks of oil to avoid speculation. Confronted with a fall in its oil stocks, a Community country on its own might try to buy all the oil available and thus ultimately provoke a rise in prices. This first challenge was met. We must now consolidate this first sign of progress.

Europe's vulnerability as regards oil remains serious. Even when its supplies are not threatened, Europe can still experience difficulties because of the movement of the dollar. Thus the price per barrel as expressed in European currencies had gone up by 25 per cent between the end of 1980 and the second quarter of 1981. This is the paradox of an oil market where the prices, expressed in dollars, are going down but the oil bill of the EEC countries as a whole is going up because of the association with the American currency.

I personally have warned the governments of the ten Community countries to remain vigilant. Some of them, indeed, behave like the grasshopper in the fable of La Fontaine: the Community, in their eyes, must assume the role of the ant, but who this time would be unselfish. An attitude of waste, provoking speculation on the price of oil and thus a dangerous loss of the financial reserves of the European countries, is no longer acceptable. All EEC countries without exception are facing serious budgetary difficulties. The economic recession is hitting hard: the capital indispensable for industrial redeployment is scarce.

A rational use of energy, the second aspect of the energy challenge, is an absolute must to enable a revitalization of European, and world, economic activity during the 1980s.

The manner in which Europe responds to the challenge of energy in particular, and to that of its dependence on raw materials in general, will have repercussions throughout the world. How can we envisage solving the energy problems of the developing nations if Europe does not make better use of its own resources?

In diagnosing the energy problem of the EEC and analysing the perspectives for 1990, the European Commission came to one crystal-clear conclusion: the level of investment is totally inadequate to answer tomorrow's economic needs. We warned the governments of the EEC countries that the present depressed economic activity does not mean that investment in energy can be postponed. It is time to act. If the economy revives, the Community countries who have not made the necessary investment will once again have to increase their oil imports. The price may rise and these rises in turn may neutralize the beneficial effects of an economic revival.

The Commission must exercise its responsibility to guarantee the vital interests of some 260 million people. It must contribute to the definition of a real energy strategy; appropriate short-term measures are no longer enough.

The size of the financial effort that the ten countries of the European Community must make between now and 1990 to meet the investment needs of the energy sector is clearly illustrated in figures. It will be necessary to get together some 500–600 billion dollars to satisfy the restructuring of energy demand and the requirements of energy supply.

This also affects the oil-producing countries. The recycling of these countries' surpluses will have to be mobilized in relation to the financial task to be accomplished. This currency surplus in the OPEC countries is estimated to be about 140 billion dollars in 1980 and about 150 billion dollars in 1981, whereas the global deficit of the OECD for the same years will be in the order of 100 billion dollars.

There are other figures which should make Europe reflect: they concern the likely energy investment of our American and Japanese competitors. Between 1981 and 1990 Europe's investment in energy should increase, in terms of the GNP, from 1.6 to 2.2 per cent. The Americans expect an annual rate of investment of as much as 4 per cent of the GNP, whereas the latest figures for Japan indicate annual rates of 3–3.5 per cent.

International experts have calculated that a 1 per cent increase in GNP going to investment would imply, for the Community, an increase of 0.6 per cent in economic growth and 0.25 per cent in employment. The dryness of the figures conceals a message for Europe: these same experts have calculated that in terms of energy saving, the same investment would bring twice the advantages in terms of employment and balance of payments if all the Community countries invested at the same time, instead of pursuing their national programmes in isolation. If the experts are right, the net creation of jobs for the Ten could reach between 300,000 and 500,000 in 1985. This is surely a beneficial European strategy. Let those who want more, make sure they do not bear the responsibility for penalizing our economy yet again. To fail to create one Europe could become intolerable.

On another level, Europe, which is so often criticized within itself, remains an attraction and a source of hope for many third world countries. The developing countries are waiting anxiously for Europe's answer to the energy crisis. Their needs as regards oil imports will almost double between now and 1990, from 4.5 million barrels a day to some 8 million.

Such a demand will increase the pressure on the oil market at the end of this decade. It is in the interests of both the industrialized nations and of the oil producers to reduce this pressure. But this must not be at the cost of falling growth in the developing countries, which in turn would undoubtedly put a brake on the expansion of world trade and thus to our own progress. For reasons both of principle and of legitimate interest, producing and consuming countries must find an answer to this vital question.

Without entering into facile propaganda, we must recognize that the European Community has shown us the road to follow: in 1980 the EEC and its member countries were, after the World Bank, the largest suppliers of aid for the development of energy in those countries poor in it, contributing more than one billion dollars.

All the interested parties – producing countries, industrialized countries and developing countries – have had plenty of time to take stock of the energy crisis and of its vital link with the world economy; if we can avoid the pitfalls of rhetoric, the elements necessary for good co-operation already exist.

Another 'dialogue of the deaf' would be fatal. As Aurelio Peccei says in *Cent pages pour l'avenir*: 'The 1980s will be decisive. The changes which are necessary and possible will call for a good number of sacrifices, but they will be less than those humanity will be forced to make if it continues in its present path.' Politics sometimes includes common sense!

The strategy of defiance: Europe and its grey matter

The difficulties of the traditional industries in the face of the formidable energy challenge and its consequences point to Europe's basic option in a changing world: specialization. This is above all a technological matter. It is clear that the two main transmitters of tomorrow's technology will be telecommunication, in the 1980s, and bio-industry in the 1990s. But we must not lose sight of the fact that in the more classical high-technology industries, such as aerospace and nuclear power, Europe still possesses considerable room for growth development. In civil aviation its production is only 10 per cent of world output, whereas it represents nearly 90 per cent of the world market.

A priori Europe is not in such a bad position. On the level of basic research the gap between it and the USA and Japan is not as large as it was at the time of the 'American challenge'. But Europe is in greater need of scientific progress than the USA because it has fewer natural resources and more serious demographic problems.

Ultimately, its applied industrial technology remains inadequate for the needs of international competition. This is, first of all, because of social and cultural reservations about the effects of technology on employment and social life. Secondly there is the fact that, despite its relative importance – comparable in some cases to that in the USA and Japan – state intervention in Europe is losing a lot of its impact by being divided between concurrent projects.

This, too, is the price of a non-Europe.

How can we deal with these two obstacles? First of all, social resistance. One should not underestimate the phenomenon or curse public opinion. In the short term, maintaining employment in traditional industries no doubt does more to reduce unemployment than creating jobs through technological development. But in the medium term there is a strong chance that the opposite will be the case. Do we realize, for example, that in the USA they are predicting that in 1990–95 the steel requirement for applied technology based on solar energy will be comparable to that for the railway and construction industries?

No one can be sure that there will be an exact correlation between jobs created in new technologies and those lost in declining sectors. The truth is probably that the relationship is more indirect than this. The gain in productivity produced by technological progress in industry and the services is the means by which our economies will achieve a better division of labour, in whatever form – a shortening of the working day, part-time work or increasing employment in the non-commercial sector.

Europe must not give way to technological malthusianism and deprive itself of its strongest card in the new international economic order, i.e. grey matter. It must associate the unions with the development of new activities, through education, information and professional recycling. Technological progress cannot and must not come about in a disorderly manner; it must be channelled and programmed by a concerted effort of governments, unions and industrialists.

How do we remove the obstacle to European technological co-operation? Clearly, Europe must co-ordinate its forces in the leading industries, and here there are two traps to avoid: on the one hand we must not confuse projects which have a Community interest with those which inevitably unite all the member states; on the other hand we must not demand European solidarity for what has been produced in a national context. Co-operation must occur around effective strong-points. The birth of an industrial network within Europe does not for a moment mean that we must do everything together, or wait until we have a project or a budget for Ten or Twelve before starting. The Airbus is the perfect example of 'good' co-operation. We can conceive of co-operating on the same basis in nuclear, space and electronic projects.

What can the European Community itself bring to the realization of such plans? The possibilities are threefold. It can provide an 'initiating market', stimulating demand, establishing European norms and standards, and encouraging public buying. Secondly it can offer real support in facing the world market, through the commercial policy of industrial co-operation and through the important financial channels which are peculiar to it, such as the European Investment Bank and the European Development Fund. Finally, it can help the co-ordination of national efforts in research and development.

The Community should thus improve the general environment for the development of small and medium-sized firms. In America these are playing an increasingly important role in certain leading sectors. Such firms face many obstacles in the field of high technology – the difficulty of mobilizing high-risk capital, the inflexibility of legislation on hiring workers, and the complexity of fiscal and administrative rules. These obstacles must be removed, particularly in those parts of Europe affected by the crisis in the

131

traditional industries and where small and medium-sized firms could provide an alternative industrial fabric.

But the principal asset which Europe has at its disposal, and of which industrialists in particular are not sufficiently aware, is the huge Continental market of the European Community. The tendency to national insularity is not the least of the dangers threatening Europe in these difficult times. As regards research and development in particular, though worldwide European activity is at a high level, it remains diffuse and inadequate within the European industrial framework.

The telecommunications revolution: opening doors in Europe

People in Europe have taken some time to realize that a new technological revolution was imminent. There is no longer any doubt, given the speed with which things are happening, that this new revolution is upon us, based on the information and telecommunications industries.

The question is whether Europeans – because this affects the whole continent, not just one or two countries – want to play an active part in this 'race' or merely be passive observers of their American and Japanese competitors. For the European Commission the answer is simple: Europe cannot allow itself to miss out on this crucial area of modern technology. If it does, it must henceforth accept a subordinate role. Our actual autonomy is in question.

We have already been widely criticized – wrongly, in my opinion – and sometimes accused of destroying industry. Europe is accused of allowing the disappearance of, or even contributing to the dismantling of, the steel industry, the shipyards and the textiles industry in Europe.

Faced with the harsh realities of a constantly evolving world, the European Commission has simply fulfilled its function, which is to consider the common good, and to try to guarantee the future of a whole continent. Confronted with this phenomenon of 'folding up', the Commission has also come up with a more positive strategy, that of defiance. The telecommunications industry falls into this latter category, as do aeronautics, the car industry and other sectors which remain growth sectors. As regards telecommunications, action on the European level is all the more essential because the fate of the citizens of Europe for the last two decades of the century is at stake, in the fields of employment, the type of society they will live in, and their individual protection against the abuses which can always accompany a new form of technology.

Action on the European level would not require prior approval of any interesting projects by ten governments, nor would it require that they be the result of joint action by *all* the industrialists concerned. We do not intend to place restrictions on industry. The idea is to make use of a true European market, a common market which will first of all make it possible for our industrialists to operate in conditions similar to those enjoyed by their American and Japanese competitors.

In fact what we favour is not a European solution at all costs, nor a national solution at all costs. The general public, confronted with an economic crisis for nearly seven years, would not allow Europe and its member states to waste public money in the new technological industries.

Having said this, we will have, to make the operation succeed, to release certain bolts which are preventing this market from opening up; national monopolies, strictly national state control and disparate technical standards are among the constraints which are preventing the development of our market, and thus the real economic growth which we need. Sociological barriers are also important; innovation is resisted because it is seen as a threat.

The telecommunications market brings hope, because of its sizeable growth (in the order of an average of 15 per cent per year). With the help of a spectacular effort to train people, this market should make possible the creation of numerous new services and facilities, which will in turn create other new jobs.

Some people wonder why the European Commission is getting

involved with telecommunications. They believe that everything seems to be going smoothly in the telecommunications market and that industrialists 'are managing well without the Brussels technocrats'. This is precisely the point: Europe is 'managing'. In reality this means the following: the European component production represents only 10 per cent of world production in this field, whereas the EEC represents 25 per cent of the world market. This quite clearly means that even if we see considerable annual growth in this industry, the gap will continue to widen between us and our competitors. As regards computer science, even though Europe has an enviable position in this field, our share of the world market had fallen from 33 per cent in 1973 to 25 per cent in 1978.

The greatest danger for Europe lies in not analysing these figures and abandoning ourselves to euphoria. The truth is that Europe's industry, even in a state of growth, covers only a fraction of its market. Governments, industrialists and the European Commission are all agreed that Europe's industry must aim to provide one-third of the world telecommunications market by the end of the 1980s. This is an ambitious target, but one which it can reach. Some people will be sceptical. They wonder how we can compete with the Americans, whose policy of public control of the industry is far more efficient than that of the European public authorities. But are we sure of this?

European state expenditure represents 35 per cent of the world market in telecommunications. In the market for telecommunications materials alone, public expenditure in Europe in 1978 almost reached total American public expenditure – one billion dollars for Europe, against 1.1 billion dollars for the United States.

What puts us in a weak position is not the level of expenditure, but the way in which this money is spent. This, once again, is the cost of a non-Europe.

The European strategy proposed by the Commission has certain priorities. In fact, what is involved is catching up. First of all we must increase Europe's share in world production of integrated circuits from the present 6 to about 12 per cent by 1984–85. This first operation for gaining ground is all the more indispensable because in world consumption of integrated circuits Europe's share is 25 per cent. As regards the 'chip', we run the risk of being even more dependent on outside countries for this technology, which constitutes a kind of 'raw material'. In comparison we must note that with a lower public expenditure than Europe (slightly less than $240 million in Japan, as opposed to about $470 million in Europe), the Japanese have acquired in four years about 40 per cent of the world market for integrated circuits and caught up with their American competitors.

The action proposed by the European Commission will involve co-ordinating national programmes; studying new possibilities in the fields of ideas and computer-assisted experiments; and promoting a European equipment industry. This last is without doubt the most urgent. At the present time the bulk of this key industry is in the United States. The fragmentation of the European market has not helped the development of specialist firms producing new materials and equipment.

The danger in such a situation is obvious: the technology for the production of these is generally acquired under licence or bought from America several years after the American companies already have it. Indeed sometimes a new generation of equipment arrives on the American market while buyers in Europe are acquiring material from the preceding generation. This has the same effect as if European industrialists in the machine industry could not rely on the back-up of the machine-tool industry.

Finally, in the telecommunications sector, we must progressively create a European market for the new generation of equipment. Electronic mail, video, the transmission of figures: all the gamut of new services rests and will rest on an efficient and economical system of communications. If Europe maintains its national distinctions in terms of techniques and telecommunications networks, the installing of most of the new services will be practically impossible.

It is clear that a technological revolution such as telecommunications will involve changes in employment, working conditions and professional relationships. I think it is perfectly legitimate for the unions to ask questions about the future; the European Commission waited for no one's advice before associating those responsible in the working environment in the formation of its strategy.

Having said this, it seems to me risky to see the problem solely in terms of employment figures. In other words, if we let our competitors divide up between them the growing telecommunications market it is a sure bet that they would be happy to flood the European market with 'new machines' without creating any new jobs in our countries. We must not ignore history's lessons: in every era, industry has been able to adapt to new circumstances, including a new awareness of social matters.

A central problem, in the eyes of the European Commission, is that of professional training in telecommunications. The Commission has undertaken to prepare, on a Community level, a summary of the needs in professional training resulting from the introduction of the new technology. We have suggested that on a national level the countries of the European Community should come to a considered diagnosis of the evolution of the structure of employment.

The answer to the technological challenge lies not in a refusal to accept the 'machine', but in the wish to tame it. To those young people who are preparing for a professional career I would like to address a simple message: one should no longer see a 'career' as a job which one does without changing until retirement. The speed of the changes linked to the introduction of new technologies requires a virtually permanent process of professional adaptation. To make such adaptation possible, to make such professional education versatile – this is the challenge offered by telecommunications to those responsible for economic, political and social life within the Community.

If telecommunications and its various applications is the major area of technological, scientific and human activity during the 1980s, the biological revolution brought about by the explosion of the new 'technology of living things' will be, in the opinion of all the specialists, *the* challenge from the 1990s onwards.

Well before man discovered the existence of germs, he was already, without realizing it, using their synthesizing powers to produce or conserve, through fermentation, free of cost and without consuming any energy, his food and drink. This has given birth, in the twentieth century, to a 'miracle' product extracted from mould, penicillin, which made it possible to conquer various fearful diseases.

Today man has achieved an understanding of the way in which a living cell functions: he can tame this and put it to his own uses. 'In a single cell, weighing less than one hundred-thousandth of a milligram, there is more chemical genius than in all our factories and all our laboratories put together', we are assured by the Nobel prize-winner Christian de Duve. From this we can imagine the huge field open to bio-technology.

The economic effects of this bio-industry are undeniable. With new forms of energy and economies in energy, with information technology and before the large-scale exploitation of the oceans, bio-technology can be the motor force behind a new growth during the next few decades.

The road to growth is therefore not closed to us, but this growth, less energy-demanding and based on the technologies of information and biology, on the precise work of micro-processors and micro-organisms, will without a doubt force us to reconsider man's work, its duration, its role as a factor in subsistence, and even its meaning for the development of the human personality.

This field is particularly crucial for the European countries. In international competition we have neither the price advantages which some of our competitors have because of their low wages, nor of substantial reserves of raw materials. More than any other continent, Europe is condemned to innovation.

The 'new frontiers' of tomorrow's Europe are those in which the world of science will play a more important part in everyday life. The dream I cherish, and it is rather a bold one, is of a Europe in which the effects of science, thoroughly understood because they have been well explained, will silence the present-day apostles of 'what's the point'. The worst enemy of Europe is the doctrine of the alibi. Since it is never our fault, we can combine passivity with indifference.

What we need is a Europe modelled on the Netherlands in the seventeenth century: a Europe in which the spiritual heirs of Locke, Descartes, Spinoza and Galileo would be gathered around a certain Christian Huyghens, man of letters and science, and the inventor of two instruments – the telescope and the microscope – which have made it possible for twentieth-century man to pursue his thirst for knowledge of the infinitely great and the infinitely small. A society in which scientific creativity and industrial inventiveness will once again live happily together.

Part IV
Independence and dependence of the smaller countries

7 Benelux: unity in diversity – a pattern for Europe?

Jan Tinbergen

The structure of Benelux

As is well known, Benelux stands for the combination of Belgium, Netherlands and Luxemburg. Even the three countries together (which co-operate in a special framework within the European Community), with their twenty-three million inhabitants, are a small unit surrounded by the medium-sized economies of Britain, France and West Germany. Part of Benelux's economic base is precisely this location, at the crossroads of the prosperous part of the world. This location's advantages are dwindling, however, now that the world's economic centre of gravity is moving to the Pacific.

Yet, of the European countries, Benelux is still the area with the highest foreign trade (as a percentage of total income): exports being about half of national income. A high population density around two big ports reflects this, together with a real income per capita of about two-thirds of the American figure. Tax fraud, as estimated by the Belgian expert Professor M. Frank[1], amounts to some six per cent of national income. Social security and assistance are high, probably too high when compared with other north-western and central European advanced countries.

Alongside these important common features there are also differences, some of them rather pronounced. The frontier between Catholic and Protestant Europe runs through the Netherlands, making that country clearly religiously mixed and Belgium–Luxemburg Roman Catholic – apart from a considerable portion of the population of both areas which is described as non-religious. Whereas for Holland that religious division, now on the decline, is characteristic, Belgium has its language problem: north of the line Dunkirk–Liège, Flemish (officially identical to Dutch) being the language, and south of it Walloon (officially identical to French), with Brussels as a bilingual island in the Flemish area. Completely different from Switzerland's peaceful language coexistence, the Belgian model is one of armed vigilance mainly because before World War I it reflected a social conflict in Flanders, where the upper classes spoke French.

The two countries' industrial history is also completely different. Belgium is the oldest continental industrial country, whereas the Netherlands were latecomers. Early Belgian industries were the heavy industries of coal and steel, and steel-manufacturing industries in the francophone part; they are at present in great difficulties, as distinct from the newer industries in the Flemish area, with a more diversified pattern, including pharmaceuticals. In Belgium, industry was financed by the banking system. Dutch industries, also rather diversified, had agriculture, transportation and trade (food industries, shipbuilding, aircraft) as their technical and financial base. Electronics have been added from the beginning of the twentieth century. Two of the large transnational enterprises are joint Anglo-Dutch (Shell and Unilever), reflecting an affinity of the Dutch to their previous rivals, the British.

Holland is an exception – connected with its Calvinist traditions – from the rest of Europe in the high percentage of women not in the (official) labourforce. In social matters as well as in their relations to the Third World, Holland is closer to Scandinavia with which it has a linguistic link as well. The Dutch also share with Germanic countries their concern about environmental issues and nuclear energy – a situation very different from that in France.

Belgium has energetically taken advantage of its location to attract to Brussels the EEC administration and, after France, in its search for a more independent international policy, left NATO, the latter's secretariat.

Economic trends after 1950

After World War II all Western European countries witnessed a rate of economic growth never experienced before; it amounted to about 5 per cent per annum for real gross national product, whereas for long periods, such as 1870 to 1914, it had been about 3 per cent. The USA grew somewhat more slowly, but typically was the pioneering economy; Japan for the period 1961–80 showed a growth rate of over 7.5 per cent per annum.

Western Europe had been 'put on its feet' with the aid of the Marshall Plan, and its further growth was due to several other favourable factors: (1) reconstruction of war damage constituted a powerful demand pull; (2) liberalization of foreign trade by a succession of negotiating rounds, conducted under GATT, contributed to productivity growth; so did (3) a considerable expansion of education; and (4) the low energy prices prevailing until 1973.

The change in educational attainment of the labourforce in the Netherlands is illustrated by Table 1, which may be taken as roughly characteristic of Western Europe.

Table 1 **Percentage distribution of the labourforce of the Netherlands over levels of educational attainment**

	Elementary	*Extended elementary*	*Secondary*	*Semi-higher*	*Higher*
1960[a]	56	34	7	2	1.4
1977[a]	31	39	16	8	3.0
1985[b]	23	41	23	10	3.5

[a] SOURCE: Central Bureau of Statistics, Pocket Year Books 1966; 1980.
[b] Forecast.
SOURCE: Central Planning Bureau (*The Dutch Economy in 1985*, p. 94), 1981.

During World War II Holland was hit much more severely than Belgium – in contrast to World War I which hit Belgium very badly. As a consequence, Dutch policy between 1945 and 1955 had to be very strict, maintaining for some time rationing of consumer essentials as well as the allocation of raw materials. A very restrictive wage policy was accepted – to the amazement of their Belgian colleagues – by Dutch trade-union leaders for whom unemployment had first, and the wage level second, priority. For some time Holland was a low-cost island, attracting exports of industries (printing as one example) and making up for the gradual reduction in income from its former colony Indonesia.

After 1960 the picture changed and the Benelux situation became more homogeneous. Wages rose more than productivity, and the relative scarcity of some types of labour, would have justified. Relative scarcity of highly skilled labour declined, whereas that of unskilled, heavy or dirty work rose. The best response to the changing relative scarcities would have been a relative reduction in the incomes of the professions, and of managers, both private and public, and a relative rise in wages for heavy or dirty work. Market inertia being what it is, the actual response was different. Looking back we must conclude that it was an error to 'import' migrant labour for the heavy and dirty jobs, instead of raising the relative wage rates. A host of difficult cultural and social questions might have been avoided which now add to the problems of precisely the poorer strata of Benelux workers. Of course, this statement can only be made on the condition that migrant workers would have found employment in their homelands, which condition is not fulfilled either. All this is illustrative of the intricate pattern of world problems we are facing and only beginning to understand.

During the fifties and sixties the complex of social security was rapidly extended. Throughout Western Europe a modern welfare state became the normal structure. Because of the large number of countries in this region – in contrast to the USA or Japan – Western Europe became a collection of experiments, with somewhat differing types of welfare states, from which we have not yet drawn any conclusions about what constitutes the best version. In many respects the Scandinavian countries have been closer to the optimum than most others. In a general way northern Europe has been more socially oriented and more forward-looking than southern Europe, where feudal elements have often been conserved, serving the rich rather than the disadvantaged.

Although a careful in-depth comparative study of the effects of differing implementations of a welfare society has, to my knowledge, not yet been made, one provisional conclusion regarding the Dutch version seems to me to be that social assistance there is somewhat too generous. Unemployment benefits amount to more than 80 per cent of previous income for a period of one year, and then fall to 75 per cent for another year. In Germany these figures are 68 and 58 per cent respectively. Public expenditure (including social-security contributions) as a percentage of the trend in gross national product are shown in Table 2.

Table 2 **Public expenditure (incl. social-security contributions) as a percentage of GNP**

	1962	1975
Netherlands	34.4	51.2
Sweden	32.7	49.4
United Kingdom	34.2	44.4
Belgium	30.7	43.2
West Germany	33.6	42.1
France	36.3	40.3
USA	29.5	34.0
Japan	19.0	23.4

Another piece of evidence seems to be that Holland's competitive situation on the world market has deteriorated, at least until 1980.[2] The subject of an 'optimal order' will be taken up again later.

Cyclical movements around 1980

During the 1970s a new pattern of short-term economic movements, or business cycles, has developed known as 'stagflation' – a word reflecting the combination of stagnation (in production and employment) and inflation (in prices). Before 1970 the usual picture was that the cyclical downturn was accompanied by a fall in prices, mostly followed by a fall in wages. The latter fall was even considered as part of a mechanism which brought about, after some time, a cyclical recovery.

Since the price rises in industrial countries from 1973 onwards could be partly attributed to the rise in oil prices imposed by OPEC, economists wondered whether perhaps after a while the usual impact of unemployment on wage rates would make itself felt; this is one of the reasons why no clear and unanimous recommendations to governments were formulated. Evidently a structural change in the mechanism of price-formation within industrial western countries has occurred; later we shall try to identify it.

Apart from OPEC policy, Western Europe and the USA also experienced the impact of increased Japanese competition. After becoming the world's main shipbuilders, the Japanese were successful also in increasing their share in the motorcar market – where rising oil prices caused a shift towards small cars – and introducing a number of new products. Thus, anti-pollution equipment, railway rolling stock, and a number of components of computers and computerized machine-tools were supplied. It is true that Japan did not permit some of its public or semi-public corporations to buy equipment from abroad, but this attitude is also characteristic of France and Germany.

Contrary to general belief, the total effect of trade with low-wage developing countries did not damage employment in Europe. Imports from these countries did reduce employment in a number of labour-intensive industries such as clothing, textiles, leather and leather-ware, and woodworking, but simultaneously exports to these countries rose and increased employment. The net effect on Dutch employment was slightly positive; this also applies to other countries.

Most of the loss in employment is due to two main factors. First, the oil price rises have accumulated very considerable amounts of 'petro-dollars' in the OPEC countries, part of which is hoarded or used for financial investment in western economies. To the extent that the former owners of these enterprises are not reinvesting the proceeds, these financial investments add to hoarding. Total demand for goods and services in Western economies accordingly shrinks. Compensatory deficit spending in the Keynesian sense has not been undertaken at a rate sufficient to maintain demand. This attitude is due to fear of further inflation, especially strong in West Germany.

For Benelux the second main reason for the decline in employment is high production costs, themselves due to high wages in comparison to other western economies (though in 1980 some improvement in the competitive position occurred).

Prices continued to rise in 1979 and 1980, for the EEC as a whole by 9.9 and 13.8 per cent respectively. The latter figure is the average of all member countries, with the maximum in Italy (21.2 per cent) and the minimum in Germany (5.5 per cent). Figures for Belgium and Holland are shown in Table 3; in this respect Benelux did not perform too badly, but not satisfactorily either.

Table 3 **Price rises in 1979 and 1980**

	Belgium	*Netherlands*	*EEC*
1979	6.0	4.2	6.5
1980	7.0	6.5	13.8

Probably the main cause of the phenomenon of inflation in the seventies and since, is to be found in the intensified unionization of almost all social groups. Not only workers, but also farmers, other employers, the professions, and various types of managers have, one after the other, organized themselves and, on each appropriate occasion, put forward their claims. Western societies have become, if not 'worlds of monopolies' (to use a phrase of Joan Robinson's[3]), at least 'worlds of oligopolies'.[4]

The end of stagflation has gradually become the top priority of socio-economic policies. None of the official forecasts so far is able to mark the end, however. Prospects are indicated as gloomy.[5] Though for a somewhat longer period, Samuelson expresses himself in a more optimistic way.[6]

Attempts at forecasting

Economic forecasting is a highly risky activity: the reliability of economic forecasts is low and comparable with weather forecasting in areas such as Benelux. One general reason is that in both disciplines the number of variables is very large. Moreover, such non-economic phenomena as international politics and technological changes have an obvious impact on socio-economic development. The unstable relationship between the world's superpowers and the armaments race constitute one complex of uncertainties. The acceleration in technological development, especially of micro-processors, is another.

As a consequence, any forecasts are highly conditional. With regard to the most uncertain factors, assumptions are made which eliminate them. No international conflicts of major importance are assumed to occur. In an official Dutch publication[7] it is assumed that 'the political preparedness of the industrialized countries jointly to consider the structural problems is assumed not to diminish'. One is inclined to add that since that political will is close to zero, this assumption is warranted. In that same publication hardly any mention is made of the impact of micro-processors. This may be understandable, since no quantitative estimates of that impact are available. Qualitatively, opinions diverge between, as a maximum, important reductions in the employment of office workers and, as a minimum, sufficient inertia to the new technological possibilities so as not to affect employment until 1985.

One of the most important attempts to discuss future socio-economic development has been the famous OECD publication *Interfutures*. Its proud title adds to *Facing the Future*, the eloquent phrase *Mastering the Probable and Managing the Unpredictible*.[8] This rhetoric sounds fine; the prospects of this becoming the attitude of member countries' governments are dim, however, to judge from which we know today. Rightly, the editor of a Dutch economic weekly[9] concludes that 'the plea for an "overall co-operation" and a "new dimension in international co-operation" seems to be based on wishful thinking rather than on a sense of reality'.

These difficulties of socio-economic forecasting have usually been dealt with in recent literature by the 'scenario approach' (i.e. alternative assumptions about some of the key exogenous variables). *Interfutures* presents six scenarios, characterized by alternative assumptions about the 'value system' (materialism or not, consensus or not); technology (converging or diverging productivity trends); international co-operation or absence of it; international trade (worldwide or 'block'-wide); development strategy (traditional or radical); and growth rate (high or medium).[10]

Yet the question has to be posed, whether not another approach to the future is more promising. Forecasting in whatever form is too passive an approach, typical for those who consider themselves outsiders or onlookers. A better approach is an active one, implying the setting of targets and the use of instruments by institutions (governments or other policy-makers) which have the power to act. For these reasons we shall consider some alternatives, mainly under the headings of 'inactive or active policy scenarios' for (1) the EEC, and (2) the trilateral group (USA, EEC and Japan, i.e. the members of OECD).

Inactive policy scenarios: two alternatives

In this section we assume that no change in the socio-economic, political orientation of the Benelux governments will occur. In particular this implies that no joint EEC or OECD policy is assumed to be undertaken, or, if undertaken, it is of insufficient impact. As in the 1930s, there is a tendency, with governments and parliaments, not to think in the correct order of magnitude. Even if, in some cases, qualitatively the correct measures were taken, the dimensions were up to ten times too small. This assumption of what I call inactivity is not far from the policies of the governments in office at the moment of writing (April 1981). It also reflects the spirit in which, in the Netherlands, the Central Planning Bureau shows the prospects for the period up to 1985;[11] in particular the necessity of a supra-national policy at least at EEC level is not discussed at all. Probably it is not discussed since it is not considered politically feasible. But this is not a good reason for not discussing it, in contrast to Messrs Shishido, Fujiwara, Kohno, Kurokawa, Matsuura and Wago,[12] who did study the effects of a joint policy at a higher than national level.

As a consequence the picture produced for the period studied is gloomy, if not grim: an increase towards half a million official unemployed, which is one-tenth of the labourforce.[13] If the non-official unemployed (some categories of women and those 'partly able to work') are added, one in eight of the labourforce will be jobless. In line with these prospects the government emphasizes the need for considerable reductions in public expenditure and is forced to keep incomes under control, even though in principle such control is not adhered to. The situation in Belgium does not basically differ very much from the Dutch picture.

Although the Benelux situation justifies a pressure on incomes, in view of the over-high cost level, the attitudes of both public authorities and the business community lack vision – with a few favourable exceptions. A widely debated report on a revitalization of the Dutch industrial community published by the Scientific Council for Government Policies (WRR, in Dutch abbreviation)[14] mentions this lack of vision. Too little attention is given to the innovation of products and production processes, comparing unfavourably with, for instance, Japan. In Belgium also too much protection of non-competitive industries is advocated. An example of a favourable exception is the reorientation of a textile factory towards the export of looms to developing countries (Picañol, at Ieper).

An alternative scenario of the inactive type in our sense, is one where the application of micro-processors is added to the picture as a means to restore profitability. Considerable expertise is concentrated in the Dutch-based electronics transnational, Philips; thus a role of some importance may be played in the near future. Important questions arise when we want to know what sectors will be affected and to what degree employment will be threatened. What the economist wants to know is the type of new services that can be rendered (especially in financial service sectors), and what the cost reduction and the elasticity of demand for the new services will be. A number of case studies of comparable previous cases of automatization could be of considerable help. There is a need for this type of information, of which there is little so far in the economic literature. Only when this type of knowledge becomes available can the necessary changes in working hours be discussed more concretely. Again, however, all this should be combined with a more active supranational recovery policy, which we propose now to discuss.

Active policy scenarios

Our interpretation of active policy alternatives refers to the political will to organize a recovery and to do so at a higher than national level. The Benelux countries have a good reason to take initiatives at higher than national level, since more than any other developed countries their prosperity depends on exports. Again two alternative active policies will be discussed. Their common element is that highest priority is given to the execution of the recommendations of the Brandt Report.[15] This report, whose subtitle is 'A Programme for Survival', rightly emphasizes the common interest of developing and developed countries in reducing the welfare gap between rich and poor countries, and discusses the policies needed to attain this goal. Reduction of the welfare gap is a must if we want to reduce the number of 'illegal immigrants' into the rich countries; and both reductions are needed in order to preserve political stability – internal and international. Among the policies required, internal policies of the poor countries are of paramount importance ('self-reliance'), including a policy of reducing population growth; but these will not be discussed in this essay. The goal of reducing the welfare gap will not be attained unless the developed countries simultaneously reorient their policies. Two main areas are particularly relevant: trade policies and the transfer of financial means to the developing countries, especially the poorest. Trade policies should imply free access of industrial products from developing countries to the markets of developed countries; regulation of the unstable markets of raw materials and agricultural products, and a price level of staple foods sufficiently high to induce the poorest countries to produce more food.

Financial transfers should be increased in order to accelerate the development of the Third World – differentiated according to the nature of the recipient countries. The common interest of industrialized and developing countries (including the newly industrialized among them) in the policies recommended by the Brandt Report may be illustrated by the consequences of an accelerated development of Third World countries for the metal-working industries in the rich countries whose order portfolio will be favourably affected and constitute the beginning of a recovery. Another contribution to such a recovery will be either a recycling of the oil revenues of OPEC countries, or a compensatory – and temporary – deficit financing in the Keynesian way. (We will return to this later.)

The North–South dialogue is in fact the most urgent political question we are facing. We should not forget that most of the Brandt recommendations were already made ten years earlier in the Pearson Report to the World Bank[16] and may also be found in the RIO Report to the Club of Rome.[17] The almost complete neglect of these recommendations by the governments of the large and the medium-size industrial countries was not only a slap in the face of the authors of these reports: advisers have to live with such experiences. What is more important is that the Brandt Commission is composed of experienced politicians. A continuation of the negative attitude of the industrialized countries would display a degree of myopia by the western world's political leadership reflecting a *testimonium paupertatis* of today's western leadership. It would reflect the absence of statesmen in Churchill's sense: those thinking of the next generation instead of the next election.

Part of the Brandt Commission's recommendations is the necessary restructuring of western economies, a clear longer-term interest again of both the western and the southern world. Such a restructuring is easier to carry out in a phase of cyclical recovery, and this is also an element of the strategy to be followed. (We will return to this when considering later the second alternative of an active policy.)

It seems appropriate to sketch out the longer-term development aims that should form the framework of our socio-economic policies. These are imposed by some other aspects apart from the reduction of the welfare gap mentioned; the most important of these are the energy problem and the environmental issue. As a consequence our long-term strategy must be characterized by:

(*a*) the need for an accelerated growth of the Third World, combined with a moderate, or even slow, growth of the industrialized world;

(*b*) a shift from too materialistic and detrimental consumption patterns to a 'new life-style' where, among other things,

(*c*) quality will become more important than quantity, and

(*d*) a less unequal distribution of incomes will prevail, in line with the changed supply/demand situation on labour markets. In German terminology a less unequal income distribution in most western countries will be *marktkonform*, in conformity with the markets.

The Federal Republic of Germany may be the country whose policies are crucial in the immediate future. Its contribution to the East–West dilemma as well as to the North–South relationship has put it in a unique position. If Germany were to follow the example of those smaller industrial countries which attained the 0.7 per cent of GNP for official development assistance (ODA), an important political pressure could be exerted on the large industrial countries, from France to Japan, to follow this example. With its present government this can hardly be expected from the USA.

European integration

Closely connected with our second alternative of an active socio-economic policy scenario, is the other problem confronting Western European countries generally, but Benelux in particular. It is the loss of momentum of European integration as visualized by its founding fathers and their creation, the Rome Treaty. Benelux seems to be in a better position to take some necessary initiatives than the other small members, and unfortunately the medium-sized countries are not blameless.

The present attitudes and policies of the Council and the Commission are not in accord with the spirit of the Treaty of Rome. The Luxemburg Agreement to accept a veto by a member country if it considers its 'vital interests' to be at stake, constitutes a deviation from the Treaty of Rome, and should be abandoned. The Commission should act more independently in favour of the interests of the EEC as a whole and the Council should decide by a qualified majority vote. There is some hope that the present, directly elected, parliament will continue the independent policy it has pursued since its election.

The EEC should understand the important socio-economic role it can play on the world stage because of its economic importance as a trading partner and its social importance as a more advanced type of society than both the USA and Japan. In both respects the EEC may contribute to the creation of a more positive atmosphere, especially *vis-à-vis* the developing world. Expectations on that side should not be disappointed.

A really significant role for the EEC should imply the willingness to reconsider the present policies, especially agricultural, but also industrial restructuring policies. Agricultural production in some sectors should be reduced; and its system of income minima for farmers, revised. The application of the Multifiber Agreement leaves a lot to be desired, not to mention the extensive use of escape clauses or bilateral arrangements of so-called voluntary export restrictions by developing countries.

A difficult problem remains the question of what languages to use in the European parliament. Reduction of the number of working languages may be attained by training courses for members from small language areas.

The optimal scenario

I now propose to discuss the second alternative of an active socio-economic policy scenario. In it, the high priority of the execution of the Brandt Report recommendations remains. As argued earlier, this accelerated development policy would help employment in the metal-working industries (and that implies an improvement in the steel sector). Yet, the reduction of import impediments to industrial products from developing countries will affect somewhat negatively employment in a number of industries, mainly labour-intensive or stabilized-technology industries (in the technology-cycle theory's sense).

It would be appropriate, therefore, to add some further stimuli to employment in the industrialized countries. In order to facilitate, at the same time, the restructuring already mentioned, additional encouragement should be given to activities in which industrialized countries have comparative advantages. Such advantages are to be expected in capital-intensive activities, where capital means not only physical, but also human, capital. Chemical and pharmaceutical industries may be eligible, but these will not offer an important increase of employment; moreover, the environmental byproducts of many chemical industries require caution.

Human capital offers better possibilities. As illustrated by Table 1, the labourforce of the Netherlands – and this applies to all industrial countries – shows a rapidly increasing degree of schooling. Activities requiring considerable highly qualified labour seem to be the best candidates for stimulation. The choice proposed is to expand research activities; and bearing in mind what was said about thinking in the right orders of magnitude, I propose doubling research activities. As shown elsewhere,[18] this may generate a considerable volume of employment, especially if we take into account the Keynesian multiplier.

The strongest argument in favour of expanding research to such an extent, however, is less on the supply than on the demand side, or rather, on the side of the need for research. The number of very urgent problems the world is facing is so large and the necessity of knowing solutions so strong, that there is an immediate need for accelerating research. Some examples of problem areas in need of additional research are the following. How can we step up considerably the use of solar energy, in order to avoid a higher concentration of carbon dioxide in the atmosphere? How can we conserve a sufficiently large area of wildlife (including tropical forests) so as to maintain a gene reserve for food crops, which is vital to the world's food production. How can we recycle industrial wastes, so as to reduce the future scarcity of a number of metals? How can the increasing population of the developing world be employed to a much higher degree than transnational enterprises have been able to? How can the management of the globe – politically, socio-economically and ecologically – be improved? How can the common interest of all nations, and especially of the superpowers, in avoiding a nuclear conflict be given a solid juridical framework?

Only by intensified research can we hope to avoid a number of conflicts now dividing public opinion, national and international. As an illustration take the views of those in favour of the use of nuclear energy and those unconditionally opposing it. To prevent the operation of these nuclear-energy plants, while at the same time France is operating a whole network of such power-stations, is hardly a solution if we don't indicate alternatives. The coal alternative adds to the carbon dioxide content of our atmosphere, and hence is unattractive.

Doubling the research activity therefore seems an excellent way to satisfy a crucial need for more knowledge. It is not meant to be monopolized by the developed countries. If the Third World wants to participate they are welcome. But the number of qualified individuals they have to offer will be relatively low.

How should this additional research activity be financed? Here it seems that part of the funds proposed by the Brandt Report can be used: it is a world interest that this research effort be made. Thus, part of the oil dollars now hoarded may be recycled for this purpose.

Is there not a new threat of inflation if more money is brought into circulation? The safest answer is that an incomes policy should be among the means to be used. Several countries already, in various periods, have felt forced to introduce an incomes policy – not only for wage-earners, but even more for salary-earners, the professions and even managers. Here we touch on a much wider problem than that of an organized recovery. It seems worthwhile, as a conclusion, to give some attention to this wider problem of what socio-economic order should we be aiming at.

Problems of an optimal social order

For more than a century the industrialized world has been caught up in a controversy about the socio-economic order. In the middle of the nineteenth century the belief in the self-regulating capitalist order was challenged by Karl Marx, who taught to his followers the dynamics toward a socialist society as he saw it: an order in which the ownership of the means of production would no longer be private and in which the 'anarchy' of free competition would be eliminated by centrally planned decisions. In the beginning of the twentieth century the ideas of socialists started to diverge; alongside orthodox Marxists, reformist ideas developed. After the establishment of regimes considered Marxist, in Russia during World War I, in various Eastern European countries during and after World War II and finally, in 1949, in China, experience accumulated. In Western Europe, as already observed, experience with reformist policies built up. At present we have reached the situation where theories can be tested with the aid of observations of really existing forms of socialism.

This may suggest that we add to our list of urgent topics for research one called searching for the optimal socio-economic order for communities of different cultural backgrounds and different levels of development. Quite clearly a multidisciplinary approach recommends itself, where sociology, pedagogics, biology, technology, and several other disciplines may contribute, along with economics. The mixed societies of western countries have a number of common features as the result of democratic decisions in the western sense, which we consider the 'least bad' process of decision-making; and hence these features are likely to approach optimality. Some countries – including the Netherlands – have overdone social-security provisions. All the countries mentioned are faced with rising delinquency, indicating common mistakes in education or in the operation of law and order. If parents and teachers fail, the police are the victims in the sense that they have to use more violence, a second-best solution at most. All countries, too, are reconsidering the position of women; and some feminist proposals for change are overlooking what child psychologists teach us: the need for the protection and safety of young children.

The search for the optimal learning process – formal and informal – is continuing, and debates about the comprehensive school have not yet finished. Another unsolved problem is what can and should be done for various types of handicap? Fortunately our high level of prosperity enables us to deviate from more primitive animal species which apply cruel solutions.

The most fundamental of all our problems is the need for a revision of our own value system. Not only is delinquency increasing, but also near-delinquent attitudes, illustrated by increased self-centredness, divorce, alcoholism and drug-addiction. Fortunately, the awareness that we are moving in the wrong direction has increased. Some have drawn the conclusions and attempt a better quality of life. Shall we succeed?

Notes

1 M. Frank, *La fraude fiscale en Belgique* (Editions de L'Université Libre de Bruxelles, 1977).
2 Central Planning Bureau (of the Netherlands), *De Nederlandse economie in 1985* (The Hague, 1981), p. 135.
3 J. Robinson, *The Economics of Imperfect Competition* (Macmillan, London, 1933).
4 W. Michalski, 'Facing the Future' (A summary of the Interfutures project), *Economisch Statistische Berichten*, 65 (1980), pp. 568–72.
5 Central Planning Bureau, op. cit., p. 139.
6 P.A. Samuelson, 'The World's Economy at Century's End', *The Japan Economic Journal*, 10 March 1981, p. 20, and 17 March 1981, p. 20.
7 Central Planning Bureau, op. cit., p. 64.
8 OECD, *Facing the Future, Mastering the Probable and Managing the Unpredictable* (Paris, 1979).
9 L. Van der Geest, 'Interfutures', *Economisch Statistische Berichten*, 14 May 1980, p. 565.
10 A.H.J.J. Kolnaar, 'Problemen op wereldschaal', *Economisch Statistische Berichten*, 65 (1980), pp. 577–83.

11 Central Planning Bureau, op. cit.
12 Sh. Shishido *et al.*, 'A Model for the Coordination of Recovery Policies in the OECD Region', *Journal of Policy Modeling*, 2 (1980), pp. 35–56.
13 Central Planning Bureau, op. cit., p. 139.
14 WRR, *Place and Future of the Dutch Manufacturing Industry* (The Hague, 1980).
15 W. Brandt *et al.*, *North–South: A Programme for Survival* (Pan Books, London, 1979).
16 L.B. Pearson *et al.*, *Partners in Development* (Praeger, New York, 1969).
17 J. Tinbergen *et al.*, *Reshaping the International Order* (Dutton, New York, 1976).
18 J. Tinbergen, 'Which Sectors should be Stimulated by a Recovery Policy?' *Lloyds Bank Review*, 137 (July 1980), pp. 30–40.

8 Spain at the gates of Europe

Miguel de Aldasoro

Every war enriches some people and ruins others. World War II was no exception and when it ended the European countries which took part in it were able to take stock of the serious damage they had sustained. Four European countries remained neutral: Sweden, Switzerland, Portugal and Spain. The two former, managing to profit from their neutrality, found themselves with strong economies in 1945; but this was not the case with the Iberian peninsula and Spain in particular, which in 1939 was emerging from a long and bloody civil war which lasted three years and whose end coincided with the beginning of World War II.

The United States realized in 1945 the danger implied for its hegemony by Europe's ruined economies and it was because of this that the Marshall Plan was born. However, it excluded all countries on its blacklist, in particular Spain, which remained under a personalized and authoritarian regime. It was not until 1959 that Spain obtained membership of the OEEC and by that time the plentiful resources of the Marshall Plan had already been entirely absorbed by the other needy European countries.

During the 1950s European political thinking realized the need to create a stronger structure with a clear identity and an outlook on the future. The Treaty of Rome gave this idea a name and a shape, and included nearly all those European countries which had suffered the most from the convulsions of the last war.

Some countries joined in right from the start, some later on and some, less numerous, kept out, like Norway, or were unable to join because of their commitment to neutrality, like Austria, or because of their vocation, like Switzerland or Sweden. Spain also stayed out, even though she had for many years been knocking on Brussels' doors asking for admission. The Spanish had been told in 1945 that Spain could not be part of Europe until her political system was adapted to the model of western democracy. Franco died in 1975, and in 1978 the people voted in a constitution with a freely elected parliament, which today, with her constitutional monarchy, puts her in line with the rest of Europe. She continues to appeal to Brussels, hoping for the support of her Western European neighbours.

The recent past

The economic autarchy of the Franco regime, as a result of World War II and Spain's political isolation, decided by the United Nations in 1947, gave rise to an industrial development based on premises which were untenable in the long run and which led the country into a chaotic financial situation, forcing General Franco in 1959 to sign, for the first time, decrees with which he did not agree.

The economy then became freer, Spain substituted a multiple exchange rate of the peseta for its real value of single exchange on the international market; the frontiers were thrown open to tourism and trade, and Spain became integrated into the International Monetary Fund, the World Bank and the OEEC.

Modern Spain grew closer to Europe and began to restructure its economy by adapting it to new horizons and new standpoints. It was the period when Spanish emigrants sent home the currency they earned in the rich EEC countries, when foreigners were beginning to invest, attracted by the general conditions in a country in which tourism was booming and, consequently, the free development of political ideas began to open rifts in what had previously been closed territory.

Thus in 1973, at the beginning of the present worldwide crisis, successive governments did not dare to implement urgent and much needed economic measures on the eve of a political transition which seemed imminent in view of General Franco's age and health. This explains why in 1975, when Franco died, Spain entered one of the most difficult periods of its history. The political transition, though so long awaited, was delicate and called for a constant consensus of the parties, while drastic measures were required in the economic field.

If in 1958 the plan for economic stabilization was successful in a watertight political context, the same was not the case in 1975. Everything happened at once and it was necessary to change the country, its political system and its economy in the midst of a worldwide economic crisis and in a new political environment which, though enthusiastic, was weak and lacking in the necessary authority to implement an effective economic plan.

It is not necessary at this point to analyse the international events which affected all countries to a greater or lesser extent. The roots of these were various and very complex, but the end-result was a spectacular rise in the price of oil and to a lesser extent of all raw materials, giving rise to the recession-inflation phenomenon.

In summing up we can say that these international events had two effects on Spain. Firstly, a direct effect caused by the increase in the price of oil and raw materials; and secondly, an indirect effect on the country's export sector, as a result of the upsets suffered by the economies with which Spain maintained strong economic links.

The internal or domestic causes of the crisis are also various but they are interlinked, and the process can be described thus:

(*1*) When the economic crisis began in 1973 the country's productive structures were less prepared than those of other western economies to confront it.

(*2*) On a political level the country found it had exhausted the model it had followed, and a process of change had begun which was to make itself evident years later, but only after great tensions.

(*3*) It was precisely this second point, as we mentioned earlier, which made it impossible to act in time to soften the effects of the energy crisis. The delay in taking the necessary measures, which have still not been taken in some sectors, had a cumulative effect on productive structures, giving rise to a serious economic deterioration.

This situation landed Spain's economy in a vicious circle, creating a series of problems of which two were fundamental: unemployment and inflation. A third, on the political level, was terrorism, but it was closely linked both to the economic situation and to the political development of regional autonomy.

Levels of unemployment

At the present economic juncture in Spain the most worrying problem is unemployment. We can identify the various aspects of this problem:

(*a*) The potentially active population increases yearly during the period 1976–80 by an average 1 per cent.

(*b*) The registered active population, that is that which is available for work, has declined from 1977; in the INE (National Institute of Statistics) quarterly enquiries, part of the active population registered as non-active because of the lack of opportunities for finding work. If one takes into account the incidence of this, the active population in 1980 becomes about 13,718,000 people instead of 12,860,000 and consequently the number of active people unemployed becomes 2,478,000 and the level of unemployment reaches 18.1 instead of 12.6 per cent.

(*c*) Unemployment has increased by 923,000 people between 1976 and 1980, the yearly progressive evolution being from 135,000 to 286,000. In 1980 the level of unemployment went from 5.3 to 12.6 per cent.

(*d*) The predictions on unemployment for 1981 seem to indicate that things are getting worse; unless measures are taken immediately, unemployment could reach about two million by the beginning of 1982.

Because of this, one of the first measures taken by the new government, announced in parliament at the time of the failed *coup d'état* of 23 February, consisted in facing this problem head-on. The present President and his economic ministers have conducted negotiations with the employers' organizations, the trades unions and the public administration, and this has already begun to produce positive results. A certain confidence is re-appearing, in the form of a greater willingness to invest, even though it is a bit early to make prognostications.

The rate of inflation

Table 1 gives the level of increase during the inflationary period beginning in 1973. Two-figure inflation began in 1973, even though the price of petrol did not have an inflationary effect that year since the price rise only happened in November. The increase in prices occurs in three stages: 1973-74, years of increase; 1975-77, higher increase; and 1978-80, slightly more moderate increases on similar levels. These three stages are separated by years in which the rate of inflation fell – 1975 and 1978. The level of inflation in 1981 is expected to remain the same as in 1980, due mainly to a rise in the price of energy and food.

Table 1   **Percentage annual increase in prices**

	1973	1974	1975	1976	1977	1978	1979	1980
Average levels	11.4	15.7	16.9	14.9	25.4	18.9	15.7	15.4
December levels	13.9	17.9	14.1	19.9	26.3	16.6	15.5	15.1

Having briefly analysed the two most important problems facing the country's economy in 1981, we must also examine the evolution of the balance of payments and the public-sector budget.

The balance of payments

Under this heading we examine the main indications of Spain's economic relations with the outside world.

The figures in Table 2 reflect a deterioration from 1978 onwards, a year which had shown a clear improvement on the preceding years. The balance of trade continues to register a growing deficit because of the oil bill.

Table 2 **The Spanish balance of payments**

	1976	1977	1978	1979	1980	1981[a]
Balance of trade (in thousand pesetas)	−490,468	−524,847	−312,038	−500,058	−924,355	−1,100,000
Current balance (in thousand pesetas)	−267,481	−204,656	125,363	−53,686	−427,749	−450,000
Market balance (in thousand pesetas)	−126,638	14,499	247,299	114,850	−153,825	−200,000
Foreign reserves (in thousand dollars)	4,952.1	6,132.4	10,015.4	13,116.6	12,358.1	Decrease
Foreign debt (in thousand dollars)	10,235	12,959	14,727	16,621	20,958	Increase
Exchange rate of peseta against the dollar	66.90	75.96	76.67	67.13	71.70	83–85

[a] Estimate.

The current account cannot be balanced despite the sub-balance of services and transfers, and apart from 1978 when there was a notable positive balance, the other years have all registered a net deficit, reaching rock-bottom in 1980 and leading one to foresee a serious deficit in 1981.

The market balance shows better results, even though in 1980, despite the strong entry of long-term capital, there was a record deficit of 153,825m pesetas.

For the period under consideration, foreign reserves grew every year at the same pace as the surplus on the base balance, except in 1980 when they fell. A fall in relation to the 1980 level is predicted for 1981.

The foreign debt, for the period considered, continued to grow steeply, doubling in four years. The difference between foreign debt and foreign reserves continued to grow, reaching the figure of 8,600m dollars in 1980. An increase is also predicted for 1981, given the expected application for credit.

The rate of the peseta after devaluation in 1977 went up slightly until 1979 and the beginning of 1980, but in March that year a continuing depreciation began which is still going on, increasing its rate of exchange to 85 pesetas to the dollar. A slight drop is predicted in mid-1981 and the yearly average is expected to fluctuate between 83 and 85 pesetas to the dollar.

The public-sector budget

During the last two years the deficit in the public sector has been the subject of debate and discussion between the different political groups. Debates took place in September 1980, during the December discussions on the budget, and at the time of the investiture of the president in February 1981.

The figures available show that although in 1980 the deficit reached a proportion of GNP similar to that of those OECD members who do not pursue inflationary policies, it is also true that the public-sector deficit in Spain has risen rapidly since 1977. In 1980 loans from the Bank of Spain compared with 1979 had increased by a fector of 2.1 and the public-sector deficit was well over 3 per cent of GNP.

It is not the record of past years which gives cause for concern so much as the predictions for 1981 and 1982, and the continuing deficit. It is essential to contain the public-sector deficit within certain limits. This will require more efficient fiscal management and a limit on the current expenses of the administrative machine.

Finally, and in order to give a global view of the main macro-economic indicators, Table 3 shows the real growth of the GNP

Table 3 **Annual growth in GNP in real terms** (%)

1961–73	1974	1975	1976	1977	1978	1979	1980
7.6	5.9	1.0	3.0	2.6	3.1	1.4	1.5

in percentages. Nearly all the figures indicate, for 1981, a slight rise in the rate of increase of the GNP based on exports and public investment.

Economic policy

Introduction: the institutional features

From an analysis of the essential institutional features, one can see that the public revenue, employment, trade-union and public administration systems have all succeeded in aggravating certain problems without solving others.

To begin with, the present system of public revenue has been severely distorted by the volume of contributions to social security, which is a retrogressive tax with a negative effect on the creation of jobs and on exports. The weight of contributions to social security (about 50 per cent of the total public revenue) shows a marked disparity with the structure of public revenue in other OECD countries.

The maintaining of a fiscal sub-system, based on the payslip and having an effect on the expenditure of social security is, to say the least, open to criticism, given the fact that it is not viable in the medium term.

Secondly, the system of labour relations is just beginning to move away from the norms and habits stemming from Spain's former corporatism, but this *rapprochement* to the models of Western Europe remains slow and difficult. This has been encouraged by the promulgating in 1980 of two important laws: the Workers' Statute and the Fundamental Law on Employment.

Thirdly, the present trade-union system, which on paper resembles those of other Western European countries, in fact functions very differently: rivalry between unions, weak affiliation and a high rate of abstention in union elections mean that the unions are weak, badly organized and have insufficient means for accomplishing their tasks.

Fourthly, the system of public administration – including the state administration, autonomous organizations, local administrations and the administration of the law – entails complex problems, together with low efficiency and productivity.

Economic policy: the government's economic programme

The economy was the main subject of the President's investiture speech in February 1981. His views on the economy assumed a dialectical tone: the seriousness of the crisis was accentuated by specifically Spanish factors concerning the country's deficient economic institutions and the assumptions on which the economy was based.

The government's economic programme was formulated in an international situation which had become even worse since the last quarter of 1979: the price of oil had risen again and all the countries of the OECD had reconsidered their plans for growth and reduced their aspirations. Spain's internal plan, within the renewing of the Accord Cadre International, brought with it an increase in the wages budget which, despite the efforts of all parties and its incontestable stabilizing effect, was unable to contain inflation; equally, the physical climate in 1981 could seriously affect agricultural production and the energy balance, given Spain's high dependence on hydraulic power.

In these conditions it is flexibility and liberalization, already in evidence in the 1979 programme, which will guide the economic programme, but they should take the form of more concrete measures.

First of all it is important to control the rate of inflation and the deficit in the balance of payments, and, to achieve this, to control the deficit in the public sector within the prescribed limits.

Given that the level of deficit in terms of the GNP is not too terrible (the public deficit, borrowed from the Bank of Spain, plus the issuing of securities on interior and exterior debts, represented in 1980 about 3.06 per cent of the GNP, a percentage similar to those recorded by other OECD countries), it seems more than justified to contain the public-sector debt within limits which, if the increase in liquid reserves is about 17.5 per cent, will leave a margin of 2-3 points increase in the credit of the private sector. If, despite a strict policy on the part of the government, the deficit accelerates, any interference could involve uncontrolled increases, incompatible with the aim of containing the rise in prices and restoring the balance of payments.

Thus controlling the public debt implies putting a brake on the current expenses of the administrative machine, a revision of the policy of transferring funds to sectors and firms which are in crisis, and an increase in public revenue by enforcement of the tax system. This last point necessarily entails reform of the system of public revenue which has been distorted by the financing of social security.

This reform could be achieved in two phases:

(*1*)   Raising the base scale for contributions to compensate for a lowering in general contributions, thus mitigating the effects of social security on small and medium-sized firms which generate more employment.

(2)   The introduction in Spain of Value Added Tax. This operation consists of altering the tax on firms' wages bill by the imposition of a tax of goods and services, thus adapting the tax system to that of the EEC.

These measures must in turn be accompanied by the containment of price increases using various means: flexibility in the labour market; the regulation of all contracts by the Workers' Statute; and the participation in this policy by all unions, through negotiations conducted between the government, the employers and the unions (which are already taking place).

Moreover to combat unemployment it will be necessary to resort to professional training, to unemployment benefit for people with family charges over a certain age, to the normal period of tax collection and to a system of voluntary early retirement.

The government's economic programme contains one chapter dealing with the energy problem. The aim is to achieve the maximum amount of independence in the supply of energy, the maximum amount of security, and prices similar to those in other European countries. With this in view, the problem is clear: today nuclear energy is the only realistic way forward of reducing dependence on oil, given that the capacity for hydraulic production has almost reached its peak.

It goes without saying that in these circumstances it is essential to speed up and intensify the research into alternative sources of energy, such as solar energy and wind power, which provide Spain with the most favourable hopes of producing energy.

The other guideline for the economic programme concerns the policies for industrial restructuring. For this reason particular importance is being attached to the co-ordination of the various incentives and assistance which already exist, and whose application by different administrative centres has been uneven.

It will be necessary to act in market sectors or sub-sectors on the principle of equality, making sure that the aid given does not create more distortion than already exists in the market. It will also be necessary to see if existing instruments of the law (such as the concession of fiscal moratoria or of social security) are sufficient, or whether it will be necessary to make them so.

But none of these measures can be carried out unless exports increase at the same time. The Spanish economy needs to export more, both to create more employment and to finance the import of crude oil. Exports cannot be increased without adopting a policy of complete liberalization. Any delay in the opening up of the Spanish economy could be very serious for the future of exports.

This policy of liberalization must be applied not only in the trading of goods but also in the financial market, and by the elimination of industrial interventionism from various sources. A policy to encourage exports is based not only on trade fairs, missions and export credit, but must also imply liberality and flexibility in the financial system.

Monetary and financial policy

The new administration of the fiscal system began in 1981 with the publication of plans for the freeing of the interest rate and bank dividends, and for longer-term financing by savings banks.

These measures have already contributed positively to the development of a market economy, since adequate measures have been taken to facilitate a more important transfer to the financial system. The new system will involve a clarification of the real cost of credit.

The two main problems with the present financial situation are the fall in credit and the lack of long-term financing.

As regards the fall in credit, thanks to measures which have been taken to regulate the role of the middleman in the money market and to increase the number of financial entities entitled to acquire Treasury Bills, it will be possible to encourage competition and thus reduce the costs of banking intermediaries and consequently to re-float credit, though only in the medium- or long-term perspective.

Given that the problem of financing is already alarming, one could in the short term adopt measures such as a greater reduction in the compulsory rate of investment or else a greater profitability for these operations. These measures might make it possible to reduce the cost of banking loans and this would have the effect of making credit less expensive.

However there is also general agreement that long-term financing will only provide a limited solution to Spain's needs and besides, according to the OECD, it is costly and rudimentary. Thus for example during the past five years a slight reduction in long-term credit has come about, in favour of credit granted for more than 90 days and less than 18 months. At the moment, credit of more than 18 months represents only about 14 per cent of the total credit in the private sector. In recent years the return on capital has begun to drop, and this makes for a short-term increase in the weight of the total debt of the enterprise sector. This implies that funds are being obtained in the short term for use in long-term investment projects.

From this one can guess at the difficulties created by long-term financing. Its limitations are, besides, the consequence of a poorly developed financial system which is failing to create sufficient means for adjusting savings to investment.

To remedy this situation, long-term financing should be encouraged by adopting measures to stimulate better development of the financial system, partly by the creation of new financial assets and the expansion of secondary markets, and partly by the consolidation of variable-interest-rated credit.

The ministerial decree of 17 January 1981 took account of this question and the authorities showed their willingness to promote credit with variable interest rates. What is needed then is a commonly accepted interest rate to serve as a point of reference and to prevent wild fluctuations in the value of money. The stability offered by the market is positive in this sense and if this trend continues it should be possible to reach a widely accepted reference rate of interest.

To resume, the measures which have been taken could encourage the banking organizations to find formulas for longer-term financing and discourage them from holding inactive funds. But even though these measures are positive they would best go hand in hand with other structural reforms of the financial system. These reforms would involve a greater development of the financial system by converting short-term saving into long-term investment by means of better guarantees of reimbursement offered by the borrowers and by a better policy for stabilizing the position of the banking organizations, thus palliating the problem of insolvency.

Budgetary policy

In contrast to the relatively acceptable evolution of monetary policy, we must now look at the poor budgetary policy during 1980 and its negative influence on the basic economic variables.

The most striking characteristics of the running of the public sector during 1980 were a sharp rise in current expenses, a drastic reduction in public saving, a large budgetary deficit and considerable borrowing from the Bank of Spain.

A prices and incomes policy seemed to be the objective for 1980, as well as moderating the increase in current expenditure so that the expected increase in current revenue would provoke sufficient public saving to expand public investment without substantially affecting finance for the private sector.

The information available seems to indicate that these objectives have not been met. In fact according to the figures available, the state deficit, brought about by the execution of the budget, extra-budgetary operations and other Treasury expenses, has increased to 380,211m pesetas.

The budget deficit is about 312,676m pesetas. Budgetary receipts have increased by about 24.3 per cent in comparison with 1979, while the increase in expenditure is about 30.6 per cent. Budgetary receipts have implied an increase in fiscal pressure of about 1.06 per cent, thus reaching nearly 13 per cent of the GNP.

The financing of the total state deficit has been arrived at by:

(*a*) An internal debt of 67,654m pesetas.

(*b*) Foreign loans to a negative total of 24,028m pesetas, to pay off former debts, and a practically non-existent total of loans received.

(*c*) Net variation in financial assets of 5,026m pesetas.

(*d*) Application to the Bank of Spain for 341,611m pesetas.

The general budget for 1981 will include boosting economic activity and stabilizing public finances, with the following aims: an employment policy; fighting inflation; solving the problem of the town councils' lack of funds; transferring the functions of central government to local government; putting in hand fiscal reform; restructuring the Civil Service; industrial reconversion, an energy policy and assuring the future of enterprises in a state of crisis; and reserving credit for firms once the state has reduced its deficit by issuing new securities on the public debt.

The key point in the budget is the assumption of economic

growth of 2.5 per cent in 1981, but at the present time this percentage seems doubtful and the prognostication optimistic.

The administration has done its utmost to achieve this growth, putting forward a budget where investment is set to rise by 31 per cent, though it will be necessary to spell out this percentage in specific terms for those towards whom the investment is intended.

In the general state budget for 1981 the predicted expenses for the central administration and social security come to 4,114,193m pesetas, spread almost equally between the two institutions. It is notable that of the two, it is social security which shows a continuing tendency to spend more than the central administration. In 1958 there was a ratio of 3 in favour of the state, in 1966 of 3.15, in 1970 it fell to 1.58 and in 1974 – at the time of the crisis – it fell to 113. In 1977, as in 1981, they were of an equal magnitude.

This increase has been basically due to current expenses, in other words to social services (pensions, health allowances and education), which make up about 57 per cent of total public expenditure.

As regards the prediction for real investment in the 1981 budget, it comes to 322,190m pesetas for the two organisations, about 7 per cent of the total budget expenditure, capital transfers being the most important part of capital expenses in the central administration budget.

The volume of revenue in current operations for the central administration and social security is similar, together making up about 99.4 per cent of total receipts. Contributions to social security are by far the heaviest public burden and their relationship to the mass of wages means that they do little to stimulate employment.

The economic structure

General factors

The seriousness of the energy crisis for Spain can be measured in a few dramatic figures. In 1981 the oil bill cost the country the work product of 800,000 working people, whereas at the beginning of the 1970s it only cost that of 300,000 working people. The oil required by the economy represents 60 per cent of total export goods. The impact of the energy crisis on the Spanish economy has been, one way and another, far more serious than on most of the other OECD economies.

But energy is not the only structural weakness. Spain is a country with a serious technological deficit, which affects industrial growth even in the most widely based sectors. Its industrial structure has developed and considerably improved since 1974, but since then it has been faced with international difficulties due to the change in the relative prices of labour and energy, and to its insufficient technology.

In general, the process of modernization in the Spanish economy – which in the 1950s was very backward, and plagued with archaic equipment, a paucity of firms, lack of specialization and very low productivity – has brought about a great change in the importance of the various subsections of manufacturing industry, a process of specialization in production, a great increase in the productivity of labour, and an intensification in the degree of capitalization.

This modernization has been accompanied by a greater enmeshment within the world economy, in particular with the developed industrial economies, which has improved the position of Spanish industry in relation to the outside world. This improvement is reflected in the increased importance of Spanish industrial sectors in world exports and the fact that the sale of Spanish goods has a better preferential and therefore less residual quality. The greater homogeneity with the European Community, despite the persistence of noticeable differences, is the result of these two processes (modernization and external links).

Hand in hand with the process we have described comes the other characteristic of the Spanish economic structure: dependence on abroad. The dependence on imported raw materials, machinery and new technology has grown up over the years. As a result of the measures taken to liberalize foreign trade, imports of intermediary goods greatly increased. Spain's dependence in the field of energy is well illustrated by the events which have taken place since 1974 (in 1980 crude oil represented 46.1 per cent of Spanish imports. In 1979 the price of a ton of crude oil was 9,016 pesetas; by 1980 it had risen to 16,276 pesetas.) What emerges from these problems is Spain's heavy technological dependence stemming from, on the one hand, the dictates of the world market and the indisputable hegemony of a small number of production centres and, on the other, from Spain's lack of adequate scientific and technological policies.

Spain has an extensive and poorly yielding agriculture, which weighs heavily on its economy. Finally, it is a country whose most important service industry, tourism, for many years the main engine of growth, has become strongly consolidated, but now offers only modest growth prospects.

Distribution of revenue

In 1970 profits accounted for 43.6 per cent of the net national revenue available, whereas wages came to 46.97 per cent. In 1978, the last year for which figures are available, the shares were respectively 39.07 and 53.28 per cent. This increase in the share of wages is due to an increase in the wage-earning population and stronger social pressure for higher wages.

The sectoral aspect

(A) Sector shares in total value added
From 1974 onwards a series of changes has taken place which denote a tendency towards an increase in tertiary-sector activity. The primary, or agricultural, sector has seen its position in the economy become downgraded. This conclusion was reached on the basis of figures covering the periods 1970–74 and 1974–79. The same was the case for the industrial sector. The relative prices of industrial products fell during 1974–79 in relation to 1970–74, so that the loss of their share in the GNP was all the greater. It was the tertiary, or service, sector which clearly profited from this process.

(B) *Industrial problems*

The economic crisis which affected the developed nations should really be called an industrial crisis, since it is this sector as opposed to the two others which has been most affected. Below are some factors which help to explain the situation:

(*1*) The developing countries, in particular those of southeast Asia (Hong Kong, Singapore, Taiwan, South Korea), have made a strong competitive entry into the international market for textiles, clothes, electrical and electronic machinery, and iron goods. Their competition highlights certain structural weaknesses in the industrialized nations which went unnoticed during the growth years. Labour-intensive industrial activity still represents an important part of European industry. The industrialization of the developing countries is logically based on the advantages of cheap labour and their natural resources. Sooner or later, countries which produce raw materials will process them themselves.

(*2*) The increase in the price of oil and of other raw materials has shifted the buying power of the industrialized nations in favour of the developing countries which produce these materials; in particular, those which export oil. However this purchasing power is no longer directed towards the same products as before.

(*3*) The gap between the public and private sectors closed rapidly during the growth years, but it could not have been expected that this spontaneous equilibrium would persist.

(*4*) New values have arisen with regard to the quality of life, the fight against pollution, and the protection of the environment and the consumer. They are characterized by a need to refer to 'public authority', which provides the investment to make towns more habitable and to protect the countryside (rivers, forests, animal or vegetable life, coasts, etc.), or which imposes conditions on enterprises and individuals. This has a dual economic effect: on the one hand it makes it necessary to find the funds to cover these new demands, and on the other many of the standards of protection affect the costs of industries and, as a result of this, their competitiveness with other countries. If one adds to this, the fact that contamination can cross borders, then the solution must be found at the supranational level. Up till now there has been no satisfactory response to these problems.

(*5*) Sectors such as aeronautics, information, electronic components and telecommunications, which offer the best prospects for growth in the developed nations, depend in large part on the role of governments. These sectors require considerable investment in research and development, and demand, generally speaking, is controlled by governments. In Europe the individual national markets are small for these services, which need to massproduce to absorb the large investment in research.

(*6*) Spain has seen, in real terms, a great increase in incomes without a parallel increase in productivity. The result is that investment in production has not created many jobs, and may even reduce the workforce by automating industrial processes and administrative systems. The increasing unemployment in the European economies is partly the consequence of the high cost of labour. Moreover, many productive processes are old-fashioned.

(*7*) The rise in the relative price of raw materials and energy also implies changes in the system of production, in particular towards finding substitutes.

(*8*) The restriction on open competition is not exclusive to the labour market. Monopolistic groups with common interests in the markets for goods and services are more and more numerous, both in supply and demand. OPEC is a good example, and it is not unique, for the phenomenon abounds on the international, national, regional and local levels.

(*9*) State intervention, which should concentrate on correcting the faulty functioning of many markets, often distorts things further. The governments of Western Europe, with the advancing crisis, have progressively adopted a more interventionist attitude. This development has been caused by such factors as the rise in unemployment, with its serious social and economic consequences, and the critical situation of many firms. It is clear that state aid and intervention do mitigate socio-economic problems (sometimes only postponing them), but they also affect economic efficiency, because they produce distortions in the market mechanism and in the optimum distribution of resources.

There is no question of not protecting the sectors in crisis at the present time. The resources which might be freed by closing or reducing enterprises in these sectors would barely be absorbed by other activities. Unemployment would increase and productive plants would remain, for the most part, unusable. If firms continue to function, they bring a certain value added to the economy, whereas unemployed and dismantled installations can only make a meagre contribution.

(*10*) Those economic policies which act basically through demand have proved incapable of resolving the crisis. The particular rigidity of our economic systems has meant that inflation is the only answer to relaunching economic activity. At the same time the failure of the classic 'demand' policies has aroused increasing interest in 'supply' policies, and in particular in industrial policy as a means of combatting the crisis.

Spain's industrial competition
It has been, and still is, said that Spain is the tenth industrial power. This is true if one considers the total net industrial production, but not if we examine other significant indications such as productivity, taxes, sales, technology, energy and wages. We will analyse each of these in turn, comparing Spain with the more industrialized countries.

Productivity. In 1978 Spain's industry was fifteenth in the ranking of output per head by the European Management Forum (EFM), with a figure of $8,621 compared with Holland's $26,668, in other words ahead of Greece ($6,173) and Portugal ($4,543).

Taxes. In 1977 Spanish firms were in a privileged position compared to most other industrialized nations. Tax on profits made up only 22.4 per cent of total taxes, and on this count Spain became the fourth industrialized nation.

Sales. Among the countries with the least capacity of sales per employee, Spain ranks third. On this scale, where the lowest value is 5.99, Spain reached 4.56, or third position, and the USA 2.80.

Technology. Spain is one of the industrialized countries whose workforce is the most opposed to the introduction of new technology to save firms money. The degree of opposition oscillates between 0, totally against, and 5.99, totally in favour. In this scale Spain registers a degree of opposition of 2.18, surpassed only by Great Britain with 1.95, whereas Japan, with 4.46, does best.

Energy. Even though Spain is in the best position in the industrialized world regarding the low cost of energy within industry, this has not helped to make her more efficient compared with other countries.

Wages. For the period 1970-79 Spain is among the countries showing the greatest wage increases, surpassed only by Greece and Ireland. The real rise for the period in question was 80.5 per cent, compared to the USA's 14.4 per cent.

According to the EFM's report, if one analyses the six points mentioned, Spain reaches sixteenth position among the 19 countries. Spanish industry is no longer the one which is growing the most, nor is it the most productive, the least costly or one of the least well automated. On the other hand, it is one of the countries with the lowest number of working hours, a low level of investment, significant absenteeism and poor solvency.

The energy problem

To confront the energy problem one must act on both supply and demand. The primary sources of energy supply must continue to be diversified, with the aim of reducing the degree of dependence on oil. It is also important not to abandon the search for oil under Spanish soil (oil deposits of an excellent quality were recently discovered on the marine platform of Tarragona during the 'Pulpo I' drilling, though without managing to identify the oilfield and thus assess its importance). At the same time, nuclear energy is the only means open to the country to substantially reduce its dependence on oil. As for the demand for energy, it is essential to reduce the unit cost of energy. The sectors which use the most energy must be restructured and adapted technologically to the new situation. This will produce the best results in countries which are entirely industrialized, like the United States, where there is still a large reducible margin in the energy budget. On the other hand, for developing countries which are only at an early stage of energy consumption per head, it is not possible to talk about wasting energy.

Conclusions

The Spanish economy, in the middle of the evolution of its new democracy, must pull itself out of its economic crisis by controlling inflation and fighting unemployment. To do this it must adapt its structures to those of the European Community, and create a climate which will attract investment and stimulate its own people.

This great task, of which a primary condition must be the eradication of terrorism, will require effective support and the willingness of its EEC neighbours to adopt firm policies. The forthcoming entry of Spain into the EEC will make many positive contributions to the Community; nevertheless an effort must be made not only by the candidate, but by both parties. Spain's admission into the Community should not have to jump through the hoop of frequent elections in the member states, an endless process which is quite contrary to the original idea of a strong and unified Europe.

The Spanish people know that to survive they cannot rely on the 'manna from heaven' of biblical times, and that to pull themselves out of the crisis will require an effort which can only come from within, and from the sacrifices of their own citizens. It is no less true that they rely, as they have a right to do, on a reciprocity and collaboration with the EEC member states, in terms of real actions going beyond mere statements of political support.

9 Incomes policy: Austria's secret weapon

Horst Knapp

By international standards, the tiny country of Austria – accounting for well below one per cent of the world's land area, population and gross national product, if for nearly one per cent of the world's exports and for rather more than one per cent of the world's gold and foreign-exchange reserves – is not much to write home about, though some Austrians, considering their country to be the centre of the universe, may be forgiven for thinking otherwise. What is not so generally known, even by some Austrians themselves, is that the country has for some time past been one of the world's richest. Of the 168 states and independent territories listed in the 1979 *World Bank Atlas*, only 23 (oil sheikhdoms included) have a higher per capita GNP, a mere 22 (with some differences) a higher GNP as such. To understand Austria's rather special position, both these aspects must be borne in mind.

While a small country does not benefit from economies of scale – and large sections of Austrian industry are handicapped by the minuteness (less than the population of London) of their home market – it can, however, grow unnoticed and unimpeded. In 1969, for example, the Austrian schilling completely escaped the powerful upward pressure then being exerted on the West German mark, despite the fact that in terms of annual imports Austria's gold and foreign-currency reserves at the end of 1968 were rather higher (60 against 49 per cent), and during the sixties had grown far faster (by 111 against 41 per cent), than those of West Germany, whose greater absolute size nevertheless weighed far more heavily in the balance.

Growth is the key to the situation. Both before and after the 1974–75 world recession, Austria was in the overtaking lane, or rather she was steadily catching up on the others. During the period 1962-74 her growth averaged fractionally more than 5 per cent annually, compared with just over $4\frac{1}{2}$ per cent for both the OECD countries as a whole (of whom she is, of course, one) and for OECD Europe, and though it has slowed down since, the growth gap between her and the latter, if not the former, has if anything widened. In (more meaningful) per capita terms, more-over, because of Austria's stagnant population, the gap was, and has been, wider still. But why is it Austria, of all the OECD countries, whose growth for most of the time has been outstripped, if by a considerable margin, only by Japan (or at times by none except Japan and Norway)? Is it because, after Japan, and more recently Norway, Austria's gross fixed capital formation (investment) – at 27.3 per cent GDP (at constant prices) in the period 1964-80 – has been the highest?

Priority for investment

If so, however, there is need for a deeper explanation. In a democratic society, if such a large slice of national output is to be withheld from (private and public) consumption, there has to be a basic consensus not only about the priority to be given to investment as such, but also about the distribution of incomes making that investment possible – in the case of public investment (which in Austria includes the greater part of house-building), about what, by international standards, is a relatively high level of taxation; in the case of private investment, about how the national income should be divided between wages and salaries, mainly used for consumption, on the one hand, and other incomes, more likely to be allocated to investment, on the other.

At the same time, to talk about 'private' investment in Austria's case is a little misleading. Much investment is in fact undertaken by (chiefly basic-materials manufacturing) industrial enterprises and by energy utilities which, though managed for the most part on fairly strictly commercial lines, are publicly owned. Mention of this comparatively high, if largely formal, degree of nationalization – resulting from measures taken immediately after the end of World War II – is necessary because it has made it very much easier for Austria's socialist-dominated trade unions to accept the overriding need for adequate investment, as a basis for future wage increases, than might have been the case otherwise.

In turn, this basically positive trade-union attitude towards investment-boosted productivity gains has rested, and still rests, on the tacit assumption that in Austria, increasingly unlike almost all other western industrial countries, maintenance of full employment should rank not merely as an economic fact of life – in 1982, for the first time since 1960, the Beveridge benchmark of 3 per cent unemployment will probably be slightly exceeded – but also as a political creed that all parties and organizations share in common.

Work sharing

This means that in Austria, to an extent perhaps equalled only in Japan, companies of all sizes still pay more than lip-service to the principle that, in the event of a drop in sales, they rather accept a fall in productivity, however painful, than rigorously cut back their workforce, a principle honoured in the observance even where the prevention of mass redundancies is not, as it is in the case of nationalized or other large enterprises on which a whole region's prosperity may depend, an object of political pressure. Thus, in 1975 a more than 8 per cent decline in industrial production was accompanied by a mere 5 per cent drop in employment, despite a 16 per cent (in dollar terms, nearly 25 per cent) jump in unit labour costs, or a 2.3 per cent fall in productivity combined with 13.5 per cent higher earnings, following a round of unusually high pay settlements. For all its conspicuous failure on this solitary occasion, it is nevertheless Austria's 'incomes policy' which distinguishes her from nearly all other industrial countries.

After all, those very settlements – which probably did rather more to mitigate the effect of the 1975 recession in Austria than her own (no less than other countries') deficit spending – were only one half of the incomes policy balancing act, the other half being the readiness of the unions, for their part, to tolerate an at least partial subsequent restoration of company profits, at the expense even of some reduction in their own members' real wages. Hence, in the three years from 1978 to 1980, unit labour costs in Austrian manufacturing industry rose altogether by only 5.2 per cent – productivity by 14.7 per cent, average earnings by 20.6 per cent but in real terms (allowing for inflation) by just 5.6 per cent, the same as their *annual* rate of increase in the period 1970 to 1974.

Before considering whether the same trick could be performed again on a similar occasion, however, one must establish why incomes policy in Austria appears to work, if far from perfectly, so much better than in many other countries – a question which in the late sixties, incidentally, had formed the subject of a special OECD inquiry.

Why 'social partnership'?

In trying to answer that question, two institutional features readily spring to mind. First, there is no other western industrial country where all employers (including farmers) as well as all workers are required by law to be members of statutory organizations ('chambers'), each representing their respective interests. Second, there are few others

(*a*)   where the proportion of workers who, in addition, are organized in trade unions – membership of whom is voluntary – is so high (about 60 per cent of the total);

(*b*)   where only union executive committees, not unions as such, are organized on political or other non-craft lines;

(*c*)   where the union structure is so clear-cut that demarcation disputes between different unions are virtually impossible – since each, with the single exception of a general salaried workers' union, covers a whole industry; and

(*d*)   where each union is autonomous, yet the central organization (trade-union congress) to which all unions are affiliated is so powerful.

If the Austrian system has been conducive to industrial harmony, or 'social partnership', rather than, as it might have been, to class conflict, this is probably because it was among other things the severe class conflict of the interwar period which cost Austria her national independence, and because for a whole decade after her independence had been restored the recovery of complete sovereignty was such an overriding national objective that vested interests were almost bound to take second place.

By 1955, when the armies of occupation were finally withdrawn, the two sides of industry ('social partners') had developed a thoroughly efficient collective bargaining machinery which they were firmly convinced was superior to open industrial warfare – until, that is, the Grand Coalition, which was the 'social partnership' system's political counterpart, collapsed in 1966.

1966 and all that

In spite, or perhaps because, of that renewed flexing of industrial muscles, it was only a matter of months before, at the turn of the same year, incomes policy came for the first time to be employed in just the type of situation – a threatened slowdown of growth and employment, combined with accelerating inflation, i.e. stagflation – where its advantage over all other economic policy instruments is most manifest. Thus it was, well ahead of West Germany's 'concerted action', that Austria's social partners, finance minister and (independent) central bank concluded a compact, or 'social contract', which enabled the country's fiscal and monetary policy, under the social partnership umbrella of price and wage discipline, to execute a 'dash for growth' which ushered in its biggest and longest boom to date – in the 'seven fat years' 1968–74 its GDP in real terms grew by 5.6 per cent annually.

Though conditions in 1980–81 were not dissimilar, except that growth and employment slowed down and inflation (if still low by international standards) accelerated rather more than in 1966–67, another such dash now is nevertheless just as impossible as a repetition of the incomes policy balancing act performed during and after the preceding recession of 1975 is unlikely. The huge growth potential, both national and international, of the halcyon years from 1945 to (roughly) 1973 is a thing of the past. A key pillar of Austria's (as of any other country's) incomes policy – namely the legitimate expectation by both workers and employers that present voluntary wage and price restraint will secure faster growth in the future – is thus in real, and probably more than just temporary, danger of crumbling. Hence, and for other reasons still to be related, there is also little chance of Austria, with regard to the maintenance of full employment during a recession, being able to pull herself up by her own bootstraps for a second time.

Incomes policy balancing act 1975–80

Just as the increase in public-sector debt due to the deficit-spending exercise mounted to counteract the 1975 recession, and little abated during the boom period of 1976–80, militates against a repetition of expansionary fiscal measures (government spending in 1975 and 1976 increased by 55bn schillings), so does the increase in private-sector debt against a repetition of the expansionary pay settlements conceded by Austrian employers in 1975–76 (when their payroll increased by 44bn schillings), if the risk of workers being priced out of jobs is to be averted. What precludes a repetition of the 1967–74 dash for growth, as well as of the 1975–80 incomes policy balancing act, most of all, however, is a massive current-account deficit and consequent drain on the country's reserves, which in 1980 also put paid to its hitherto independent interest-rate policy and is placing effective support for expansionary measures of any kind totally beyond its monetary authorities' resources.

This perhaps also helps to explain why, from the Austrian Chancellor down, public reactions to the first intimations (in autumn 1980) of the latest recession were so much more alarmist than on the previous occasion in 1974 or even 1975, despite the fact that (at least at that stage) all the indications were that in the rest of the world as well as in Austria herself the recession this time round would be rather less severe. However, the paradox becomes less puzzling when it is remembered that, having shot its bolt in 1974–75 (and perhaps fatally torpedoed its balance of payments in the process) and failed to replenish its ammunition thereafter, the country now has no firepower to ward off even a comparatively mild attack of the economic jitters.

No reserves for a rainy day

Thus, at the time the 1981 budget was being framed, an economic downturn and hence a higher than the 1980 dream (1.9 per cent) unemployment rate were already clearly on the cards. Yet, after public spending in the space of six years had more than trebled, a basically Keynesian finance minister was obliged to deflate an already weakening economy further, and to bring in what in intention at least was an unequivocally restrictive budget, in order to relieve the tight external position.

Meanwhile, an unprecedented wave of bankruptcies demonstrated the alarming toll which the period of rapid growth, followed by the profit squeeze of the 1975 wage explosion and, since 1971, by Austria's 'hard currency' policy (in effect pegging the Austrian schilling to the German mark), has taken of the internal resources of Austrian companies both large (including some with household names) and small. Unlike the previous recession, it now needs only a slight dent in order, on top of the greatly increased cost of their predominantly external financing, to push even relatively well-heeled companies into the red, with their alternated equity base no longer able to save them from plunging headlong into debt.

The number and magnitude of insolvencies, secondary insolvencies and near-insolvencies, and the serious difficulties with which others, notably the state-owned Austrian steel industry (and in particular the special-steels sector), have been struggling for years, also explain another striking paradox since around the start of 1981. This is the contrasting pictures presented by the macroeconomic bird's-eye view of Austria's situation and the microeconomic worm's-eye one. These conflicting viewpoints – the former favoured by the government and its trade-union backers, the latter by the principal, employer-backed opposition party – have also so far inhibited convergence on a joint strategy for tackling the problems.

Basic consensus in sight?

At the time of writing (April 1981), tentative moves in that direction were, however, becoming discernible on both sides. When these lines appear in print, therefore, Austria could again have something like a 'tacit coalition', if not between the two major political parties, at least between the social partners, after the traditionally good relations between employer and worker organizations had been increasingly engulfed in the growing confrontation between government and opposition of recent years.

Paradoxically again, this convergence could be made at once more and less difficult by the fact that the government party of a country which for the previous five years or so had – together with an OECD secretariat which, perhaps for that very reason, always gave it particularly good marks – ranked as the 'lost paradise' of Keynesianism is now, quietly and surreptitiously, abandoning demand management in favour of supply-side economics, the latest economic gospel after, or alongside, monetarism. Those inclined to think in sharply defined categories should nevertheless beware of expecting Austria to conduct such a doctrinal realignment in anything but her usual sloppy manner!

In fact, what Professor Hans Seidel (the former director of the Austrian Economic Research Institute, now Secretary of the Treasury) has labelled 'Austro-Keynesianism' had been anything but the pure milk of Keynesianism. And this not just because Austria, like a good many others, had during her last economic upswing omitted to run down her budget deficit with the same counter-cyclical fervour as during her previous downswing she had built it up. It is also because there is nothing typically

Keynesian either about the key importance Austria attaches to incomes policy (as there would be, not about forgoing nominal pay rises in excess of productivity, but about reducing real incomes through the subsequent, and none the less faster, rate of inflation) or about the hard-currency policy which, not least in that incomes policy's interest, she has been pursuing for the past ten years. In this, of course, the strong schilling was aimed not only at curbing imported inflation, and so encouraging wage restraint, but also, by intensifying the competitive pressure on prices, at preventing wage drift at plant level from reducing such restraint to a mockery.

Supply-side economics, made in Austria

If therefore it was a kind of pseudo-Keynesianism which had formed the theoretical basis of Austria's demand management strategy, then her conversion to supply-side economics is almost bound, in important respects, to deviate likewise from what passes for a neoclassical, or even monetarist, economic policy elsewhere. In particular, after three and a half decades during which full employment had been accorded top priority by all concerned, it seems inconceivable that any temporary, let alone permanent, effect on jobs would be shrugged off lightly, either as a voluntary sacrifice or as a scourge to be blamed on the unions. Equally, given the Austrian unions' quasi-official status and record, it seems inconceivable that they could be made the scapegoat for a restrictive monetary policy on the ground that everything in the garden would still have been lovely if only pay rises had, regardless of inflation, kept within the monetary target limits.

So the chances are that Austria's version of the supply-side economics game will mainly consist of measures to speed up industrial restructuring, with long experience entitling all those directly, or even indirectly, affected to expect to be cushioned against joblessness by appropriate countermeasures – whether through the adoption of a less restrictive fiscal policy or through the provision of various safety-nets like the early retirement of workers in danger of being declared redundant.

However, let us return to the paradox that changing from an essentially demand- to a primarily supply-orientated economic policy could make what all sides by now recognize to be a necessary (re-)convergence of the opposing political camps at once less, and more, difficult. Such a basic consensus is made less difficult, on the one hand, because a change in a hitherto mainly demand-orientated style of economic management also requires employers' protests about their profits and capital being eroded by escalating costs, including inflated fringe benefits and excessive social charges, to be taken seriously at last. On the other, it is made more difficult by 'ideological' arguments about the alternative policy instruments to be used, although in fact, given a modicum of goodwill, a system of 'direct' investment, and especially innovation, aids could be designed in such a way that whatever project satisfies the criteria laid down in advance will qualify for assistance in just the same way as it does under the existing system of 'indirect' investment incentives through special depreciation allowances and the like.

Restructuring deferred?

Rather more serious than the danger of investment direction by some government agency is the possibility that political log-rolling could, because production facilities in lieu of those to be closed down will for the most part have different and reduced labour requirements, cause a disproportionately large part of any extra funds earmarked for industrial restructuring purposes to be diverted to preservation of the status quo, when the occupational and particularly geographical mobility of Austrian workers leaves much to be desired as it is.

Yet, given Austria's intractably large (an average 2.1 per cent of GDP in 1976–80) current-account deficit and the present inability of her (more important than any other European country's) tourist industry to earn more than the equivalent of about

60 per cent of her visible trade deficit, the need for faster industrial restructuring is disputed by no one, particularly seeing that, as an industrial country, Austria has become a net importer not just of oil and other basic materials, but of manufactured goods as well.

Besides, 'traditional' industries still loom too large for comfort. Though such classifications are rather questionable – the Austrian textile and clothing industries, for example, are in part uncommonly innovative, but also include two 'growth companies' among the frontrunners of the insolvency parade – this perhaps also reflects the fact that in Austria, unlike most other industrial countries, the diversion of manufacturing operations to low-wage developing countries overseas has yet hardly begun. Such a move would also be vehemently opposed by worker organizations (including works councils) in a country where job creation and preservation has, far more than anywhere else in the West, come to be regarded as the prime function of management – a philosophy which employer organizations have, by invoking it for years in their own cause, done more than a little to foster.

The emerging new international division of labour with the newly industrializing countries could thus create bigger structural problems for Austria than for others already farther advanced along that road, and therefore perhaps far worse affected by hard-core unemployment, than she herself. It also remains to be seen whether ultimately the price in terms of lower profits paid for not indulging in the practice of hiring and firing may not have made Austrian companies less resistant to stiffer international competition normal during a slump, or during periods of stunted growth generally, seeing that they have so far been unable to discover an alternative to internally generated financing. The Austrian equity market is a virtual non-entity, and plans for supplying non-quoted companies, which in Austria make up the overwhelming majority, with risk capital are still only on the drawing-board.

Slower growth ...

All this means that Austria may – not merely for the time being, in order to reduce a current-account deficit inflated by her relative fast growth in the past, but for some time to come – be obliged to quit the overtaking lane, having omitted, like others in frailer health, to put her own house in order during all those easier years. After all, a business that makes full employment its top priority will regard lay-offs as 'unavoidable' only when on the brink of disaster. Incidentally, though Austria's otherwise immensely beneficial system of social partnership – during 1975–79 an average of just 0.6 minutes per worker per year were lost through strike action, compared with (during 1974–78) 27.2 in West Germany, 184.2 in Britain and 683.7 in Italy – is evidently not free from those and other blemishes, they apply only to what, by local standards, are relatively large businesses; small and medium-sized businesses exhibit a higher degree of flexibility in such matters.

But if, weighing her above-average past performance against the structural weaknesses now coming to light, Austria in future is likely to be seen ambling inconspicuously somewhere in the middle of the field, and may even, in order to reduce her current-account deficit, have to drop below the OECD growth average for a time, there are grounds for believing that she will still continue to do rather better than most West European countries in two other respects.

... but lower inflation and unemployment

For one thing, the key factors to which she owes her relatively low rate of inflation – a co-ordinated incomes policy, a stability-orientated exchange-rate policy – will probably remain unchanged, the latter even in the face of an external deficit which is proving extremely hard to redress. The main trouble here, after all, has been the rising price of oil, which a deliberate policy of allowing the Austrian schilling to weaken against the dollar (in which oil is, of course, priced) would merely aggravate. Besides, the rewards reaped by others who have taken this soft option are not such as to make Austria wish to emulate their example.

Secondly, it seems safe to predict that Austria's unemployment rate, if higher than in the past, will likewise continue to run below the world average. And this not just because she entered the latest recession with (in relation to her working population) far fewer jobless than most other countries, nor simply because of her different order of economic priorities. It is rather because in the event of a significant rise in unemployment, and especially at the first sign of any (in Austria hitherto non-existent) youth unemployment, her incomes policy can confidently be expected to pass its perhaps severest test through her workers agreeing to forgo real pay increases or even, should this prove necessary in the interest of school-leavers and others able and willing to work, tacitly acquiescing in cuts in real pay to make the work go round.

The memory of the mass unemployment which, before the war, cost Austria both her livelihood and independence is not something to be lived down lightly. A burned child dreads the fire...

10 The rise and fall of the Swedish economic model

Erik Lundberg

Introduction

The change in trend in Sweden's economic development during the 1970s is in many respects typical of that in other small European countries. While in the other Scandinavian countries some similar tendencies may be observed, these other countries are, unlike Sweden, in many ways atypical. Denmark is an old hand in the game of a slow-growth economy in disequilibrium; the deterioration of the balance of payments has during the last years forced the government to carry out severe restrictive policies, with high unemployment as a consequence. Finland has experienced so many ups and downs, with an industrial boom since 1978, that a trend is difficult to observe. And Norway, with permanent full employment has recently received a great push from its new oil resources, so that the development of this country is a special case.

Sweden is a good, in some respects a spectacular, case of trend reversal. This reversal is combined with serious economic imbalances that have developed since 1974. There is also a drastic change in the economic climate as well as in the socio-political milieu. All this may be examined in the context of the disappearance of the old Swedish socio-economic model that seemed to function so well during the postwar decades. But first we must take a look at the changes in economic trends that occurred during the 1970s, changes which form the economic background to the disruption of the Swedish model. This article will end with a look at the prospects for the 1980s and a discussion of policy alternatives that may imply another kind of 'trend reversal'.

Economic disturbances during the 1970s

Since the mid 1970s Sweden's industrial growth has been lagging seriously behind that of the 1950s and 1960s. Between 1975 and 1980 the country had experienced 20 per cent slower industrial growth than the OECD average. And yet this average represented a significant retardation of growth for all OECD countries. There was a similar gap with respect to the GNP – although not quite as big – due to a relatively rapid expansion of the public sector in Sweden.

There are both business-cycle and more long-term structural changes involved in this disappointing record. The Swedish economy lagged seriously behind nearly all OECD countries during the cyclical revival after the 1974–75 recession. One finds in fact a three-year lag, as the long-drawn-out recession in Sweden lasted up to the autumn of 1978. Moreover, the revival and the expansion of production from 1978 was unusually short, lasting only to the first quarter of 1980 (when the volume of industrial production only just reached its previous peak of 1974).

This recent business-cycle record is quite unique in Swedish economic history since the 1860s. The cyclical stability of the Swedish economy has generally been pronounced; even after such relatively deep depressions as those at the beginning of the 1920s and 1930s, quick and strong revivals were characteristic; and they were followed by industrial growth which in both decades was stronger than that of nearly all other countries. The records of the fifties and sixties were also better than in most countries: very shallow recessions in the form of growth retardation, followed by long periods of good expansion.

It is of interest to observe that government policy reaction to the recession after 1974 was in principle the same as in earlier recessions, including the depression of the 1930s. Keynesian-type expansionary policies had become more frequently and explicitly utilized in Sweden than elsewhere. During the fifties and the sixties the social-democratic government developed a lot of measures – including active labour-market policies – in order to stimulate investment, stabilize private consumption expenditure and expand public works during recessions. In the main, these stabilization policies were successful and for more than twenty years Sweden enjoyed balanced growth with full employment, moderate inflation and no balance-of-payments disturbances.

After the recession of 1970-71, the boom of 1973-74 was very pronounced, with high profit inflation and excess demand for labour. The severe disturbances arising from the oil price shock of 1973 hit Sweden seriously because of its very high oil dependence. The deep international recession was immediately transmitted to the Swedish economy by way of a declining export volume.

In accordance with the Keynesian tradition, anticyclical policies were rapidly and energetically applied. One important consequence was that open unemployment was kept low, between 2 and 3 per cent during the whole period up to 1981. This expansionary policy aimed to bridge over the recession and then link the economy to the next international revival (beginning at the end of 1975). The target was thus set to 'jump over' the international recession and then connect on to the following expansion. There was some partial success, as production and demand were maintained relatively well during 1974 and 1975. But the main result, paradoxically, was that the Swedes succeeded instead in 'jumping over' the following international revival of 1975-78!

The story behind this almost complete policy failure is complicated and cannot be fully recounted here. One important result of the development was a wage cost explosion during the years 1974-76 (by more than 50 per cent), which brought Sweden's costs up to an entirely uncompetitive level. According to approximate calculations, wage cost per unit of industrial production increased by 25 per cent more (from 1973) than a weighted average of competing OECD countries. The consequences were to be found in a sharp decline in Sweden's share of export and home markets, an extreme profitability crisis and a big decline in industrial investment. This is the main background to the disappointing business-cycle experience in Sweden in the years 1974-78.

The retardation of Sweden's export and industrial production during these years can be related to a significant overvaluation of the Swedish crown. The big deficit in the current balance of payments (varying between 2 and 4 per cent of GNP) is a significant indicator of this. During the time of the big cost inflation – up to 1976 – the Swedish crown belonged to the 'snake' of EEC currencies, and the crown appreciated together with the German mark. This disequilibrium was partially corrected, first during 1977, by means of depreciations of the crown; but these carried a long time-lag before they were effective and they turned out to be insufficient. An important condition for the earlier, successful economic growth in Sweden, referred to above, was the maintenance of an exchange rate that implied a substantial undervaluation of the crown. That had been the case during the 1930s (after the big devaluation in 1931) and again in the fifties and the sixties (after the 1949 devaluation).

It could be argued that the trend reversal of Sweden's economic development after 1974 is mainly a short-term cyclical phenomenon, in which inadequate government policies have played an important role. From this point of view the Keynesian expansionary policies applied in 1974–76, the following wage-cost explosion, and the lagging and inadequate exchange-rate policy would explain the main causes of the deviation from the development pattern of other industrial countries. This interpretation would imply that the disappointing development in Sweden should be regarded as accidental, a cumulation of unhappy disturbances and mistaken policies. Learning from these mistakes, and without new oil price shocks, Sweden's economy should be able to recover and regain lost ground.

The new recession – after the second oil price shock – in 1979–80 – that has developed in Sweden from the summer of 1980 is no longer in fact being met by compensating expansionary policies. Contractionary policies are dominant and wage increases limited, as will be discussed in the last section. It is quite clear, however, that there is much more behind Sweden's economic crisis of the 1970s than just a cyclical setback. More fundamental structural changes of the Swedish economy have occurred at a time at which the economic crisis itself has led to long-term imbalances which operate as lasting restrictions on economic growth.

The cyclical downturn has been aggravated by serious structural crises. Since 1973, a number of industries have been hit by over-capacity breakdowns coupled with demand failures and profitability crises. This has happened to iron ore, steel, shipyards, textiles and to some extent also to the timber and woodwork industries. We find here a number of related issues: international over-investment during the boom years of the sixties and the seventies, stagnating demand development especially in investment branches, keen international competition from newly industrialized countries. But something serious seems to have happened also to the comparative advantage and cost situation of the Swedish economy. So much of Sweden's rapid industrial development has depended on the relatively cheap supply of electricity and raw materials, from ores and forests. Now these comparative advantages belong mostly to the past – with reserves of cheap water-power eliminated by environmental resistance, narrow restrictions on forest supply and new, cheaper supplies of iron ore from other countries.

Government policies during 1974–78 of protecting employment in a number of corporations within these fields have caused a slowing-up of the adjustment process; and there has not been sufficient compensation in the form of expanding fields such as engineering. Strong and growing resistance to labour mobility, not only as between regions but also between firms and types of jobs, has seriously slowed down the process of structural adaptation.

The most important structural change is the tremendous growth of the public sector. The decline and stagnation of the private sector of the economy has been compensated by a rapid expansion of public consumption. This development is partly an effect of the Keynesian policies of 1974, referred to above, but it mainly refers to a strong trend factor. Since 1974 the rise of employment in the public sector has absorbed the whole of the increase in the total labour force as well as the decline in industrial employment. This is the main explanation of the fact that unemployment has been kept down to around two per cent during the whole crisis period. One result is that the share of *total* public expenditures in the GNP has increased from about 40 per cent in 1970 to 68 per cent in 1981 (this gross figure includes all transfer payments from the public sector to households and enterprises).

This rapid growth of public expenditure implies a number of structural changes to the Swedish economy, and has important consequences for its functioning. The 'right-wing' or 'bourgeois' government (in power since September 1976) has been 'forced' to socialize corporations (especially in steel and shipyards) to an extent that the previous social-democratic governments had never dreamt of during forty-four years of rule. High and rising tax rates are an important aspect of the public-sector expansion. The record level of direct taxes in Sweden that has been attained during the seventies (with marginal rates of 60–90 per cent) has serious negative effects on incentives to work and save. The absorption of employees into secure and agreeable jobs in the public sector has had negative effects on the supply of labour to the industrial sector. The rapidly expanding social services, with generous payments for sickness, unemployment, pensions and all kinds of subsidies for housing, regional employment, public works and vocational training – the sum of all this has also meant incentives to work less, avoid overtime and take more leisure.

Significant distortions of the economy during the 1970s seem thus to be caused by the large and rising level of public expenditure and the high tax payments. The combination of high marginal tax rates, high interest rates, and large and varying inflation has been followed by distorted investment activity. Financial investments of all kinds have shown much higher returns than long-term productive investments in industry. There are in Sweden good incentives for expanding 'black' and 'grey' market activities. One important result of all this is that the industrial sector has become too small, due to loss of manpower and five years of very low rates of investment. We shall return to this problem in the last section.

Finally the rapid expansion of government expenditures during the seventies and continuing during 1980 and 1981 has not been matched since 1976 by a corresponding increase of incomes, in spite of rising tax rates. The big rise in the government deficit, which to a large extent has been due to the stagnation of economic activity in the private sector, has taken the shape of a structural imbalance. The deficit corresponds to about 12 per cent of GNP – a level previously attained only during war years; it creates a severe restraint on government policy and has serious effects on credit markets, the money supply and inflation.

The working of the 'Swedish model'

I have so far given the economic background, the tendencies in economic development as they have appeared especially during the 1970s. But there seems to have been a break in development also on a socio-political level referring to the broader issues of the 'Swedish model'. Here we encounter fundamental changes in the conditions that have to be considered in any evaluation of future development alternatives.

The concept of the 'Swedish model' has had several connotations. In a more narrow sense, the concept has primarily been applied to conditions on the Swedish labour market, reflected by the ability of employers' and employees' organizations to reach reasonable wage settlements while under an obligation to keep labour disputes at a minimum.

The parties were supposed to share a common social outlook regarding the value of free collective bargaining, exempt from government interference, but not from an inherent responsibility for the country's general economic development. This outlook included a positive attitude towards the competitive conditions of a market economy engaged in free international trade, combined with full acceptance – also by the Confederation of Trade Unions – of the necessity of sufficiently high profitability in private enterprises. In a broad sense, the Swedish model also embodies aspects of overall trends in society, such as progressive social development including high employment levels, continuous income equalization and rapid expansion of the social-security system and the rest of the public sector, accompanied by increases in direct and indirect taxes. All this was exhibited during the decades between the end of the Second World War and the early 1970s.

A basic condition of the working of this Swedish model is of course the efficient functioning of the labour market. The premise shared by the parties in the Swedish labour market – and by successive governments – has been the preservation of the competitiveness of Swedish industry in relation to foreign production, in the domestic as well as the export market. The equilibrium condition ultimately concerned the balance of payments. As exchange rates were fixed (according to the Bretton Woods system) up until the beginning of the 1970s, in the last analysis there was a clearly limited margin for wage increases in the sectors most exposed to international competition. All political parties were in agreement on this point.

Towards the end of the 1960s, the labour-market organizations' economic experts – the EFO group, in which the Confederation of Trade Unions, the Central Organization of Salaried Employees and the Employers' Confederation are represented – interpreted the margin for wage increases as corresponding to the sum of the rise in productivity and the price increases for export goods,[1] both measured in annual averages. The EFO model may be regarded as a fairly good description of, and explanation for, real wage and price formation and also as a *norm* according to which wage policy should be formulated. This EFO model appears to have performed rather well during the decades prior to the troubled 1970s, to some extent by means of variations in wage drift. The average increases in unit labour costs did not exceed the limits necessary for maintaining balance-of-payments equilibrium, although a tendency towards deterioration could be discerned at the end of the 1960s.

This EFO formula determined the principal course, with annual deviations. Years in which the increase in unit labour costs was too high were followed by corrections which resulted from more or less automatic repercussions in the economy, supported by stabilization policy. It should be emphasized that balance-of-payments equilibrium during this period was not achieved at the expense of significant deviations from the goal of full employment. Wage formation seemed to be guided by an invisible EFO hand. The export industry set the standards, leading wage development – in conformity with the parties' common ideology – whereas wages in the non-tradables and public sectors were adjusted accordingly. One of the harmonious notions fundamental to the EFO model – which was, in fact, the economic nucleus of the Swedish model – was the prerequisite of satisfactory profit margins. Acceptance of this condition was implied by the EFO model's wage-policy norm. Sufficiently high industrial profits were a necessary condition for investments and expansion and, as a result, for the sharp rise in productivity which provided the scope for a rapid rate of increase in real wages (by approximately four per cent per year during the 1960s). Of course, the labour unions could never explicitly proclaim the necessity of maintaining satisfactory profit margins as one of their goals. In collective bargaining, it was always self-evident that the labour unions would try to squeeze out as much as possible. But, at least in the long run, employer opposition, combined with the corrective effects of wage drift, did produce results which more or less adhered to the EFO norm.

There was more to this part of the Swedish model than just this type of wage adjustment. The goals presupposed a generally restrictive monetary and fiscal policy which made it difficult for firms to compensate for increased cost under constant exchange rates. A squeeze from labour cost in conjunction with a solidary wage policy – with uniform increases throughout, regardless of the financial strength and productivity of individual firms – would, in fact, bring about a general rise in productivity. This would occur along several paths. Firms would have to implement rationalization measures in order to cover cost increases at given, internationally determined prices. The uniform cost squeeze would also force weak firms and subsectors to cut back or discontinue operations, and thereby relinquish production resources to expanding and profitable firms and subsectors. The structural transformation precipitated by the labour-cost pressure would be – and actually became – an important cause of the rapid rise in industrial productivity during the 1960s (about 7–8 per cent per year).

The deterioration of the model

A number of serious disturbances to the Swedish model appeared during the 1970s. The international inflationary upswing,

accentuated by the oil price shock in late 1973, was too great a
disturbance for the EFO model. The excessive profits of 1973 and
1974 were regarded as signifying 'undershooting' with respect to
possible pay increases. But the ultimate result – partly attributable to the international recession in 1974–75 – was such a tremendous 'overshooting' in the development of wages that the
Swedish economy was hit by a profound cost crisis, as mentioned
above. This profitability and cost crisis could not be rectified easily.
The deviation from the norms of the EFO model with respect to
the share of profits and indeed profitability was so large (the total
of companies listed on the Swedish Stock Exchange did not show
any net profits in 1978) that union and also political leaders came
to regard a complete recovery of profits as unacceptable.

The efficient operation of the EFO model up until the beginning of the 1970s was implicitly based on the condition that
nominal wage increases would lead to a satisfactory rise in real
wages – even after taxes. This relation was disrupted in the
seventies by the combination of an increase in the inflation rate
and a steep rise in direct taxes. The marginal tax level – elevated
by inflation – had widened the gap between wage increases before
and after taxes. The 'conversion rate' for the average industrial
worker during the latter half of the 1970s was cut down to about
60 per cent, i.e., a nominal wage increase of 10 per cent did not
yield more than a 6 per cent rise in income after tax. In order for
the purchasing power of wages to remain unchanged when the
consumer price index increased at the rate of 10 per cent per year,
wages would have to rise by 17 per cent. When the subsequent
acceleration of expected price increases is also taken into account,
wage demands would need to be at least 10 per cent higher. Thus,
the dynamics of inflation forced the government to intervene in
wage determination on several occasions through fiscal policy
measures; it was not until direct tax rates were lowered that an
increase in real wages (after tax) could be achieved. Thus, wage-
policy conditions have undergone fundamental changes, deviat-
ing drastically from the EFO norm.

It is important to stress that there were many other changes of
conditions in the 1970s other than those involving the mechanics
of the EFO model. A kind of socio-psychological change of

climate took place which incorporated both political and economic dimensions. It seems as if the very success of the Swedish model during the 1950s and 1960s may have triggered off counteracting forces which impaired its efficiency.

Rapid and steady economic growth throughout a quarter of a century created an attitude whereby such expansion was thought to be self-evident and inexorable. It was taken for granted and, in effect, became an integral part of prevailing social mechanisms. Problems related to the rapid growth of the public sector and policies of income equalization seemed affordable and caused a minimum of social friction as long as this growth appeared to be self-perpetuating. There was no reason for concern about the possible negative impact of how resources were utilized, indeed about the prerequisites for growth, until growth itself came to a standstill. But before that, an uninterrupted rise in the level of GNP resources led to attitude changes and new demands. Since the mid 1960s, the original and simple economic policy goals (full employment, stable prices and rapid growth) have been reoriented towards more ambitious welfare aims. Price stabilization, however, was relinquished as an objective because other goals were given priority. It seems as if annual inflation amounting to 7–10 per cent has become an acceptable rate.

What were once simple growth and employment objectives have been consistently differentiated and supplemented. Security and equity aims have taken precedence at the same time as welfare costs associated with high productivity and effective resource allocation have been regarded as increasingly serious. It became desirable to consider whether the price of rapid growth and full employment was too high. One example is the intense reaction to the high labour mobility which prevailed during the decades of rapid growth. Labour legislation during the 1970s reflects demands for job security, and employees have become more closely tied to their employers. There thus appeared mounting criticism of the one-sided emphasis on growth; rising productivity claimed many victims through lay-offs, unemployment and forced retirement. Demands for environmental protection and improvements in the working environment gained momentum owing to the negative effects of rapid growth and high GNP. Forces demanding a more equalized distribution of income and wealth have also grown. This is made evident by greater efforts to improve the position of low-wage groups and by more progressive taxation. Leading politicians and the organizational bureaucracy have come to be much less inclined to accept a high level of corporate profits – the level of the 1960s – arguing that these are a source of the uneven distribution of power, income and wealth.

The Swedish economy suffers from imbalances which may be interpreted as stemming from insufficient access to productive resources and fears that GNP growth during the 1980s will be too slow. There seems to be a kind of political and social schizo-phrenia, i.e. distorted attitudes both within individuals them-selves and between different groups of people. On the one hand Sweden has achieved such a large total supply of resources (GNP per capita) that there is plenty of – and perhaps even more than enough – room for high levels of welfare and quality of life, as long as given resources are utilized and distributed in a reasonable way. On the other hand, prevailing serious imbalances of the economy and the threat of potential conflicts of interest imply that now, more than ever, an increase in GNP and growth are necessary prerequisites for arriving at a more or less harmonious solution to economic problems. The old Swedish model was based on simple rationality and an optimistic outlook for the future which no longer exists. The new schizophrenic attitudes are seriously influenced by genuine uncertainty about future prospects.

A fundamental prerequisite for the satisfactory working of the old Swedish model was also the fact that a *consensus* on mutual values took precedence over special interests. The EFO model was based on this consensus and on a reciprocal outlook, which was deeply rooted in the labour-market organizations. The objective, of course, was to apportion the growth of the 'pie' in a rational way, so as to preserve the conditions favourable to continued growth. There was also a secure political basis for this overall perspective. At the time, the relatively strong Social Democratic government (or the dominance of Social Democrats during the coalition years) created a kind of acceptable political balance whereby various aspects of the Social Democrats' welfare

policy were offset by the maintenance of the market conditions
for a free-enterprise system. Since the mid 1970s, these conditions
are no longer given. Governments have been weak and, after
1976, headed by a Liberal–Conservative coalition. Conflicts of
interest and issues related to income distribution are at the fore-
front, and the common outlook has receded into the background.
It has become increasingly difficult to concentrate on effective
stabilization and growth policies, due to discordant views concerning both means and aims.

Prospects for the 1980s

In Sweden we would have to go back to the latter half of the
1920s to find a parallel to the current widespread polarization
and disintegration of common interests. The severe crisis of the
1930s actually helped the country to find effective, unifying
solutions (it was then that the foundation for the Swedish model
was established). Perhaps a profound crisis would once again
create the conditions for effective solutions based on some kind
of consensus about a new Swedish model. So far, governments
have on the whole been successful only in their efforts to disguise
the crisis, keep unemployment low and prevent it from substantially affecting ordinary citizens.

However, politicians, trade unionists and entrepreneurs are at
present quite aware of the imbalances in the Swedish economy
and the uncertain prospects. The Government Committee on
long-term projection (report published in the autumn of 1980)
accepted as its optimistic alternative an annual GNP growth rate
of 2.5 per cent per annum on average during the 1980s. This
rate is thus substantially lower than that prevailing during
the 'golden decades' of the fifties and sixties when GNP growth
in real terms varied between 4 and 5 per cent. But by now those
decades are being regarded as quite exceptional. This break of the
growth trend will involve a much more serious change in the
growth of real wages and private consumption standards. In fact
the report projects that up to 1985 there will be hardly any

resources left for a rise in private consumption, and a slightly declining tendency for real wages per employee. The reason is that the projected rate of growth requires a rise in the share of investment and saving, and a sharp reduction of the present big deficit in the current balance of payments. The pressure on the consumption standard of the working population is further increased by the rising share of disposable resources going to an expanding number of retired people.

The predominant problem at present concerns, however, the prevailing imbalances in the Swedish economy which may lead to severe difficulties in achieving the new 2.5 per cent growth target. The present international recession should be passing. But in order to attain the conditions of balanced growth there is also need for a radical change in economic policy, and in this respect too, a trend break is occurring. The old type of Keynesian expansionary policies, still applied in the 1974-76 recession, will not do any more. There is quite general consensus about that. But there are sharp conflicts about what types of policy will be adequate to solve the short- and long-term disequilibrium problems of the Swedish economy. There is not the space here to deal at length with the prevailing policy conflicts. In these concluding remarks something must be said about alternative policy prospects, as this issue clearly belongs to a 'reversal of trends' discussion.

As mentioned above, there are a number of unresolved imbalances in the Swedish economy.

(*1*)   A big balance-of-payments deficit, at present corresponding to about 4 per cent of GNP. This is much more than the average of the OECD (1-2 per cent) and seems to be more persistent than in other countries. This imbalance can be expressed as an insufficient rate of saving in relation to investment.

(2)   A total government deficit corresponding to 12 per cent of GNP. This implies a state financial crisis. The financing of a deficit on this scale (of which one-third is met by borrowing abroad, 'thanks to' the balance-of-payments deficit) tends to imply inflationary financing with too much money creation.

(*3*)   The rate of inflation – at around 10-12 per cent per year at present – is much too high for an effective functioning of the economy.

(*4*)   As mentioned above, public-sector expenditure has been increasing too rapidly, especially during the 1970s. The record high levels of expenditure and taxation are causing inefficiencies in the working of the economy.

(*5*)   The industrial sector has become too small due to the decline in employment and investment during the 1970s. The main problem is that this sector cannot generate the extra volume of goods needed to solve the balance-of-payments problem. This problem is aggravated by the fact that Swedish industry is only expanding abroad. The big transnational companies have an increasing share of employment, and investments occur in countries other than Sweden.

(*6*)   The deficit in the balance of payments implies that 'Sweden is living above its means', as is often maintained. But it is equally true that the country is producing below its capacity. The big retardation of production – both in relation to other countries and as compared to earlier performance – should mean the existence of a 'production gap', i.e. the potential for a higher production level. This is the great issue of *supply-side economics*, topical in so many countries. Better incentives for work, investment, enterprise and risk-taking are suggested as ways of mobilizing potential resources.

In principle most of these imbalance problems could be solved by a bold, radical policy combination, a kind of complete recasting of policies and policy attitudes – a big devaluation of the Swedish crown (an insufficient devaluation occurred in September 1981), combined with a stabilization of wages during a long enough period (2–3 years), plus a reduction of public expenditure and the lowering of the scale of progressive taxes. The essence of this type of policy strategy would be to attain an export-led growth under effective market conditions. The restoration of profitability and work incentives could 'in theory' create wonders if demand expanded in harmony with the increased elasticity on the supply side. Examples from other countries which have carried out policies of this kind (Portugal, Finland, Japan) illustrate the possibilities.

However, the political and ideological conditions in Sweden exclude any clear and persistent effort of finding solutions along such lines. In this sense there is a *political* crisis. The 'bourgeois' governments have made weak, and in the main unsuccessful, efforts in this direction. There is not much support from the trade unions or the social democrats for a return to an efficiently working market system with adequate profitability and a good incentive system. The egalitarian spirit is in the way.

In essence there is a confrontation as to the choice of economic system – and therefore a kind of *system* crisis. Leading groups of trade-union officials and social democrats maintain that the 'mixed system' of the Swedish economy – the Swedish model – supported by a functioning market system and free trade has failed during the 1970s. They try to show that high profits do not effectively stimulate investments in production and expansion of production in acceptable channels. But the argument can be turned around. High profits lead alternatively to over-investment in certain lines, to exaggerated rationalization and too much financial investment. The effects on distribution of income and wealth from sufficiently high profits cannot easily be accepted. The target of a much more even income distribution is in conflict with the target of improved incentives. The socialist solutions are, instead, found along the lines of 'fund socialism': government or trade-union-owned investment funds – covering branches of industry and regions of the country – supply savings and become planning agencies; obligatory wage funds mean growing collective ownership and lead to the increasing control of corporations; the supply of savings from such funds will lower the dependence on profits. Planning of investment will be done with more attention to employment goals and regional balance, with only certain reasonable profit criteria as restrictions on expansion.

These are but vague indications of the lines of social-democratic and trade-union thinking in reaction to the present crisis. The failures of the bourgeois government and the growing strength of the social democrats will mean that there is going to be much less of a renaissance of a market economy system in Sweden than in other countries. The trend change will perhaps be most evident in this respect.

However, when the prevailing policy confrontations with re-gard to overcoming the crisis have settled down, the Swedes are usually good at finding workable compromises. The trade-union leaders and many of the social democrats have a traditional respect for the working of decentralized markets and are unlikely to want to go too far with their fund experiments. There should, therefore, ultimately appear a reasonable compromise between a free-enterprise system and a centralized, collective organization.

11 Switzerland:
once again a special case?

Francesco Kneschaurek

The Swiss, they say, are different from everybody else – and, some would add, they would still be different if they were the only people in the world. But now, on top of her peculiar political set-up and neutralist foreign policy, she has also since the start of the seventies been something of a loner in the economic field. At a time when other western industrial countries have been vainly battling against a mounting tide of unemployment, she has been scraping the barrel of her manpower resources, with a few thousand (in 1980 below 0.3 per cent of her working population) registered jobless far exceeded by the number of unfilled vacancies. Boasting the lowest inflation rate of all industrial countries, she has not been racked by the kind of monetary starvation diet to which many others have been treated in order to keep their inflationary pressures at bay. And while those countries have been recording current-account deficits of ever dizzier heights (in 1980 these nudged $60bn), she has been notching up one handsome surplus after another. Yet in the world slump of 1975–76 her gross national product in real terms, like her level of employment, had fallen by 10 per cent – more than that of any other OECD country – and her growth rate in the last few years has been lagging behind most of the rest. To explain those apparent contradictions, Switzerland's economic history since World War II – in which, as usual, she played no part – needs to be examined a bit more closely.

Sea-change of the seventies

The most striking feature is the decisive change in all major economic indicators – summed up by the trend of the gross domestic product – which took place in the early seventies (see Table 1). Thus, from 4.6 per cent in the fifties and 4.7 per cent in the sixties, the average annual growth of Switzerland's GDP during the seventies slowed down to just 1 per cent, and this not primarily for any short-term reasons connected with (say) the pattern of the business cycle, but because of fundamental changes in the economic environment.

Table 1 **Switzerland's real GDP 1950–80** (at 1970 prices) (Sw Fr billion)

Average annual growth	*1950–70:* 4.7%		*1970–80:* 1.2%
	1950–60	*1960–70*	*1970–80*
Average annual growth (%)			
Number employed	1.5	1.3	−0.4
Productivity	3.1	3.4	1.6
Real GDP	**4.6**	**4.7**	**1.2**
Absolute change (No.)			
Number employed	+357,000	+423,000	−140,000

Since the economic fortunes of land-locked Switzerland are, despite her splendid political isolation, closely tied up with those of the rest of the world, from whose recurring troubles she has long served as a trusted refuge, it is with the principal external aspects of that environment that this examination can perhaps most fittingly start.

The socio-economic context

Political clouds

For the western industrialized countries, Switzerland included, the 1970s saw, in the first place, a distinct worsening of the world political climate. First, with new power centres proliferating, each increasingly intent on pursuing its own political goals, there was a growing number of potential international flashpoints over which the West, and the United States in particular, could no longer exercise effective control. Secondly, the Soviet Union adopted a more blatantly expansionist policy aimed, through the well-tried weapons of political subversion, ideological infiltration and social revolution, at destabilizing, and thus detaching from the West, more and more countries previously integrated into the western economic system and in which a lot of western capital had been invested. Lastly, North–South relations were marred by an intensifying struggle for a 'new world economic order' seeking to swing the balance in the developing countries' favour to such an extent that the West so far has been reacting in a predominantly defensive manner and the North–South 'dialogue' has been overshadowed by rhetoric, rancour and suspicion, to the economic detriment of all concerned. All this has, by comparison with the immediate postwar period, cramped the international style of Swiss industry in no uncertain terms.

Social tensions

The 1970s also saw the international propagation of attitudes diametrically opposed to what until then had been almost universally accepted social standards and aspirations. In particular, they saw a rising criticism of the economic growth philosophy, of a market economy based on private ownership and private enterprise, of a society with performance-related rewards and incentives, of traditional western Christian or 'bourgeois' values, and of belief in the possibility and efficiency of scientific and technological progress. Obviously, the wider those currents spread, the more deeply they undermined the social and political foundations on which the forces of economic growth had previously resided.

Economic inertia

In addition, the West's slower growth can be ascribed to the inability, if not unwillingness, of western governments, operating within the framework of the world economic order (and its institutional backing) that they themselves created after World War II, to surmount fundamental and growing economic problems – unemployment, inflation, balance-of-payments deficits. In the words of an OECD report,[1] western industrial countries have merely been 'muddling through', more intent on evading than removing increasingly intractable obstacles faced in common, with the result that countries have again and again 'gone it alone' as soon as they saw the slightest advantage, however ephemeral, in doing so. Much of the debilitating deficiency of private industrial investment stems, after all, from a hotch-potch of Keynesian (pump-priming) and monetarist (blood-letting) measures which, far from getting to the root of the trouble, has merely intensified the general business uncertainty.

The outsize welfare state

At the same time, the modern welfare state has been developing an ever more powerful momentum, far in excess of the growth of productive capacity. The added burden thus imposed on industry's back has crippled entrepreneurial initiative and aggravated stagflationary tendencies. After years when the whole subject had been enveloped in a conspiracy of silence, it has only just begun to dawn on many that the welfare state has become too big. Appropriate action to cut it down to size, however, has yet to be taken.

Progressive hardening of institutional arteries

This feature of outsize growth has manifested itself in many countries and at various levels: in a rampant growth of bureaucracy, swamping economic and social institutions and progressively draining them of their vigour and flexibility; in economic policies directed towards maintenance of the status quo, leading to a reduction in risk-taking and mobility, the ossification of outworn structures, the perpetuation of existing hierarchies, etc; and in the increased difficulty of translating divergent social aspirations into effective political action. This has increasingly strained the relationship between individuals and the state, undermining the confidence which, in a western democracy, they must have in order to display personal initiative and assume personal responsibility in the general interest.

Oil price explosion

1973 constitutes a milestone in world economic history by marking the transition from a period of relatively declining oil prices – during which all western industrial countries had allowed themselves to become oil-dependent, not to say oil-addicted, to a dangerous degree – to a period, whose end is not yet in sight, of explosively rising ones. The consequences for the oil-importing countries have, of course, been worsened terms of trade and mounting payments deficits (hence continuous currency problems), rising inflation and diminished growth, an increasingly threatened world monetary system and a perilously high susceptibility, particularly at the hands of the Arab countries of OPEC, to economic and political blackmail. Not least, the giant task of recycling the OPEC countries' swelling petrodollar surpluses is in danger of cutting the entire world economy loose from its financial moorings.

Currency floating

For Switzerland, the replacement of fixed by floating exchange rates represented a decisive turning point because the Swiss franc had previously been grossly undervalued. Together with the availability, until the mid-sixties, of a plentiful supply of cheap (if mostly unskilled) foreign labour, this had led to the building up of production facilities. These plants were incapable of holding their own even under properly balanced, competitive exchange-rate conditions, and they were plunged into a life-and-death struggle when the pendulum for a time swung to the opposite extreme and speedy conversion to more competitive products and services proved impossible.

Growing protectionism

Since 1975, industrial countries, in response to high unemployment and rising imports and in some cases perhaps also for security reasons, have increasingly resorted to protectionism. Developing countries have also done this on the long-established principle of sheltering infant industries. This tendency has been aided and abetted, moreover, by the modern state's greatly enhanced powers and bureaucratic machinery. The old lesson that protectionism tends to feed on itself, to the detriment of all concerned, is thus having to be learned afresh.

World economic trends

For the western industrial countries, Switzerland included, all this has produced a fundamentally changed world economic environment, notably:

(*1*) *Slower growth*, combined with wider growth differentials between countries and regions. From over 5 per cent in the 1960s, the western industrial countries' average annual real GNP growth declined to less than 3 per cent in the 1970s. The slowdown in world trade growth – from an average annual rate of over 10 per cent in the 1960s to less than 6 per cent in 1972–80 – has been greater still, partly because over 70 per cent of the western industrial countries' export trade is conducted among themselves, and partly because their slower growth was nowhere near offset by relatively faster growth on the part of OPEC and Communist countries, which towards the end of the seventies, moreover, slackened likewise.

(*2*) *Faster inflation*, combined with a widening of inflation differentials which increased the risk of the chronically sick infecting the relatively healthy.

(*3*) *Increased payments imbalances*, whose destabilizing effect after 1973 was aggravated by the steep rise in oil prices.

Impact on Switzerland

Naturally, these changes in world economic conditions had a profound impact on Switzerland's exports of goods and services (including, of course, tourism), whose average annual growth rate slackened from 7.1 per cent in the sixties, after 7.5 per cent in the fifties, to just 4 per cent in the seventies. But this was much less than the deceleration – to just a fifth of what it had been before – in the growth of Swiss domestic demand (see Table 2), pointing to a remarkable adaptability on the part of Switzerland's exporters, particularly when, as already mentioned, the Swiss franc at times rose far above its proper level.

Table2 **Average annual growth of Swiss exports[a] and domestic demand**

	1960–70	1970–80
Exports	7.1%	4.0%
Domestic demand	5.1%	0.9%

[a] Goods and services.

Among the domestic factors which were thus paramount, three in particular stand out. First, what until 1970 had been an abnormally rapid population growth (1960-70 increase 900,000) has all but petered out since (1970-80 increase only 65,000) and, in some years, been replaced by an actual decline. This has particularly affected the demand for building: the number of new dwellings completed under 'boom' conditions in 1980 (40,000) was barely half what it had been in 1973 (82,000), yet exceeded the projected medium-term requirement. Accordingly, since 1972-73 the building industry's capacity has been cut by a quarter, in house-building alone by half – a process which cannot be reversed.

Secondly, after a period of mounting budget deficits, Swiss fiscal policy has if anything gone to the other extreme, with the authorities in the latter half of the seventies increasingly compelled[2] to curb spending growth, rather than raise taxes, in order to restore budgetary balance. Public expenditure as a proportion of GNP has thus, since 1977, been on the decline.

Thirdly, Switzerland, if so far to a lesser extent than her neighbours, has been subjected to social tensions which, together with a polarization of public opinion and the spread of anti-growth, anti-industry attitudes, are seriously cramping private initiative and imposing political rather than scientific constraints on technological progress. Fierce opposition to the building of additional nuclear power stations and, more recently, to the wider application of computer and microprocessor technology is a case in point.

But, it may be asked, how can a greater slowdown than any other industrial country has suffered be reconciled with Switzerland's (so far) continuing full employment and persistent current-account surpluses? If, to start with the labour market, in 1975-76 a 10 per cent drop in the country's level of employment only led to a modest and brief rise in its number of jobless, this was because two-thirds of the jobs lost had been occupied by foreign ('guest') workers who went back to their own countries, while of the remainder a fifth had been held by older workers, some of whom were pensioned off early, and 80 per cent by women, most of whom withdrew from the labour market without claiming unemployment benefit.

As for Switzerland's continuing trade surplus, its industry, having long had to hold its own in the rough and tumble of international competition, has moved swiftly up the quality range into areas where price is not so critical and has learned to be highly adaptable. Also, Switzerland has little of the heavy industry most vulnerable to competition from the newly industrializing countries, while its exporters are, by international standards, mostly small businesses commanding a high degree of skill and technical know-how. Again, after its massive offshore lending and investment during the 1970s, it now enjoys a rapidly growing foreign investment income. Last but not least, its high productivity and relatively low per capita consumption of energy (under half of the German, less than a third of the American and British) help to keep down its imports of oil and petroleum products.

Prospects for the 1980s

So much, then, for some of the factors behind the trend change of the 1970s. How about the outlook for the current decade?

The world economic environment is not likely to improve greatly. On the contrary, existing political tensions could well be exacerbated. From a demographic point of view, too, Switzerland's working population will increase little, if at all, with a slight rise in the first half of the 1980s expected to be followed by a fall from 1984-85 onwards. Apart from an immigration policy intent on stabilizing the number of foreign workers, Switzerland has an ageing population – a growing army of old-age pensioners and, following the drop in the birth rate from 1964-65 onwards, a diminishing band of school-leavers who, in the second half of the 1980s, may hardly meet the labour replacement demand, let alone allow the number of those willing and able to work to grow.

Hence the country's growth potential during the 1980s will be restricted to possible increases in output per worker, or productivity gains. Since these, for a variety of reasons, cannot be expected to match the pace set in the 1960s, growth will be at best about half the average 4.7 per cent of that decade.

The Swiss are sufficiently realistic to recognize that in these circumstances they will still have their work cut out to maintain full employment. Given the likely continuing strength of the Swiss franc, the growing danger of protectionism and more aggressive selling on the part of the old industrialized countries in the face of increasing competition from the newly industrializing ones, the exorbitant demands of the welfare state, and above all the diminished growth prospects in those countries which have been Switzerland's best markets hitherto, their success in this venture can by no means be taken for granted.

Accelerated structural change

In the absence of that powerful demand pressure which, in the years before the first oil price explosion, had kept even laggard industries reasonably busy, Switzerland will therefore be facing an increasing need for industrial restructuring. With a growing number of industries likely to be unable to hold their own, those made redundant will be increasingly hard put to it to find suitable alternative jobs in the vicinity. Accordingly, labour mobility and retraining will be at a greater premium than ever, a challenge whose possible political repercussions could drive the government to adopt makeshift, but misguided, policies to preserve the status quo.

So far, of course, the Swiss government has firmly resisted any pressure to that effect. With the sole exception of agricultural policy, which is something of a special case, its industrial policy has been extremely liberal, concentrating in the main, even when the going was exceptionally difficult, on smoothing the way and relieving unavoidable hardships, despite vigorous demands – including some from quite a few liberal economists who accused the government of allowing Swiss industry to bleed to death[3] – for protectionist measures. However harsh it may have seemed at the time, that policy in the end, especially since 1975, has done much to accelerate the adjustment process and, in the private sector, to mobilize those forces of resilience and vitality which distinguish Switzerland from other industrial countries less favourably placed.

In all this, the co-operative attitude of the Swiss trade unions – rightly claimed, not because of any weakness but because of their leaders' consistent sense of realism, to be among the most sensible anywhere – has played a vital part. There is no knowing, of course, what might have happened if in 1975–76 as a result of the world recession Switzerland's unemployment rate had been rather higher. Suffice it to point out that, on matters of manpower redeployment, the Swiss trade unions' response is an eminently constructive one.

Conclusion

The reasons why in the 1970s, in a world increasingly up against it, Switzerland managed to lead a seemingly charmed life may be summed up as follows: a social, legal, political and economic system which is both stable and liberal; a well-educated, exceptionally hard-working people; excellent industrial relations, shown among other things by the absence of strikes and other labour disputes; an up-to-date, relatively efficient infrastructure and, despite Switzerland's system of political devolution and direct democracy, a minimum of red tape; a still relatively low level of taxes and social charges – despite a tendency until the mid-seventies to emulate the example of others; a unique measure of international confidence; an outstanding talent, among the country's still predominantly small and medium-sized businesses, for innovative adaptation; a technological capability in keeping with the country's size and ambitions; concentration on high value-added and relatively price-insensitive goods and services; comparatively low interest rates and high savings; and a strong and efficient banking system.

These factors should, in spite of growing obstacles, continue to operate to Switzerland's advantage, enabling it, as before, to make the most of its chances. The real danger lies elsewhere – in the widespread recourse to short-term expedients, the prevalence of selfish national interests and the lack of a responsible spirit of international co-operation, whose damaging consequences are already plain to see. The events of the 1970s have revealed the extent to which the West's disunity, fragmentation and complete preoccupation with short-term economic problems have undermined both its political power and its economic dynamism. A solution of the problems thus swept under the carpet requires a greater degree of international solidarity, calling in turn for a better understanding of their worldwide ramifications and of the urgent need for all countries to work together. For Switzerland, much will depend on how successfully that task is accomplished.

Notes

1 *'Interfutures', Facing the Future* (OECD, Paris, 1979).
2 In Switzerland, all fiscal – including tax – proposals have, as before, to be put to the people in a referendum.
3 Cf., among others, R. Erbe, *Helvetia, schrumpfe Dich krank* (Basle, 1976).

12 The Greek economy in crisis

George Krimpas

Introduction

Economic growth at an average rate of seven per cent per annum is a heady state of affairs. The volume of output and expenditure doubles roughly every ten years, while above-average items, such as motorcars, television sets or foreign travel, grow at effectively astronomical rates. Looking at the Greek experience it is not immediately obvious which items of expenditure were expanding at less than the average growth rate, so much does everything seem to have grown. Between 1948 and 1973, output and expenditure grew over tenfold in real terms, with per capita incomes reaching averages of the order experienced in the advanced Western European economies in the middle 1960s (the pitfalls of translating per capita incomes by applying exchange-rate valuations are especially great in the case of Greece, so that apparently precise numerical comparisons are better avoided).

The economy's structure had effectively been transformed in the postwar years. A previously poor and overpopulated agricultural sector was replaced by a labour-scarce countryside where the old outnumbered the young. Massive migration to the major urban centres was accompanied by an accelerating foreign migration, which at one point caused the natural rate of population growth to become nil. The share of agriculture in total output fell from over 60 per cent prewar to about 15 per cent in the 1970s. Slow-growing productivity, despite the great fall in numbers, further reduced the relative position of per capita agricultural output, while agricultural incomes were increasingly dominated by public and private transfers, in other words subsidies and emigrants' remittances.

The secondary sector presented the obverse picture. Its share in total output grew from less than 20 per cent prewar to nearly 40 per cent in the 1970s, its share of exports rising from virtually zero to over 60 per cent while agriculture's shrank from over 90 per cent to less than 30 per cent by the end of the rapid-growth era. The qualitative change in industry was equally impressive. Productivity in the secondary sector grew rapidly, only a shade less rapidly than output, so that the sector's employment share increased rather little. By the end of the period of rapid growth one could clearly observe a modern industrial sector where very little existed before, some parts of which were increasingly competitive in the international market. In retrospect, and ignoring the problems of 'structure' which will be examined later, the strides in productivity growth were not surprising. When virtually all machinery and equipment were imported, it was natural to expect that internationally best-practice technology should have been installed. This, given the small initial size of Greek industry, and even though industrial investment was never very great, inevitably represented a significant increase in modern productive capacity which pushed average industrial productivity quickly upwards. However, manufacturing industry was not the most important factor in secondary-sector expansion or in the economy's qualitative advance. The public sector, both in terms of the volume and of quality of investments, was the real engine of growth, despite severe ill effects related to the socio-political structure which will be examined later. Public works and the utilities increased spectacularly, so that by the 1970s the economy's infrastructure was no longer underdeveloped (railroads being the notable exception).

Yet the true (if double-edged) success story of the Greek take-off was the service sector. State-sector services (as well as dis-services) increased considerably faster than national income; and the concentration of state consumption and transfer expenditures in the largest urban centres (mainly Athens) was paralleled by the massive growth and concentration of private-sector services in those urban centres (again mainly Athens). A significant proportion of the service economy was 'productive', in that service exports commanded an increasing share in the balance of payments; but 'productiveness' was ever more necessary, as the fastest growing item in the national accounts was the negative balance of trade. 'Unproductiveness' was the more powerful force in an economy whose viability had gradually come to depend on earnings of Greeks abroad, whether in the merchant marine, which was rapidly becoming the largest in the world, or in Western Europe, particularly Germany, which had provided employment to more Greek workers than their own country's industrial sector.

In brief, the present crisis in the Greek economy is the culmination of a process whereby the dominant growth of services determines the growth of incomes, outstripping the growth of competitively saleable output. The transition from 7 per cent growth to zero growth, coupled with nearly 30 per cent inflation, has been quite dramatic and is proving very painful. The global economic crisis makes the adjustment all the more difficult, while there is also regret for the opportunities missed, when the world economy was experiencing the prolonged postwar boom. We will look at the causes which acted cumulatively to produce the downturn, then describe the structural features which now amount to an unviable economic system, and finally examine the particular institutional and socio-political features which distinguish the Greek economic crisis in the context of the European economy.

The crisis of the 1970s

The original as well as the ultimate cause for the Greek economic crisis is the failure of policy. Two aspects of this should be distinguished, failure in development policy and failure in management policy. It is useful to start with the latter, particularly since in Greek policy discussions the short run and the long tend to become confused. The word 'Keynesian' has been used in two senses, firstly (and usually as a misnomer), to mean a policy whereby public investment has been used as an engine-of-growth variable since private investment has been persistently inadequate to achieve feasible growth rates, even in the eminently speculative housing sector, and, secondly, in the stricter sense of short-period demand management. It is interesting to note that for a relatively long period (approximately the first half of the high-growth years) stabilization policy had been used sparingly and not with notably stabilizing effects. The inauguration of an openly Keynesian expansionary short-term stance in fact marked a break from a long-held insistence on currency stabilization, which was justified in the immediate post civil-war years but was maintained as an ill-matched partner during the public investment-led growth policy for nearly a whole decade.

The first instance of successful reflation occurred in 1964–65, when increases in pensions and other benefits not only improved the distribution of incomes but also gave a much-needed boost to domestic consumer goods manufacture. This was multiplied-up throughout the economy to restore a flagging growth rate without aggravating the balance of payments or disturbing price stability, which remained remarkable (less than 2 per cent inflation) until 1966. This policy was politically motivated: it coincided with the end of a prolonged spell of conservative government and the inauguration of liberal/social-democrat reform. But this phase was short-lived. The second Keynesian injection of 1966–67 was even more clearly politically motivated: the return of the conservatives (after a *coup de palais*) being deeply unpopular, the government attempted to gain popular favour by using the liberal methods, only more so. But this time the effort went over the top, inflation got underway, the balance of payments deteriorated sharply, and the growth of the public-sector borrowing requirement forced the government to raise taxes, thus spoiling the exercise. A third Keynesian injection followed the colonels' coup in 1967. This was aimed at counteracting the recession which was triggered off when the impropriety of the regime worried investors (a proper royalist dictatorship was expected and it took some time for them to realize that there was to be a boost for profits).

The colonels' junta made extensive use of mortgage credit (and town-planning measures), which brought quick profits to contractors and land speculators. A housing boom resulted, which gave immense impetus to the growth of the Athenian conurbation and the proliferation of services there. Inflation was curbed for a time through a most effective form of incomes policy which banned trades unions and made strikes illegal. By the end of the seven-year dictatorial period the share of wages in the national income had fallen by nearly ten percentage points, while the share of profits had risen correspondingly. Output growth was back on trend, with agriculture lagging behind and industry slightly above average, while the services gradually became dominant. For political and economic reasons alike, an expansionary policy was maintained regardless of the deterioration in the balance of payments, whose prospects looked alarming. Despite efforts at price control price stability eventually gave way. Costs were uncontrolled in the numerous fly-by-night enterprises which were mushrooming with open or hidden subsidies, while major importers, thriving in a vigorous sellers' market, engaged extensively in speculative stock-building and raised markups. In the midst of unprecedented official corruption, various scandals were uncovered (rotten meat imports being a notable instance). In a very disturbed economic climate, where spending was obviously exceeding the growth of productive capacity, the first oil crisis struck. Prices immediately responded with a 15 per cent jump within a year, with inflation finally running at over 30 per cent.

The restored parliamentary regime of 1974 had to cope with a complex of problems which the centre-right coalition government was too short-lived to face. The conservative government which followed the 1974 election gave way to a wages' explosion, which was essentially a catching-up after the long virtual freeze on wages. An investment downturn soon followed, 'normal' profit having suffered a fall to pre-junta normality. The government thus came to face the general European stagflation problem, how to induce expansion in real output while restraining the growth of money incomes. The years from 1975 to date have witnessed successive failures of policy to attain any goals whatsoever, so that by now the economy has sunk into zero growth, massive foreign deficit, plus inflation and growing unemployment. The structure of the crisis in recent years must now be documented.

1974 was a crisis year in every sense. GDP *fell* by 1.8 per cent, and GNP twice that, compared to averages of *plus* 7.4 and 7.8

per cent respectively over the previous decade. Investment and income from abroad virtually collapsed that year and so did industrial production. The recovery was all the more remarkable for being swift, yet its *structure* weakened longer-term prospects. This must be seen in some detail in order to appreciate the magnitude of the present crisis.

Recovery was complete by the end of 1976. GDP was already up 5.1 per cent in 1975. The recovery would have been more marked had it not been accompanied by the beginning of a crisis in agriculture. As it was, the pace-setter was industry which turned round from an over 10 per cent fall to a nearly 10 per cent increase two years later. However, services were the dominating feature, growing faster than GDP in 1976, 1977, 1979 and 1980, by which time they accounted for nearly 55 per cent of output. Public expenditure led private consumption with increases of around 12 per cent in 1974 and 1975, by which time private consumption, static in 1974, recovered to stable levels in relation to income. Significantly, the savings propensity had fallen.

Despite massive public spending, investment took longer to pick up. The dramatic fall (by a whole quarter) in 1974 in total fixed investment was not reversed until two years later, the government finding it easier to spend on current account as well as politically more necessary. In fact total public investment fell over two consecutive years (1974: − 20.1 per cent, 1975: − 6 per cent) and grew by only 2 per cent from a low level in 1976, only to be curtailed again in 1977 (− 10.2 per cent). For four successive years, 1974–77, there were reductions in capital spending by public corporations, which are responsible for nearly half of public investment. Private investment, which had also fallen by over a quarter in 1974, responded more rapidly to the usual semi-Keynesian stimuli. Easier mortgage credit boosted the house-building sector, which accounts for about 40 per cent of private investment. This led by 1977 to an immense building boom, which was a crucial factor in the renewed wave of inflation which is still going on. Other forms of investment, related to machinery and equipment, including transport equipment, were slow to respond, partly because of delayed public-sector expenditures and partly because of administrative hold-ups. Starting from a low point, big purchases of transport equipment were carried out, but much of this investment was met by imports. Imports initially grew less rapidly than exports, the latter also a considerable factor in the pick-up. Net factor income from abroad also turned round sharply from two years of serious decrease to well above long-term trend, contributing by 1976 about half of a percentage point to GNP. Till 1979 this, as well as autonomous capital inflows (largely destined for real-estate investment), made the balance of payments less of a constraint on growth, despite the serious imbalance in commodity trade. Inflationary pressures were however close to the surface. The savings rate, which had fallen below trend since 1974, had not recovered. The recovery of consumption was strongly directed to imported durable goods, motorcars figuring prominently. Machinery and particularly manufacturing investment accounted for a low share of fixed capital investment, in contrast to housebuilding which had increased its share of national savings. The distribution of personal income was very unequal, reflecting the high proportion of self-employed who were also more immune to personal income taxation. This found its counterpart in items of consumption which were generally imported. The composition of private consumption progressively favoured the growth of imports.

The post-junta recovery was thus based on the, by now, traditional mixture of fiscal expansion and over-accommodating monetary policies. Apart from increasing items of government expenditure which had lagged way behind, such as education and health, the fiscal-monetary stance was channelled through house-building, partly because of the ease of such a policy and partly because of its high multiplier value for the rest of the economy. Short-term policy was thus unaccompanied by longer-term supply measures which would be necessary to match the long-term implications of demand-side management. In spite of considerable efforts at legislation there was no clear-cut development policy designed to overcome structural weaknesses and promote longer-term industrial development.

With the economy relatively fully employed, the public-sector borrowing requirement remained high and the need for a slow-down was becoming apparent. This however was not easy to do.

Table 1 **The structure of crisis, 1974–80**

	1980 (bn drachs, 1974 prices)	1963–73 average	Percentage change from previous year						
			1974	1975	1976	1977	1978	1979	1980
Private consumption	319.0	7.0	0.6	5.7	5.6	5.1	6.1	3.1	-0.2
Public consumption	68.5	6.2	12.1	11.9	5.1	6.5	3.5	5.8	-0.4
Gross domestic capital formation	90.1	10.8	-25.6	0.2	6.8	7.8	6.0	7.9	-8.3
Public-sector deficit as % of GNP			6.3	5.6	4.2	4.8	5.2	6.2	9.7
Foreign current-account deficit as % of GNP			5.8	4.5	4.0	3.9	2.9	4.7	5.3
Agriculture	60.6	2.6	4.8	5.7	-1.3	-7.4	7.0	-5.0	11.5
Industry	133.5	11.8	-11.1	5.8	9.3	4.8	6.4	5.6	-2.9
Manufacturing	88.9	11.7	-2.8	5.5	10.0	1.4	6.6	5.2	0.0
Services	223.1	7.3	2.6	4.5	6.4	4.9	5.3	4.6	2.5
GDP (at factor cost)	417.2	7.4	-1.8	5.1	6.1	2.9	6.4	3.7	1.9
Consumers' price index			100.0	113.4	128.5	144.1	162.2	193.0	241.0

SOURCE: National Accounts Service and OECD.

Most items of expenditure were inelastic, tied as they were to contractual forms of pay. Coupled to this, revenue had the built-in inelasticity derived from the structure of taxation. Taxation out of personal income was low, at about 2.5 per cent of GNP, compared to three or four times as much for most Western European countries and a mere one-eighth that of Sweden. In particular, profits taxation was exceptionally low, so that the bulk of revenue came from indirect taxes on goods and services. Without VAT, this was heavily regressive as well as inelastic with respect to the growth of income. The problem was structural in that the tax base could only be enlarged by taxing incomes. Excluding the 'black' economy, which started flourishing during the years of dictatorship, the virtual constancy of entrepreneurial and property income in total income should imply that the number of people entering the tax net ought to be increasing with the growth of income. The fact that income-tax receipts were persistently sluggish therefore meant that tax avoidance and evasion had become institutionalized into the system. A final aspect of this problem relates to the great difficulty of implementing a prices and incomes policy when so much of the economy's activity depends on small economic units which are very cumbersome to monitor. All these problems made themselves more apparent in the period following the first oil crisis.

Rapid growth, which had almost put the economy back on trend, was succeeded by slump in 1977. The primary cause was a fall in exports, due to the slowdown in world trade. The balance of payments further deteriorated, due to a rapid increase in the propensity to import. Inflation, though somewhat subsided, was running at twice the rate in Western Europe. Yet the authorities decided an expansionary stance was more than ever necessary. With supply lagging behind demand, particularly of internationally competitive saleable output, all policy had to be short-lived. 1977 in fact inaugurated a style of sharp, annual stop-go-stop swings. GDP swung from a low of under 3 per cent growth in 1977 to more than double that in 1978 and down to half as much again in 1979, by which time the policy was out of hand, with inflation now the outstanding and dangerous factor. Stop-go thus gave way to plain stop, with virtual stagnation in

1980 and no expectation of recovery in 1981, at least with respect to endogenous factors.

1977 is thus a significant turning point in several respects. Inflation passed the threshold where painless measures could cure it. Unit labour costs were rising rapidly, which coupled with the slump in world trade made Greek exports uncompetitive, despite the effective devaluation of the drachma. One-third of the rate of inflation could be accounted for by increases in labour costs. Money wage claims had never really slackened since the post-junta recovery. With sluggish productivity growth, reflecting slow industrial investment, this was bound sooner or later to affect prices. Coupled to this, government policy made it possible for firms to maintain mark-ups and often increase them. As the composition of incomes and consumption favoured the upper end of the market, mark-ups at that end tended to spread downwards, much as wages traditionally do to maintain differentials. Another one-third of the renewed inflation could thus be accounted for by the ability of profits to gradually recover their share after the fall which was experienced immediately after 1974.

A particular form of profits inflation was directly due to the boom in the housing market. By 1977, and increasingly for another two years, house prices rose rapidly. The housing boom, which was heavily concentrated in the Athens area, made development land sufficiently scarce to push the return to developers from under one-fifth of the value of the finished building prewar, to over four-fifths at the peak of the boom. Tax evasion in the housebuilding industry was very widespread. Legislation favouring house ownership at the expense of people living in rented accommodation, coupled with a sudden insurge of wealthy refugees fleeing the Lebanese crisis, gave a sudden twist to rents. These were also widely untaxed, since contractual agreements were often fixed at below the true value, to the mutual interest of owners and tenants. As with consumers' goods, the upper end of the market dictated developments elsewhere. Increased rental charges were in turn a serious factor in keeping money wage claims well above the growth of productivity. The policy response to inflation was thus itself inflationary.

The personal savings ratio fell, revealing a preference for nonfinancial asset holdings. Commodity speculation was widespread and was strongly related to the multiplier effects of the housing boom. This was particularly marked in the building trades following the upsurge of private investment in housing. But even private consumers engaged in a form of commodity speculation, as is shown by the virtual doubling of motorcar registrations over two years of inflation, following immense increases in car prices due to the imposition of special taxes, a curious policy which resulted in capital gains to the owners of secondhand cars as secondhand prices adjusted to fresh imports. By contrast, investment in manufacturing declined continuously. No major manufacturing projects were underway, a factor which became progressively more important. Investment was mainly destined for replacement rather than the growth of productive capacity. Yet the traditional manufactures which had until then achieved competitive advantages in world markets (mainly textiles, clothing, footwear, furniture, cement and processed raw materials) were approaching their natural limits. The domestic market was equally saturated with the domestic product mix, so that manufacturing output growth inevitably fell, from 10 per cent in 1976 to under 2 per cent in 1977. The crisis did not immediately reach the labour market, despite the return of immigrants and the continuing if diminishing outflow of labour from agriculture. Labour was generally absorbed. A factor in this (other than the great statistical inadequacies) was the reluctance of employers to shed labour in the short run due to high severance commitments. Nonetheless pressures of unemployment started to be felt among overqualified youth entering the labour market for the first time. The balance of payments was more worrying. In accordance with the expansionary stance of policy, imports accelerated ahead of exports. Above-average inflation was reflected in the foreign sector, with export prices rising while the volume of exports was stagnant, causing diminished competitiveness in all markets. Yet imports did not fuel inflation, despite the continued fall in the exchange rate, which was just adequate to maintain favourable terms of trade given the differences in productivity growth and relative rates of inflation. The growing reduction in competitiveness was to deepen the crisis in subsequent years.

The expansionary stance in 1977, which was an election year, succeeded in producing a short-lived boom in 1978. Consumption went up 5 per cent overall, the private sector leading, while investment went up similarly. The recovery of exports and continued capital inflows kept the balance of payments financially manageable while imports eventually responded to the punishment of special surcharges, particularly on motorcars. Agriculture had a boom year, starting from a low level, while industry and the services responded rather less. The rate of manufacturing investment, however, kept falling, its level by now one-fifth less than that reached in 1974. The housing boom continued, with 90 per cent of the increase in total investment going into dwelling construction. With unemployment low and falling, average earnings continued to rise at over 20 per cent annually, as they had done with remarkable regularity since 1974. Inflation accelerated a little to more than double the Western European average. Wage demands in the public sector made it impossible to reduce the borrowing requirement even though public investment was again reduced. Resistance to increased taxation was becoming stronger, partly in response to a rather heavy-handed package which provided for automatic assessment, using such items as motorcars and yachts as proxies for income which could not be determined otherwise. The inability to raise taxation from property income was evidence for the existence of widespread networks of tax evasion. With the public-sector deficit running at over 5 per cent of GDP under conditions of excess demand, the economy was set for explosive inflation. Unable to reduce public-sector pay or increase taxation, the government slashed public-sector investment and directed public corporations to borrow abroad. The growth of the public sector, which had hitherto been largely financed from growing personal savings, now started to impinge on the liquidity requirements of the private sector. This latest facet of the crisis became apparent in 1979.

By mid 1979 the force of the boom was spent. Agricultural output swung back into recession, reflecting the inadequacy of the infrastructure whose build-up had stopped several years earlier. Industry and the services declined somewhat, while the growth of exports fell by over a half. Private consumption was finally curbed in response to the upsurge of inflation, and investment was only maintained by the public corporations. The public-sector deficit rose from 5.2 to 6.2 per cent of GDP, through the inability to contain current expenditure, while inflation accelerated from about 15 to over 25 per cent. The economy's vulnerability to the 1979 oil price rise was unexpectedly great. The accumulation of structural imbalances had made adjustment exceptionally painful. Curiously, the upsurge of inflation was largely due to the delayed action of the authorities to reduce the food subsidies and to gradually liberalize previously administered prices, including the end of rent control. These rationalizing measures were ineptly timed to coincide with the oil price crisis as well as the world boom in commodity prices.

The virtual doubling of the rate of inflation within a year induced inflationary expectations in every section of the economy. In the structural setting of a progressively parasitic and uncompetitive economy, rising mark-ups became a feature of every type of enterprise, not just monopolistic large firms. Consumer resistance to rising prices was minimal. The fall in real disposable income instead plunged the economy into stagnation. In 1980 private consumption actually fell in real terms and there was a sharp reduction in the rate of gross fixed investment (*minus* 8.3 per cent). Industrial output growth was down, at 3 per cent, with manufacturing reaching zero growth, while the building boom suddenly collapsed, recording *minus* 15 per cent in construction output. GDP would have been growing negatively were it not for a fortuitous bumper year for agriculture as well as the growth of government services. The balance of payments was aggravated as export receipts declined from 31 to 4 per cent growth in money terms, with services following from 28 to 9 per cent. The continued rise of export prices improved the terms of trade but by now severely contained the volume growth of exports. The oil price increase put 1 billion US dollars onto the foreign deficit which, despite economic stagnation, grew from 2.9 per cent of GNP in 1975 to nearly 5 per cent in 1979 and 5.3 per cent in 1980. Public-sector borrowing abroad had to increase from 150 million US dollars in 1979 to nearly $800 million in 1980. Structural imbalances in the foreign sector were presently

235

aggravated by the prevalence of high interest rates coupled with the accumulated volume of debts to be serviced.

In 1981, the year of entry into the European Economic Community the Greek economy is thus faced with a number of conflicting objectives: how to bring inflation down while taking steps to expand the economy's competitively saleable output, how to increase productivity without creating severe unemployment, how to transform an economy progressively geared to consume out of unearned income, largely transfer income from abroad, into an economizing machine able to produce valuable goods and services. Greek society has hitherto been remarkably successful in containing social pressures. The penalty of this social stability has been the gradual transformation of all classes of society into interlocking communities of *rentiers*, who occasionally go in for capital gains through land speculation. In this social setting the public sector is less of an economic category, more a way of life. Economic stagnation is an inhospitable environment for this sort of community. Disguised unemployment, which is widespread everywhere but particularly in the service sector, is now coming into the open. The role of land in the Greek economy and its fundamental importance in the formation of Greek society by now borders on the fantastic, the value of money being progressively determined with reference to speculative land values. If an economic crisis is ultimately about people, it is not a moment too soon for Greek society to be firmly in the Common Market whose institutional challenges and opportunities will help bring about a gradual and progressive, if not altogether methodical, adaptation toward a viable economic order.

Prospects

In spite of the depth of the present crisis, this should nonetheless be evaluated in the context of an economy whose longer-term prospects are considerable. Thus while short-term prospects cannot be properly assessed, if only because 1981 is an election year, some factors which represent objective opportunities for long-term stable development must be taken into account. Should the stabilization of the price of oil persist sufficiently to improve prospects for world trade and finance, this would give the Greek economy a chance to become integrated into the advanced industrial context of the EEC. Development policy hitherto has persistently neglected the possibilities of agriculture. More than half of the cultivable land remains to be irrigated, while the spread of modern methods, which have been successful in some areas, notably in Crete, would extend the season's production and marketing and even out the strong seasonal need for labour. The climate as well as the land clearly favour up-market specialization. The major constraint in the development of agriculture now appears to be the reversal of the demographic pyramid. The modernization of agriculture could thus go hand in hand with institutional reform designed to upgrade the technological and economic status of the farmer.

On the industrial front, the Greek economy possesses two powerful areas of comparative advantage, one natural, the other acquired. Mining and quarrying have only recently come to the fore as a major growth sector, while shipping is a well-known international success story. From the mining end, major processing industries would enlarge the base of domestic value added and open up opportunities for selective industrialization in the broad engineering sector, now almost non-existent – an integrating process which will eventually link up with the requirements of the shipping industry. Financial resources for a major effort of industrialization, which would internalize the export-led (and well-nigh external) mining and shipping sectors could be drawn from the substantial savings of Greeks accumulated abroad. Some beginnings of such repatriation of funds have already been effected by locally based 'peoples' shareholdings', notably for domestic shipping lines. Reform of the financial system will in any case be needed to deflect the channelling of savings to the housing market. Even in that subsector, investments will have to be restructured so that development is spread more evenly throughout the country rather than being concentrated in the Athens area, which now holds one-third of the population. Medium-term development prospects will also depend on the

restructuring of the economy's energy sector. The overdepend-
ence on imported oil is presently coupled with serious waste of
energy, notably for household purposes. Apart from problems of
environmental pollution, which have recently become acute, the
heavy dependence on oil leaves domestic resources well below
potential use. Environmental consciousness, progressively
stronger demands for decentralization of physical economic
activity as well as of decision-taking and the important constraint
on the balance of payments, point to a restructuring of imports
towards coal and to an integrated effort to develop domestic
energy resources. Economizing measures, which also have environmental value, such as heat and noise insulation, in turn offer
considerable opportunities for industrialization on a large scale
through small, decentralized specialist units.

Mixed private-public as well as foreign-domestic forms of ownership and management have been under study for a variety of
industrial projects. The exclusive reliance on the public sector for
the launching of major development projects coupled with the
reliance on dominant foreign firms is now being questioned, while
forms of social participation in the management of industrial
concerns find wider appeal. State-sector investments in infrastructure, which have been curtailed to danger point (as was
documented above), will now be necessary – particularly in the
fields of the transport system, specifically the railways and the
ports – as well as the provision of cheap industrial land. The
escape of the public sector from financial constraints will pose a
severe political problem in that state-sector unproductive labour,
widely prevalent in the administrative apparatus, is an easily
measurable cause of inflationary pressure whereas the even more
widespread use of labour for the production of uncompetitive
goods and services in the private sector is naturally more disguised, at least in financial terms.

Political prospects with respect to administrative reform will
obviously depend on the balance of political forces after the 1981
election. There is however widespread public feeling that the use
of the state sector as a mechanism for social integration of the
unemployed has reached a dead end. There is similarly strong
pressure for reform of the state system of education which has

hitherto concentrated on the production of manpower fitted for clerical desk jobs. The technological content of Greek education will need to be augmented. Differential pay for technically trained people has in recent years provided some incentives for younger people to prepare for entry in the labour market by switching from traditional educational courses toward productive skills which are clearly in greater demand. Manpower exports in recent years, particularly to construction and technical projects in the Arab countries, have been a pointer to highly paid employment, though conditions are hard, a lesson which is beginning to be felt elsewhere as witnessed by the as yet timid return of graduates to the agricultural sector.

Medium-term development prospects depend crucially on the short-period problem of beating inflation. Recent experience has shown that a monetarist approach, which is sometimes advocated, has been ineffective as a cure of inflation although costly in terms of output and employment. The cure of inflation would seem to depend on a broad package of measures, some of which must be sustained over a long period of time. Thus apart from some price reductions (e.g., motorcars and other consumer durables), which are possible in the context of full membership in the Common Market (e.g., removal of monopoly control of trade from so-called exclusive importers) and which would be important in breaking the present conundrum of inflationary expectations, an integrated incomes policy is felt to be essential. The structural and institutional difficulties, which were examined above, make the implementation of an incomes policy more difficult in Greece than elsewhere and therefore make it necessary that such a policy should be designed in a larger context of social reforms. Money wage claims and profit mark-ups by small enterprises, which really amount to the same thing, reflect to an important extent the insecurity felt by wide sections of the population recently urbanized. Taking urban land out of speculative market forces, broadening the range of the national health service, rationalizing the system of retirement benefits, improving the free educational services provided by the state, combined with some inflation-proofing of money incomes, would seem to be the socio-political prerequisites for the acceptance of an incomes policy which has hitherto been one-sided since it has effectively monitored wages while leaving prices and profits uncontrolled. Contrary to experience in Western European countries, the successful implementation of a guaranteed social wage policy, something broader than a traditional incomes policy, will go together with the dismantling of a large part of today's centrally run administrative apparatus. The over-administration of economic life has in fact gone together with growing inefficiency, wide evasion of controls and the discrediting of incomes policy. Experience of the use of incomes policy for anti-inflationary purposes shows that the policy must be seen to work fairly. It must also not be at loggerheads with fiscal and monetary policies, which must inevitably be contained, at least for a time.

Reform of the structure of taxation is another thorny precondition for realizing potential prospects. Personal income tax has hitherto worked as a tax on wage and salary incomes which could be identified at source. Social-security contributions have distorted the labour market since they cannot be levied on the vast number of small and midget firms where occasional employment is the rule. Labour legislation has in fact led to a broadening of the 'black' economy. Here again, reform in the Greek socio-economic context may have to take a different line to established practices in Western European countries. The taxation of property, whose value can be ascertained relatively objectively, would enlarge the tax base as well as spread the tax burden more equitably than the nominally progressive income-tax net. Land taxation would be at the basis of a system of property taxation, to act as a built-in restraint on the speculative character of the land market whose operation, as was seen above, is perhaps the most important root of the inflationary process in the Greek economy. The belated implementation of value added tax, now finally due because of Common Market membership, will also serve to reduce the inequity of the present system of indirect taxation.

An important decision taken in the late 1950s was to join forces with the Six of the Common Market rather than with the Seven of EFTA. The treaty of association which has operated between 1962 and full accession on 1 January 1981 has in fact been the one unqualified policy success. The transitional period worked in

Greece's favour despite the suspension of the process of harmonization of agriculture during the years of the dictatorship. A major restructuring of trade took place, whose net effect was trade creation and thus a useful impetus to industrialization. Contrary to fears expressed at the time, association did not prevent the expansion of Greek trade with the traditionally friendly Arab world. If full advantage was not extracted from the status of association, which broadly coincided with the great boom years of the European economy, the blame must be equally shared between the disastrous policies followed during the dictatorship and the short-sighted, spasmodic turnarounds of the policies pursued since 1974.

After liberation from junta rule, the pursuit of full membership in the EEC was the only logical objective. This time, however, negotiations were carried out with a less clear aim in mind, so that the new transition period does not favour Greece, which is the weaker partner, in contrast to the safeguards provided by association some twenty years before. Inadequate preparation to take advantage of full membership, particularly as regards institutional and administrative reform, has resulted in difficulties of adaptation, some of which have been aggravated by the persistence of economic crisis in the European economy as well as the restructuring of some policies, mainly concerning agriculture, at the European level. It is nevertheless true that, despite transitional frictions and maladjustments, Common Market membership is effectively the only overall policy which guarantees the openness of the Greek economy and Greek society. The geopolitical position of Greece and its excellent relations with the Balkan countries as well as the Arab world, together with its important position in the international maritime community, make Greece a natural partner in the process of European political and economic integration.

Part V
Conclusion

13 A little silver lining on a dark horizon

Ralf Dahrendorf

The patient reader who has managed to stay the course will have observed a number of recurring themes. Foremost among them, of course, are the two oil price explosions – the first of 1973–74, which most countries somehow took in their stride, the second of 1979–80, which for many marks the real turning point. Inflation, unemployment and growth are other themes more often laboured than not. Nor do any of the contributors seem to take issue with the notion that, somewhere in the seventies, there was such a thing as a trend change.

Yet, in a brief summary, the most obvious, and hence the first, point to be made is the striking variety of the pictures that have been presented. This is partly a question of style, extending from technical descriptions to wide-ranging social analyses. But it is also a question of philosophy. Political economy cannot, after all, help being political, whatever else it is. This book conspicuously exemplifies the fact that economic commentators see life through coloured spectacles. For some it is the socialist philosophy that is out of date, for others the liberal. While Keynes finds little or no sympathy anywhere, prescriptions vary widely. Central-bank governor Emminger and finance minister Delors would make awkward colleagues; Professors Kneschaurek and Tinbergen, sitting round the same table, would be more likely to be at each other's throats than make common cause. The differently coloured spectacles of theirs and others nevertheless reveal deeper national differences which are not just matters of personal opinion. The Swedish model, Austria's secret weapon, the Swiss cat that walks by himself – these are, in their different ways, just as typical as the Italian crisis and the English (excuse me, British)

245

sickness. Though most may be just different shades of grey, the differences between European countries are still the feature that distinguishes them most.

Any attempt to summarize this book's many conclusions, and at the same time to try and take some of its argument a step or two further, is bound to lose much of what colours its contributors. The summary is no substitute for the book itself.

Nature of the trend change

That at some point in the 1970s there was indeed a trend change, and that somewhere along the line the European countries' growth curves did suffer a downward jolt accompanied almost everywhere by rapidly rising inflation and unemployment, is beyond question. But what are the factors that brought it about? The first, adduced by all of the book's contributors and in recent years cited by politicians almost *ad nauseam*, are 'exogenous' factors – i.e., factors lying both outside a country's borders and beyond its control. The main culprit behind them, however, is hard to pin down, being variously labelled the OPEC countries, the newly industrializing countries, the United States, or just other countries in general.

Thus, to pick out a few typical remarks, the second oil shock struck down the economy just as it was on the road to recovery, making an effective attack on inflation all but impossible. Export-oriented growth in Europe has been hampered by competition from low-cost countries, Japan included. One cause of unemployment is the need to adapt and re-equip. European countries' export difficulties have been aggravated by the high-interest-rate policy of the US. No country is an island; in an unhealthy world, even the best-laid plans to keep one's own country healthy are bound to fail. In a way, even co-operating with others – within, say, the European Monetary System – is to buy trouble. To crown it all, there is all this damaging talk about a new world economic order.

Such remarks could well be true, even though most do not

apply to all countries alike. Their real importance, however, lies less in what they say than in what they imply, namely (as cannot be stressed too strongly) that the many different ways in which European and other countries influence each other make it imperative to devise and observe ground-rules binding on them all. Failing this, protectionism will spread and everybody be worse off still. There must be co-operation, if prosperity and freedom are to survive.

Yet, leaving Europe aside for a moment, there is precious little of it about. A treaty between the OECD and OPEC countries, of which the Brandt Commission is only the latest of a long line of advocates, is still in the remote future. Furtive references to the protection clause (Article XIX) of the General Agreement on Tariffs and Trade (GATT), no less than vociferous demands for self-restraint on the part of the well-to-do, bode no good. A new world economic order conducive to the welfare of all is still, as Jan Tinbergen rightly points out, a pipe-dream. Difficulties of one's own making are thus, to some extent, exogenously caused. But the rest of the world remains in disarray, a dangerous place, sowing the seeds of fear and hence conflict. The unsettled worldwide economic horizon is the worst aspect of all.

For politicians, talk of exogenous factors is, of course, a ready-made excuse for doing nothing about them. Yet, as most of them know perfectly well, many of their troubles are in fact homemade. Among the causes of these, though not all of this book's contributors will perhaps agree, three groups of factors seem to stand out.

First, most countries since the early seventies have seen a dramatic change in the way in which (poor) productivity gains, (excessive) pay rises and (low) company profits are related. The reasons why, however, are hard to discern, inflation – which might be regarded as one – being both cause and effect. Perhaps those like Lundberg who speak of changes in human attitudes, governing the expectations of individuals and the behaviour of organizations alike, come closest to hitting the nail on the head.

Secondly, there has been an equally dramatic change, with far-reaching consequences, in the role of the public sector, manifesting itself partly in an expansion of the public sector's size in relation to the rest of the economy, partly in increased public spending on account of other commitments. Enlargement of the welfare state has played a key role here. Anyhow, the public sector's increased size has, for most countries, been a mixed blessing – Austria, as demonstrated by Horst Knapp, is here clearly the exception that proves the rule. High taxes discourage the individual, reducing his disposable income to little more than pocket-money. The dominant role of the state also discourages investment. This in turn fosters the growth of bureaucracy, that 'iron cage of bondage', as the German sociologist Max Weber called it, in which modern man finds himself imprisoned.

Thirdly, most European economies have not, or at least not yet, passed the test of structural adjustment. Many of this book's contributors refer to the hardening of their countries' institutional arteries, their incapacity for change. Even geographical mobility is anathema, with government welfare policies putting an additional spoke in the wheel. There are, of course, exceptions. Switzerland, according to Francesco Kneschaurek, has adapted to the changed environment reasonably well. But it has done so in part by running down the number of its foreign workers – i.e., by exploiting its special position. Elsewhere in Europe, adjustment remains the key problem yet to be resolved.

High wages side by side with poor productivity and low profits – what is needed to redress this balance is something like Sweden's 'EFO system', a 'social contract' along British lines, or 'concerted action' along German lines. Again, once the state becomes too big, its excessive spending becomes a political issue which will, it must be hoped, one day lead to it being cut back to size without the welfare of the individual suffering in the process. And as for hardening of the arteries, it should be possible, without perhaps going all the way with the Swiss, to do at least something to make flexibility rather than immobility, attractive. On all three fronts, however, it would be just as possible instead to follow the line of least resistance, with fatal consequences – cost inflation, resulting in an increasing inflation weariness; a perilously high degree of state interference; protectionism and all the rigours of the siege economy.

Are these problems cyclical or structural? Not all contributors deal with this question, but almost all argue that the new situation contains at least a strong cyclical element. To that extent, this book is rather more optimistic than its editor. Leaving aside contributions like those by Lundberg and Tinbergen, however, it seems appropriate to make special reference to two particular passages. The first is Miguel de Aldaroso's list, under the 'Industrial problems' heading, of ten changes in the economic climate (see pp. 177-9). The list is an impressive one, and it would be rash to assume that all ten factors will alter in the foreseeable future. The second passage is Francesco Kneschaurek's summary of the reasons why Switzerland has managed to lead such a seemingly charmed life (see pp. 221-2). This includes such things as 'a social, legal, political and economic system which is both stable and liberal', 'excellent industrial relations', 'a still relatively low level of taxes and social charges', and much else that others might crave but few possess. If these two things make sense, then the theory that the economic trend change of the past decade is merely cyclical, clearly does not.

Are there possible solutions?

The aim of this book, however, is not just to illumine; it is also to pave the way to solutions of the problems discussed. That, of course, is easier said than done. But if the key question remains how to preserve the basis for sustained and secure growth, then two possible solutions, touched on by Otmar Emminger and Jacques Delors, can be eliminated straightaway.

For one thing, Europe no longer has an economic 'locomotive'. Interdependent though its economies may be, there is not one among them capable of galvanizing, and so solving the growth problems of, the others. Perhaps Emminger is a shade too pessimistic on this score with respect to his own country, which he describes, right at the end, as Europe's 'still most important and relatively most stable economic partner'; but his thesis that Germany cannot, for all that, act as Europe's driving force must willy-nilly be accepted. The continuing (at the time of writing) weakness of her balance of payments, and hence the need for further restructuring of her economy, is the crux of that issue.

Again, it is no longer possible to maintain that sustained growth can be achieved simply by boosting demand, that you can, as it were, spend your way into full employment. Jacques Delors is alone in still viewing this traditional pump-priming technique with some favour. Nor does he share the aversion of other contributors to government intervention, or even to enlargement of the welfare state. His own prescription – an astonishing mixture of Keynes and Friedman, of demand- and supply-side economics, or (as he puts it) a 'judicious blend of different instruments' – must, however, be read carefully and deserves quoting in full: 'a prudent stimulus via the budget: a fiscal structure geared towards greater social justice, and the encouragement of saving and entrepreneurial initiative; an active employment policy (training, mobility, placement); a counter-inflationary monetary policy; and a more selective financing policy, particularly as far as long-term bank loans and the provision of risk capital are concerned' (see p. 68). Nevertheless, it should be noted that this approach – which, though promising, leaves open some questions to which we must return later – equally rejects the nostrums of yesteryear.

So, if there is in Europe at any rate no longer a growth 'locomotive', and if Keynesian recipes no longer fill the bill either, what remains? Well, there are at least two things, which will not have escaped the careful reader's attention.

The first is that, battered though the continent may be and clouded the horizon, there are a few bright spots. Switzerland, of course, is one; Austria, as Horst Knapp indicates, is another. That those countries have remained an oasis of price stability for highly specific reasons is irrelevant in this connection; what matters is that in the present socio-economic climate it is possible for price stability, and growth, to be maintained at all. And such success is true, as far as growth is concerned, not just of countries but of industries and indeed individual companies as well. A country-by-country analysis like the present cannot of course make this clear, and ought to be supplemented by a companion volume organized on an industry-by-industry basis. In any community, there are always some who buck the general trend. Here, as elsewhere, a uniformly grey picture is misleading.

A second – perhaps not entirely redeeming – feature, first noted in this book by Guido Carli, is the growth of what he calls the 'submerged' economy, George Krimpas the 'fly-by-night' economy, others the 'black' economy – the moonlighting section of the economy which escapes the eye of tax authorities (Jan Tinbergen candidly talks of 'tax evasion') and of official statisticians alike. To ignore or malign this, as most countries do, however, is a little unfair. These days, with so much working against them, the marvel is rather that so many people, instead of just sitting back in an armchair in front of their television screen, actually do something. They decorate first their own walls, then those of others; they repair first their own cars, then those of others. In Italy, the black economy has not only created its own class of small businesses, it also holds the 'white' economy together. Working on the side is also a stand-by for many in hard-pressed Britain. In some countries, estimates of the black economy's size range to up to 15–20 per cent of the GNP. The hope must be, of course, for a return to conditions where this kind of self-help is not required. In the meantime, however, such 'gainful' occupation is far preferable to virtuous impoverishment. Ultimately, it is living standards, not official statistics, that count.

All the same, neither individual bright spots nor the general existence of the black economy get us very far. Both are, after all, equally incapable of being produced to order – a statement more significant than may seem at first sight. To start with bright spots, the historical odds are against any country being able to pull itself up by its political bootstraps. In this respect, Mrs Thatcher's hopes – flying as they do, as shown by Samuel Brittan, in the face of a century-old trend as well as the present drift – are deceivers. As for the black economy, it indicates how treacherous has become the hope for the creation of an 'official' middle class of businessmen. Small and medium-sized businesses should, of course, be given every possible encouragement (and nothing here would be more helpful than less state interference). Basically, however, there will always be a tendency, at least in Europe, for people to do their own thing, working outside rather than within whatever official framework governments deem best for them.

If, then, it is hard to swim against the stream and officially encouraged entrepreneurial initiative remains a poor bet, does this book, it may be asked, offer any relevant guidelines whatever? The answer to that question is difficult to square with the usual political stock-in-trade, let alone any of the currently popular panaceas. It can be summed up under five, already outlined headings.

First. The way in which pay, productivity and profits are related to each other needs to be radically altered – though again this is easier said than done. To achieve both stable prices and sustained growth (and also a high level of employment, about which more later), it is necessary, first, for pay rises to be kept below the increase in productivity and, secondly, for adequate resources for investment to be provided out of profits or higher savings, or both. With regard to that end, the contributors to this work are in broad agreement. Concerning ways and means, Lundberg (on Sweden), Knapp (on Austria) and Kneschaurek (on Switzerland) perhaps hold the key. The only hopeful way of achieving a better balance is through co-operation rather than confrontation. Wielding the big stick of unemployment is not only inhuman; it is abortive. Nor, frankly, are there any magic wands to be found elsewhere. Something like a social contract will therefore be indispensable.

Second. Barring fundamental structural adjustments, Europe's economies will be not only in peril themselves but also quite unable to do anything to improve prospects for the rest of the world. Worse, they will fall prey to, and be impoverished by, protectionism. The necessary adjustment impetus cannot, however, be generated by the market alone, which provides neither training for personal adaptability nor incentives for mobility, nor yet even the basic signposts to new paths for antiquated businesses to follow. That, anyhow, is how it is in the real world of (frequently) fettered and distorted market forces. There remains then, as the only practical – and indeed widely practised – alternative, Delors's 'judicious blend of different instruments', which means in particular that economic policy-makers must forswear dogmas and ideologies of any kind, whether left, right or centre.

Third. A necessary, albeit not sufficient, condition of future price stability and growth is a reduction of the role of the state – not only of the public sector itself (though this is not of primary importance), but above all of public spending and of government intervention. This means that the welfare state must be re-appraised. Has its job not to a large extent been accomplished? Cannot European societies nowadays afford new approaches which combine minimum safeguards for all with a greater degree of self-help? Again, there is a need for a loosening of bureaucratic fetters. The black economy is an example to be applauded, rather than a deplorable breach of etiquette. Others besides the Netherlands are in the fix vividly described by Tinbergen – one can only hope that Delors's fiscal and monetary policy won't land France in the same cul-de-sac.

Fourth. A word must be added about supply-side economics, that new amalgam of (partly technical) economic measures – ranging from a reduction in government activity to tax cuts to boost savings and thus investment – which has figured prominently in many of this book's pages. Not that the next tax cut on this side of the Atlantic will necessarily be of that ilk – it could well be a Keynesian measure to stimulate demand – nor is it the availability of capital which in most European countries is the prime difficulty. Companies are slow to invest not because they are unable, but because they are unwilling, to do so. A reduction in government activity might make them less inhibited, but by itself it is not enough. The key factor in investment decisions is confidence, something with which, for the reasons enumerated by Kneschaurek, Switzerland is blessed in special measure, though other countries would be content with less. Politically, confidence means that the economic policy ground-rules should remain intact regardless of changes induced by the democratic process. This is, of course, the Achilles' heel of the British style of adversary politics. Confidence also calls for co-operation rather than confrontation in industrial relations. Creating a climate of confidence is now, for the majority of European governments, at once the hardest and the most important thing they have to do.

Fifth. We are thus brought back to the question of what makes an interdependent world, and Europe in particular, go round.

The role of the European Communities

Readers cannot fail to have been struck by the apparent indifference of most of the contributors to the exhortations uttered by the president of the EEC Commission, Gaston Thorn, in his preface. Those from the larger EEC member states write almost exclusively about their own country. For West Germany, the EEC's function is primarily political. For France, it is, with the possible exception of agricultural policy, of marginal interest only. For Britain, which joined the wrong (mainly agricultural-policy-oriented) community, at the wrong time (when business activity was on the down-swing), the EEC has been a catalogue of hopes disappointed. And as for Italy, it is the pegging of her currency to the European Monetary System instead of the dollar, and the consequent damage to her previously quite rosy export prospects, which appears to be the main worry. Contributors from the smaller applicant countries, and from newly joined Greece, still view the EEC with some degree of optimism. George Krimpas, for example, believes Greece's membership could speed up the structural adjustment the country badly needs, having only in the previous breath referred to its unpreparedness and to the possibility that membership could ultimately work out less favourably than the preceding association. Indeed, apart from Gaston Thorn's preface, Jan Tinbergen of the Netherlands is the only one to ascribe to the EEC a double role of economic locomotive and of responsibility for the Third World. What is one to make of all this?

Of course, the principal objective of the EEC, still the centrepiece of a wider framework which also embraces the European Coal and Steel Community (ECSC) and Euratom, has been and remains the creation of a Common Market. The Common Market, particularly in the field of non-tariff trade barriers (where national security considerations exert an influence), still leaves a good deal to be desired. Nevertheless it does constitute for the economies of its member states an eminently successful attempt to overcome the confines of national borders. On the international stage, moreover, the EEC hitherto has played the part of a champion of free trade, the Common Market being seen as a link in a worldwide chain, not as a free-trade oasis. All this could now be in peril, from within as well as without, making preservation of the Common Market – itself a hopeful contribution towards Europe's economic future – a prime EEC objective.

Here three points must be made. The first concerns the common agricultural policy (CAP). The EEC rests on a treaty between industrial and agricultural interests (not to say between Germany and France). Its Common Market concept recognizes that in the field of agricultural products, where it is a question, even at national level, of policies rather than actual markets, a common policy is called for. Since that policy has of course had to be financed, the European Agricultural Fund has come to be the European Communities' most important political instrument, absorbing over two-thirds of their resources and, in the course of time, radically changing their character. The CAP is thus a conspicuous, if rather expensive, exercise in the art of industrial restructuring.

The second point is the converse of the first. Just as the common agricultural policy has been and is the consequence of the non-existence of a genuine agricultural market, so the consequence of the existing market for industrial products is the absence of a common industrial policy. The EEC from its outset, and particularly in response to German pressure, has repudiated intervention in the industrial process by political means. Industrial policy, insofar as it exists at all, therefore begs for resources in vain and – except perhaps in those areas (of late, of course, notably the steel industry) covered by the European Coal and Steel Community – is dependent on the benevolence and support of those concerned. In the field of industrial products, the European Communities' contribution towards solving structural problems has thus been a rather dismal one.

This weakness has, moreover, been compounded by others,

especially – and this is the third point – with regard to the Common Market's external relations, or its common trade policy. Although it is true that in the field of tariffs, and hence in the relevant GATT negotiations, the European Communities have been playing an active and positive role, the fact remains that in the non-tariff field their member states have increasingly been going it alone. And as far as more advanced instruments of trade policy – export credits, joint ventures, trade promotion generally – are concerned, the bigger member states in particular have always been ultra-conservative in their interpretation of the relevant Article 113 of the Rome Treaty. The European Communities have thus remained anything but a champion of worldwide economic progress. On the contrary, European trade policy has been gravitating back towards splendid isolation, with each member state again increasingly pursuing its own policy. Opinions as to how far this process has already gone, vary. But the developments of the past decade suggest that a return to beggar-my-neighbour policies has been espoused rather more than the spread of free trade.

This, briefly, is the story of the European Communities' achievements and limitations. To round off the picture, there has, of course, been the drive, initiated at the Hague summit of EEC heads of government in December 1969, to set up an economic and monetary union (EMU). The concrete proposals subsequently formulated by Raymond Barre, the responsible Commissioner, on the one hand, and by a committee of the Council of Ministers under the chairmanship of Luxemburg prime minister Pierre Werner, on the other, culminated in a plan to complete Europe's monetary union by stages over a period of ten years. That this would call for quite a number of 'concomitant policies' was recognized by the visionaries with open eyes. Germany in particular, during the talks that went on in 1970 and 1971, insisted that a common currency, to wit a common monetary policy, implies a common economic policy, a claim duly endorsed when, in the spring of 1971, the first major decisions to that effect were taken. The way to an economic and monetary union was, it seemed, being paved.

Perhaps nothing could illustrate the trend change that has been the subject of this book more dramatically than the failure of that endeavour, showing as it does, moreover, that the oil price explosion of 1973-74 was not the first or only precipitating factor. The ink on the agreement to launch the first stage of the EMU rocket, and to restrict the Community currencies' margins of fluctuation, was hardly dry when on 15 August 1971 President Nixon 'shut the gold window' and so, in place of the Bretton Woods system, ushered in the regime of currency floating. True, for a time there was still brave talk of a 'tunnel' in which world currencies were somehow conjoined, and of a 'snake' of European currencies striving for still closer conjunction therein. But the 'snake in the tunnel' soon burst, and the 'tunnel' itself fell apart.

The episode is important because it marks, probably for a long time, the European Communities' farewell to ambitious plans of economic and monetary harmonization. Nothing that has happened since has matched the imagination of Barre and Werner. The European Monetary System (EMS), established through the efforts of Roy Jenkins, while president of the Brussels Commission, and others, has done something to contain Europe's refractory currencies within a common frame. But its powers are limited – no frame-breaker need stand in fear of sanctions – and it is no substitute for, and can scarcely even be called a step in the direction of, monetary union, if only because European countries remain as far as ever from co-ordinating their economic policies. Their ministers do, of course, hold regular meetings, but these are more for exchanging on views and experiences than for formulating concerted approaches. So far there is no common European economic policy, nor anything remotely like it.

The more is the pity. The sole relics of the bid to forge a European economic and monetary union are the rudiments of a European regional and social policy, which will remain starvelings under the present system of Community financing (member states' contributions not in excess of one per cent of their value-added-tax receipts). Again, whatever innovative impulses might be generated by the makings, largely a Euratom legacy, of a European research policy, have been altogether negligible so far. That leaves, as one of the Community's most outstanding achievements, a European development policy which, by providing aid without creating new dependencies, does fulfil many of the conditions that Tinbergen stipulates.

But while the Community's record is thus by no means black throughout, it falls well short of meeting what might be called the European interest. This book demonstrates both how differently European countries view their economic position and how varied that position in fact is. For all that, they share common problems, above all a number of tasks they can only solve together. Apart from the preservation of the Common Market – the right arena in many respects for essential initiatives of industrial restructuring, however cool the attitude to a common industrial policy hitherto – and the creation of a zone exchange-rate stability, European countries share much the same problems with regard to oil and other (including alternative) energy resources. A common energy policy, a common stance *vis-à-vis* the oil exporters – the European Community here, as elsewhere, can be the generator of worldwide, or at least OECD-wide, solutions. Perhaps no longer boasting a locomotive within, Europe has, after all, what it takes to set the economic pace for others. Or instead of 'can' and 'has', must one say 'could' or 'might have', reducing Europe to a place of perpetual promise, at best wishful thinking?

A glimpse into the future

All the contributors say something about the future; not all, however, look very far. This may be wise, but it does, by and large, leave the impression that current difficulties are of a temporary (cyclical) nature and will in due course be followed by a return to normality. Contrary opinions, such as Lundberg's and Tinbergen's rather more sceptical views, are the exception. Having myself intimated similar thoughts in the Introduction, it may therefore be appropriate, in conclusion, to pursue them a few steps farther.

A possibly fundamental change in the socio-economic climate can be demonstrated in two ways. One is the defunct – shattered

– world economic order, the need for and lack of, international co-operation having been a constant theme throughout. That this can be the cause of a long-term decline, as well as of unpleasant conflicts, is obvious. And if, as also seems likely, Europe chooses to bury its head in the sand, the chances are that the rest of the world will act likewise. Given that tendency towards introversion, the prospects for a new world economic order are hard to view optimistically. This goes equally, and especially, for the vital business of North–South relations, on which, after Tinbergen's masterly summary, all that needs to be added is that growing protectionism makes effective changes here unlikely. Rather, the odds are that the countries of Europe, as of the OECD (not to mention the Comecon ones), will be thinking first of themselves and only then, when it is too late, of the hungry millions.

The other straw in the wind, overlooked by none of this book's contributors, is unemployment. Some refer to the solutions adopted in their own countries – reducing the number of foreign workers in Switzerland, use of the public sector as an under-employment haven in Austria. But such 'solutions' are clearly special cases. What is striking in some countries, France and Britain obviously excepted, is their relatively low unemployment rates, coupled with the expectation that a fresh upswing will reduce them to an acceptable norm of its own accord, or else that current unemployment rates are themselves, in the Friedmanite sense, 'normal'. Yet that can hardly be the last word. If today one-tenth (and in some places, a good deal more) of those willing and able to work cannot do so, this is not only a social and political problem of the first order, but also an indicator of economic changes which, in all probability, are irreversible.

Consider the following additional facts. Current European production capacities are by no means being fully utilized. Whether an economic upswing will directly lead to the creation of a substantial number of new jobs is therefore highly uncertain. Secondly, the official unemployment statistics are incomplete. There are any number of people – including the millions who, in European countries, attend places of further education – who are voluntarily unemployed. Thirdly, many of those in work are underemployed. Their job does not stretch them. Statutory regulations and social conventions permitting, they could just as well be declared redundant. There are plenty of signs, then, that the way people work is undergoing fundamental changes. It looks, as Hannah Arendt has put it, as if the work society is running out of work.

For the organization of European societies remains as job-centred as ever. To the individual, his job is not only his bread and butter; it also establishes his entitlement to social-security benefits, including his old-age pension, as well as his self-esteem. And joblessness invariably constitutes a psychological problem. With society thus entirely job-centred with regard to its status system, its income structure and its appreciation of what is needed, it is not surprising that many politicians, in the face of the economic problems of the hour, are urging people to work harder, when in fact the needs of today's high-technology economies would probably be rather better served (as proposed by the present French government) by a shorter working week, accompanied (as the present French government perhaps does not envisage) by a corresponding reduction in pay. Though there may be no shortage of work, there is, and in the foreseeable future is likely to remain, a shortage of jobs.

If this is so, a number of things follow. Of course, the need for economic growth to create jobs and employment will persist. There are nevertheless also special problems like school-leavers, who must be trained for a world where flexibility will be at a premium, yet where what needs to be done is not necessarily in keeping with what society can afford to pay. In the society of the future, the idea of some kind of community service for all young people is therefore by no means preposterous. But flexibility, including the opportunity to organize one's own career, is equally important in later life, as some encouraging (mostly, as might be expected, American) experiments to that effect confirm. Then there is also the question – less abstract than it sounds – of transforming heteronomous work into autonomous activity, passive leisure into active living, and of all that is meant by the humanization of working conditions. This, too, is no longer just a pipe-dream, but is already in many countries being put into practical effect.

The weather change with which this book is concerned could thus be more than a temporary aberration from standard and predictable norms; it could signal more fundamental changes in climate. That does not denote a sudden diminution of the importance of economic growth, which on the contrary, however difficult, remains essential. But it does denote a gradual shift of emphasis. The social contract we need, for example, could contain a clause whereby productivity gains are translated not so much into pay and profits as into leisure and profits, thus turning unemployment from a negative into a positive concept, one which challenges us to broaden rather than to narrow the sphere of human activity.

But there the matter must be allowed to rest, because this is an essentially practical book whose aim is to provoke action as well as thought. If, in relation to the ideas outlined here, European policy-makers still appear to have some way to go, we must hope that their next steps will be steps in the right direction. The right direction is not, however, a simple extrapolation of the past, such as economic forecasters (rather than futurologists) are apt to make. At the very least the advanced European economies are today experiencing a trend change. Historians may well come to regard it as the start of a new era.

Tables – Europe's crisis: some statistical illustrations

Table 1　**Rate of economic growth**

| | Population (1980, millions) | Annual Growth in Real GDP (Per capita, per cent) | | | |
		1960–69 (average)	1970–79 (average)	1979	1980
Belgium	9.86	4.3	2.9	2.1	2.2
Denmark	5.13	4.4	2.6	0.3	−0.8
West Germany	61.56	4.7	2.7	4.5	1.8
France	53.71	5.0	3.5	0.3	1.2
Greece	9.60	5.7	4.5	0.4	1.6
Ireland	3.43	3.5	3.5	1.9	2.1
Italy	57.04	5.9	2.7	4.9	4.0
Luxembourg	0.37	3.4	2.5	2.3	NA
Netherlands	14.14	4.5	2.8	2.3	0.8
UK	55.89	2.6	2.0	1.2	−1.5
Total EEC	**270.85**	**4.4**	**3.0**	**2.1**	**1.3**
Austria	7.51	4.0	3.5	3.6	3.6
Spain	37.38	7.1	3.7	1.5	NA
Sweden	8.31	3.6	1.8	3.7	NA
Switzerland	6.37	4.2	1.0	2.6	NA

SOURCE: Economist Intelligence Unit, London (1981).

Table 2　**Inflation: Annual growth in the consumer price index**

	1960–69 (average)	1970–79 (average)	1979	1980	1981[a]
Belgium	2.6	6.7	4.4	6.7	7.2
Denmark	4.1	8.0	9.6	12.3	12.2
West Germany	2.4	4.6	4.1	5.5	5.6
France	3.5	8.3	10.7	13.3	12.8
Greece	1.8	11.8	19.0	24.9	24.0
Ireland	3.9	11.8	13.2	18.2	17.1
Italy	3.4	12.0	14.7	21.2	20.6
Luxemburg	2.1	6.0	4.6	6.3	7.8
Netherlands	3.6	6.6	4.2	6.5	6.5
UK	3.3	11.7	13.4	18.0	11.7
Total EEC	**3.1**	**8.8**	**9.8**	**13.3**	**12.6**
Austria	3.1	5.6	3.7	6.3	6.8
Spain	5.5	13.6	15.6	15.6	14.9
Sweden	2.8	7.8	7.3	13.7	13.1
Switzerland	3.0	4.6	3.6	4.1	6.0

[a] Estimate.
SOURCE: EIU (1981).

Table 3 **Annual growth in industrial production (per cent)**

	1960–69 (average)	1970–79 (average)	1979	1980	1981[a]
Belgium	4.6	2.3	4.4	6.7	−3.6
Denmark	4.6	2.3	4.3	0.0	−1.7
West Germany	4.7	2.3	5.3	−0.8	−0.8
France	4.6	3.0	5.4	−0.9	−3.0
Greece	8.6	6.8	6.1	0.9	−3.9
Ireland	6.6	4.3	6.2	−1.7	−2.9
Italy	6.3	2.8	6.6	5.6	−4.7
Luxemburg	2.4	0.4	2.8	−2.7	−9.2
Netherlands	6.2	2.8	2.8	0.0	−4.4
UK	2.7	1.7	2.5	−6.7	−7.2
Total EEC	**5.2**	**2.9**	**4.6**	**0.0**	**−4.1**
Austria	4.7	3.5	6.2	5.0	−2.9
Spain	10.5	6.2	0.2	1.4	−2.5
Sweden	5.5	1.3	6.5	3.1	−3.9
Switzerland	4.4	0.6	0.9	5.6	−0.5

[a] Estimate.
SOURCE: EIU (1981).

Table 4 **Unemployment: Number unemployed as % of the labour force**

	1960–69 (average)	1970–79 (average)	1979	1980	1981[a]
Belgium	3.5	6.3	10.9	11.8	13.8
Denmark	NA	4.1	6.0	6.9	8.6
West Germany	1.0	2.9	3.8	3.8	4.8
France	NA	3.2	5.9	6.3	7.7
Greece	NA	NA	0.9	1.0	1.0
Ireland	6.1	9.5	9.3	10.3	13.3
Italy	5.2	6.4	7.7	7.6	8.7
Luxemburg	NA	NA	0.7	0.7	0.8
Netherlands	NA	3.1	5.1	5.8	8.1
UK	1.9	4.1	5.4	6.8	10.4
Total EEC	**2.7**	**4.2**	**5.6**	**6.1**	**7.8**
Austria	2.9	2.0	2.0	1.9	1.7
Spain	1.3	4.1	9.2	11.8	13.9
Sweden	1.7	2.1	2.1	2.0	2.0
Switzerland	NA	NA	0.4	0.3	0.2

[a] Estimate.
SOURCE: EIU (1981).

Index

agriculture: EEC and, 154, 255;
France, 49; Greece, 223, 224, 227,
228, 230, 234, 235, 237, 241; Spain,
176; state intervention, 79;
Switzerland, 221
Albert, Michel d', 61
Alt, James E., 5
alternative economy. 9–10
Arendt, Hannah, 260
Australia: taxation, 78
Austria, 182–94; currency
movements, 182, 188; current-
account deficit, 191, 193; economic
growth, 182–3, 186, 193, 265; and
German tourism, 23; GNP, 182;
incomes policy, 184–5, 186–8, 190;
industrial restructuring, 192;
inflation, 186, 190, 193–4, 265;
investment, 183–5, 191; production
growth, 266; productivity, 184,
185; supply-side economics, 189,
190–1; taxation, 78; trade unions,
184, 185–6; traditional industries,
192; unemployment, 184, 188, 193–
4, 266; work sharing, 184–5

balance of payments, 217; Britain,
76; Greece, 224–5, 226, 227, 229,
231, 233, 234, 235; Italy, 108;
Spain, 164–8, 169; Sweden, 197–8,
202, 208, 209; West Germany, 26,
31, 32–5
Bank of Spain, 166, 169, 173
Barre, Raymond, 58–9, 62, 63, 256,
257
Belgium: currency policies, 63;

economic growth, 265; industrial
history, 142; inflation, 265;
linguistic conflict, 142; production
output, 266; public expenditure,
145; taxation, 78; unemployment,
266; see also Benelux
Benelux, 141–58; and developing
countries, 151–3; economic
forecasts, 147–9; employment,
143–4, 146–7; and European
integration, 153–4; exports, 141,
151; inflation, 147; post-1950
trends, 143–5; price rises, 147;
public expenditure, 145;
stagflation, 145–7; structure of,
141–2; unemployment, 150
black economy, 251, 253; Greece,
240; Italy, 111; Sweden, 200
Bonn Summit (1978), 26, 27
Brandt Report, 7, 151, 155, 247
Bretton Woods, 13

Callaghan, James, 89, 93
Cambridge Economic Policy Group,
75–6
Canada, taxation, 78
Centre for the Studies of Prices and
Incomes (CERC), 50
Cepremap, 54
chemical industries, 155
Clegg Commission, 89
Club of Rome, 'Limits to Growth', 7,
8
Comecon, 12
commodity speculation, Greece, 232–
3

Index

Index

Portugal: taxation, 78
prices policies, France, 49, 60, 61–2, 64
production output, Austria, 266; Belgium, 266; Britain, 72–3, 75, 266; Denmark, 266; European growth rates, 266; fall in OECD countries, 53; France, 48, 53, 54, 266; Greece, 224–5, 266; Ireland, 266; Italy, 112, 266; Luxemburg, 266; Netherlands, 266; Spain, 266; Sweden, 197, 209, 266; Switzerland, 266; West Germany, 266
productivity: Austria, 184, 185; Britain, 94; France, 48; Greece, 224; Italy, 102–3, 104, 111–12; pay and profits and, 252; Spain, 175, 178, 179; Sweden, 203; technological progress and, 130; Switzerland, 219; Greece, 226, 227, 231, 239
profits: Italy, 101, 103, 105; pay and productivity and, 252; Sweden, 203, 204, 206, 210
protectionism, 7, 8, 14, 34, 121, 217, 220, 247, 252, 259
public expenditure, 74–7, 247–8, 253; Belgium, 145; Benelux, 145; Britain, 76–7, 145; France, 145; Greece, 228; Italy, 104; Japan, 145; Netherlands, 145, 150; Sweden, 145, 199–200, 209; Switzerland, 218; USA, 145; West Germany, 145
public-sector deficit, Austria, 187; Britain, 88; Greece, 234, 235; Spain, 166–7, 169, 173–4; Sweden, 208; West Germany, 36–7

raw material costs and availability, 121; France, 49; Italy, 102, 113; Spain, 175–6, 177, 178; Sweden and, 199
Reagan Administration, and the OECD, 13–14
research activities, 155–6, 178, 257
RIO Report, 152
Robinson, Joan, 147
Rostow, Walt, 8

Samuelson, P. A., 147
Sautter, Christian, 59
savings, 11; Greece, 229, 232–3, 237; West Germany, 37, 41
Schmidt, Helmut, 26, 62
Scientific Council for Government Policies (WRR), 150
Seidel, Hans, 189
service economy, Greece, 224–5, 227, 228
shipbuilding, 122
shipping, Greece, 237
Shishido, Sh., 149
Simons, Henry, 83
social benefits, 5, 115, 248; Benelux, 141; Greece, 226; West Germany, 37; *see also* welfare state
Social Democratic Party (Britain), 98–100
social structure, Britain, 81; France, 49–50, 51
Spain, 160–81; balance of payments, 164–8, 169; budgetary policy, 172–4; economic growth, 86, 265; economic policy, 167–74; economic structure, 174–81; energy problems, 170, 174–6, 180–1; and the EEC, 160–1, 181; exchange rate, 161, 166; exports, 162, 170–1; and German tourism, 23; gross national product, 167; imports, 175–6; industrial competition, 179–80; industrial problems, 177–9; industrial restructuring, 170; inflation, 164, 168, 169, 265; international competition, 177; long-term financing, 171–2; monetary policies, 171–2; production growth, 266; productivity, 178, 179; public administration, 168; public-sector budget, 166–7, 169, 173–4; revenue distribution, 176; state intervention, 178; taxation, 78, 179; technological weakness, 175, 179–80; trades unions, 168; unemployment, 163–4, 170, 179, 266; Value Added Tax, 169; wages, 180
special interest groups, 83–6

Index

wage levels, Benelux, 144; Britain, 87, 93, 98; Greece, 232, 239; Italy, 102, 103, 105; Japan, 35–6; productivity and profits and, 252; Spain, 176, 180; Sweden, 197, 202, 203, 204; West Germany, 36

Wages Council system, 97

welfare state, 114–15, 215, 253; Benelux, 144; France, 50; Netherlands, 115, 157; Sweden, 200; West Germany, 38, 41

West Germany, 21–43; adjustment of domestic demand, 35–8; balance of payments, 26, 31, 32–5; competitiveness, 29–30, 32–4, 38–9; current-account deficit, 25–7, 31, 43; decline in exports, 30; economic growth, 23–5, 85, 265; 'economic miracle', 21–2, 35–40; economic outlook, 40–3; and the EEC, 22–3, 254; effect of Japan on, 27, 29, 33; effect of oil prices, 27–8, 32; employment, 24, 41; energy costs, 32, 39; exports, 33, 39, 40;

external constraints on, 30–1; foreign travel, 23, 32, 38; growth differential, 26–7, 28–9, 32; import restrictions, 34; imports, 29, 32–4, 43; imports of EEC goods and services, 23; industrial restructuring, 39–40; inflation, 24, 41, 265; interest rates, 31; international corporation plants, 73; investment, 74, 75; price stability, 24; production growth, 266; public expenditure, 145; public-sector deficit, 36–7; reduction of real incomes, 35–6; share of EEC's GNP, 22, 23; state intervention, 79; strength of the mark, 21–2, 29–30, 32, 33, 34–5, 38–9; taxation, 37–8, 77, 78; unemployment, 97, 266

work sharing, Austria, 184–5

World Bank, 161

Yugoslavia, and German tourism, 23

274